# The Foundations of Property Law

This Revision Guide covers the basics and fundamentals of Land Law & Equity/Trusts.

Muhammad Gangat

The Foundations of Property Law

Copyright: Muhammad Gangat 2019

ISBN: 9781092928007

Edition: 1

All rights reserved. No part of this publication may be reproduced, stored in any retrieval system or transmitted in any form or by any means, electronic or otherwise, without written permission of the publishers.

Author: Muhammad Gangat

The Foundations of Property Law

| Contents: | Page No. |
|---|---|
| **Foreword** | **4** |

# Land Law

| | |
|---|---|
| **Introduction to Property Law & Locke's Theory of Property** | 7 |
| **Recognition & Property Rights** | 13 |
| **Introduction to Personal Property** | 19 |
| **Communal, Private & State Property – Property & Ownership** | 23 |
| **Property Economics** | 36 |
| **Property Economics Hypothetical** | 45 |
| **Property & Common Law** | 49 |
| **Property Title, Possession & The Law of Finding** | 56 |
| **Adverse Possession** | 62 |
| **Leases & Licenses** | 67 |
| **Co-Ownership** | 76 |
| **Leasehold Covenants** | 85 |
| **Non-Leasehold Covenants** | 90 |
| **Easements** | 103 |
| **Unregistered Interests in Land** | 114 |
| **Registered Interests in Land** | 124 |

# Equity & Trusts:

| | |
|---|---|
| **Property Equity** | 135 |
| **Trusts** | 139 |

# The Foundations of Property Law

| | |
|---|---|
| **Express Trusts** | **143** |
| **Implied Trusts** | **166** |
| **Trusts of the Family Home** | **174** |
| **Unincorporated Associations & Rules against perpetuity** | **182** |
| **Charities** | **191** |
| **Formalities & Proprietary Estoppel** | **196** |
| **Doctrine of Notice & Overreaching** | **205** |
| **Trustees Powers & Duties** | **215** |
| **Breach of Duty & Fiduciary Duties** | **228** |
| **Proprietary Remedies & Tracing** | **241** |
| **3rd Party Liability – Personal Claims** | **252** |
| | |
| **Recommended Readings** | **265** |

The Foundations of Property Law

### *Foreword*

This book is written by a student, for students seeking to understand the concepts, tenants and proponents of Property Law in the United Kingdom. Covering all aspects of Land Law and Equity, this revision guide provides a comprehensive collation of the key ideas needed in order to do well in your exams, be that for your Law LLB or GDL.

The idea behind this book is to speak directly to the reader & the method of writing is completely different to all other revision guides and textbooks out there; you read this as though someone is talking to you. The method of writing, with humour and informal language (banter innit), is designed to keep you, the reader, engaged.

This book seeks to give you a detailed step-by-step logical guide on how to answer the exam, and more importantly, the logic that one should follow in order to consolidate your knowledge in preparation of the exam. The use of tree-diagrams and easy examples is highly encouraged, as this most certainly helps to structure your understanding.

I would like to thank all those, friends and family, who have tirelessly proof-read this material, supported me in putting this together and encouraging me to actually publish this. This wouldn't be in existence without you and this is for you guys.

I hope you have an enjoyable time engaging with this guide and I am very keen to receive any feedback.

Muhammad Gangat

September 2019

# The Foundations of Property Law

The Foundations of Property Law

# Land Law

Introduction to Property Law & Locke's Theory of Property

Recognition & Property Rights

Introduction to Personal Property

Communal, Private & State Property - Property & Ownership & Bentham

Property Economics

Property Economics Hypothetical

Property & Common Law

Property Title & Possession & The Law of Finding

Adverse Possession

Leases & Licences

Co-Ownership

Leasehold Covenants

Non-Leasehold Covenants

Easements

Unregistered Interests in Land

Registered Interests in Land

# Introduction & Locke's Theory of Property

  I.   What is property?
  II.  Locke's Theory of Property

## What is Property?

Property isn't actually by definition a thing. Rather, it is the rights you have to a thing. Property doesn't necessarily need to have value either but rather, it is usually something which is scarce & has a demand, allowing for it to be owned. Likewise, it doesn't strictly have to be tangible, but something which is not intangible may be difficult to own, such as air! But then on the other hand, shares in a company aren't exactly tangible but are still property.

The rights one possesses over a piece of property, should allow one to do whatsoever one wishes to do with it. Think of it as a bundle of rights; you are the possessor of a bundle of rights over property & you then have the right to use those rights however you wish; be this by taking advantage of the property yourself, lending a few rights from the bundle to someone else, or selling the whole bundle on. Obviously, this isn't strictly true with the ideas of absolute possession discussed later & how we aren't really capable of owning something in such a way that we can do whatsoever we wish with it, solely because of the external restrictions by which we are tied down & limited by.

You never actually own the property but rather, you own a collection of rights regarding that property.

## Locke's Theory of Property

John Locke was a 17th century philosopher who was a key political theorist for the development of liberalism. He was a key advocate of 3 core rights; a right to life, liberty & property. It was in his most famous works, *Two Treatises of Government* wherein he defined these rights and further defended the claim that men are, by nature, free & equal beings rather than being subject to a monarch.

## The Foundations of Property Law

This was the basis for his argument, writing against the work of Robert Filmer in his book, *Patriarchia*. Here, he suggested 3 ideas:

I. Government is the divine right of a father - patriarchy
II. There is a divine right for Kings
III. There is divine Law

This suggestion of divine rights led to a debate of 'natural law' which roots from the Declaration of independence, wherein it is stated that "All men are created equal" in the eyes of God suggesting that law and rights cannot & should not be derived from the monarch, but rather they are inherently divine.

Filmer had a set of arguments which can be summarised as:

I. Land was bestowed from God to Adam.
II. Once Adam died, the successor of this gift from God was the monarch.
III. This led to the monarch having exclusive rights over the land as he/she held all land.
IV. Thus, anyone else who had property, had it at the grace of the monarch. This was at a time where the monarch would gift land to certain people (aristocrats) as a method of bargaining and appeasing them.
V. Subsequently, this all implies that land can be taken back by the monarch at their will as they are the ultimate owners.

Locke, who felt this was completely out of order, argued that property was most definitely not derived from the grace of the state/monarch and rather there was another basis for property. In arguing against this, he developed what became his theory of property which in turn was the foundation for protecting individuals from the supremacy of the state. His theory developed a number of assumptions/points:

I. We all have an element of property in our bodies in the sense that they belong exclusively to us & us alone. This means that this element of private property, cannot be owned by the state/monarch & thus not all property is owned by them.

# The Foundations of Property Law

II. We all have a right to preservation such that we have a right to eat & drink to enable ourselves to grow and we can do this using that which is provided to us by naturally by nature.

III. There is a commons/state of nature

Commons is the idea that God has given us access to us the state of nature; meaning that as human beings, we have a right to make use of anything we want, so long as it is in the realm of the state of nature. We can, as humans, go and for instance, to a forest, hunt a deer or pick a piece of fruit & eat it without any restrictions on us! No one in the world can stake a better claim to that piece of property, unless they've got it before you – first come first served!

This is underlined by Locke's key belief in the idea that once labour is added to an object of nature, the individual who has invested his/her labour into it, has effectively taken it from the state of nature and into their direct possession. The notion of labour adds value to a thing, which is often far greater than the value of the thing alone. He states, *"For being a beast that is still looked upon as common and no man's private possession, whoever has employed so much labour about any of that kind as to find and pursue her has thereby removed her from the state of nature wherein she was common, and hath begun a property."* In English, what he is saying, is that once you add labour into something which is in the state of nature, you have staked a claim to call that yours.

There is an argument which arises from this in relation to consent. Finner is of the opinion that in order to take something from the state of nature, you are required to get permission/consent from every individual who has a right to it. Locke argues against this because he says that consent is 'compact' in the common which means that everyone is aware that it is there to be used which in effect works as a consent. He also suggests that if you tried asking everyone who had a right to it, it would become an impossible task to do so & would eventually lead to death, because you simply would not be able to eat until consent was achieved – it is unrealistic to expect someone to receive consent from absolutely everyone in the world!

However, Locke goes beyond to argue that okay, if it isn't common consent alone that provides the justification for something coming into the remit of exclusive/private property, the thing that can definitely justify it entering this realm (as in allowing something from the commons/state of nature to become private property) can be the labour expended on the thing received from the commons by the recipient. This is because, the labour is the only thing that adds something (some sort of value) to what nature has provided & is essentially the only thing that distinguishes this thing from all the other things in the common; the value of one's labour.

This is based on the condition that natural resources in the common are quite simply useless to us, until we make effective use of them & in order to make use of them, labour will have to be put into it; be that of an intense or un-intense nature, labour alone adds value - 99% worth of value to that thing according to Locke.

This can be put in religious terms as Locke does: God provided mankind with natural resources so that people would work to improve them to produce sustenance to preserve their lives; labour being a virtue in itself, and private property being both the reward and the compensation for the expenditure of labour and the means by which God intended natural resources to be developed so that they could sustain humans.

Alternatively, we can put it in economic terms - natural resources can be exploited to their fullest extent only by people working on them, and people will choose to undertake the necessary work if they are rewarded by the allocation of private property in whatever is produced by their work; this is the just reward theory. If I put work into anything, as a human being, I naturally need and want to somehow be rewarded for it, in order to justify the exertion of my effort (why would I do something for free pls?)

However, in order to combat exploitation, Locke does set limits on how much can be taken from the state of nature, by declaring two rather significant & important provisos:

I. The sufficiency proviso – this is the idea that you must leave enough for others to take when there is an abundance of resources, don't be greedy! Commentators are keen on suggesting that what this means, is that it is justifiable to confer ownership of a thing onto a person who initially mixes their labour with it, in the sense that they will be deemed as the rightful possessor of that private/exclusive property, but only if they leave enough of the same/like thing remaining in the common for others to be able to 'appropriate' those things too. You need to make sure that there are enough resources left so that others can engage in the same labour and gain the same benefit as you did; you cannot self-impose a monopoly on the commons.

Nozick argues, quite simply, that this then rules out all those things in the world which are finite regardless of how much there may be. A more adequate interpretation of this proviso could be that as long as it leaves others with sufficient opportunity to provide for their own subsistence and preservation by labour, even if this then involves labouring for money to acquire property by exchange, rather than labouring to appropriate property from the commons.

II. Spoilation proviso – This is the idea that you can take as much as you wish from the commons, but you cannot allow for anything you take to become spoilt & thus ruin it for others – again, don't be greedy! This links in wholly with Locke's belief that God is the provider of all things to humans for their sustenance & that any appropriation which leads to a waste of resources is illegitimate, regardless of whether it diminishes the supply or the prospects available for others because religiously, it is seen as a sin. In Locke's view, God gave people resources to use, not to waste, and so even the consent of all the commoners or even a limitless supply would not be a legitimate justification of an appropriation of more than you can use for yourself or pass onto others by means of exchange.

Locke was keen to follow up on the spoliation proviso; there is always a risk that things will be spoilt due to the nature of man & thus Locke acknowledged that money such as gold & diamonds give value to a thing and though they are not necessary life, they have value because people are enforced to look after it. Thus, this money can be exchanged for potential things which would otherwise be spoilt; the money is paid for the labour added to the thing in order to derive it.

All in all, for Locke's theory of property, we can declare two things. We feel that Locke is of the idea that adding Labour to a thing gives enough justification for that thing to then become exclusive in your private property possession. Secondly, we can say that his argument mostly works as well whether we believe that natural resources were provided by God for the benefit of humankind, or whether concern for the environment and the proper relationship between people and the world leads us to adopt a similar position on the uses to which natural resources may legitimately be put. In other words, although Locke believed in a Christian God, his argument need not be confined to property rights arising in a Western Christian society. It is equally applicable to any society that accepts that everyone has a liberty to make use of unappropriated natural resources and an obligation not to waste them, whatever the origin of that liberty and obligation is thought to be.

The Foundations of Property Law

# Recognition & Property Rights

I. Recap of Locke's theory of property
II. Hegel & Philosophy of Right – key concepts
III. What is recognition?
IV. Recognition & its relationship to property ownership
V. Bentham's Views on Property

Recap of Locke's Theory of Property

I. A person has property within their own body
II. Each person has a right to maintain/sustain their body making use of the resources which can be found in the commons/state of nature
III. As soon as one adds their labour to anything from the state of nature/commons, that thing becomes their private property

Hegel & Philosophy of Right – key concepts

Who was Hegel? A philosopher prominent in Western philosophy and the concept of the dialectic method.

This is the concept of the self-thinking individual vs the other. A thesis vs an anti-thesis. In a mathematical sense, A vs B = C. This is him attempting to define that everything in existence has an opposing force.

This led him to then develop his own theory of property which he summarised in 3 key points;

I. There is no natural self-ownership; we do not have property within ourselves
II. Appropriation of things gives rise to personality – this is developed through the notes, but as a brief, property promotes recognition such that actual appropriation is a root cause of personality (developing a personality.) Hegel is of the belief that a person takes a hold of/appropriates themselves once they have appropriated external thing. People recognise as by the property we have for example, "That's Matthew's car/house" etc.

III. People need property to become full/complete humans – this suggests that people who do not have property are not actually complete humans. Historically, women, ethnic minorities were not referred to as full humans; the famous "Ain't I a woman?" speech by Sojourner Truth wherein she stated, *"That man over there says that women need to be helped into carriages, and lifted over ditches, and to have the best place everywhere. Nobody ever helps me into carriages, or over mud-puddles, or gives me any best place! And ain't I a woman? Look at me! Look at my arm! I have ploughed and planted, and gathered into barns, and no man could head me! And ain't I a woman? I could work as much and eat as much as a man - when I could get it - and bear the lash as well! And ain't I a woman? I have borne thirteen children, and seen most all sold off to slavery, and when I cried out with my mother's grief, none but Jesus heard me! And ain't I a woman?"* highlights her disapproval of the inferiority given to women.

But here the term property is used very vaguely in the sense that it doesn't only refer to property as in property of car/homes etc. but can also refer to internal properties/qualities such as ones handwriting or one's ability to do something.

Hegel summarises his expansion of actualisation into 3 key steps:

I. Step 1 – Hegel believes that a person begins as an entity which has free will that has no property & no properties/personality, like a piece of mould which is just roaming the streets, opposed to the external world & only really bothered with one's internal self. There is no regard to anyone in the outside world. They are internal, self-conscious & relate to themselves on an individual basis, because we declare ourselves to be wholly internal & not at all related to the external world.

II. Step 2 – Next, a person begins to actualise themselves – this is done by actualising one's personality to be able to project themselves to the real world as they begin to externalise themselves too. Hegel postulated that in order to actualise/realise your own personality, you must project yourself into the external world.

The Foundations of Property Law

III. Step 3 – Once fully actualised, they then become externalised into a thing & that thing becomes property. They are able to appropriate things as property. This actualisation happens because a person through their own will attempts to make it their own. Effectively, in this step, the externalised will that is developed in step 2 appropriates itself in the form of property meaning that if a person has occupancy or possession of something, that thing becomes a form of property solely because that individuals will/thoughts are that they are associated themselves with that thing & thus they associate their being with it, thus it is property. This is actually quite difficult to comprehend properly & I can't really explain it as well as I should be able to ☹ Let me try this... If my Dad gave me a watch which he stole from you & then he passed away, I would love that watch so dearly & see a part of myself in that watch such that it becomes attached to me in a way that some people will think that watch is me & I am that watch; we become so intertwined with each other that my will & passion for that watch constitutes it being my property because of my attachment to it. But this can give rise to a conflict which is discussed below.

In paragraph 40 in his Philosophy of Right, Hegel states, *"Right is in the first place the immediate embodiment which freedom gives itself in an immediate way, i.e. (a) possession, which is property-ownership. Freedom is here the freedom of the abstract will in general, or eo ipso, the freedom of a single person related only to himself. (b) A person by distinguishing himself from himself relates himself to another person and it is only as owners that these two persons really exist for each other. Their implicit identity is realized through the transference of property from one to the other in conformity with a common will and without detriment to the rights of either. This is contract."*

Here he is eluding to the problem which arises if two people identify themselves with one particular thing. This would cause a conflict & in order to settle this conflict, Hegel suggested that it is resolved through a contract. This may seem simple through the notion of the self-identifying owner and the other person agree that the thing actually does belong to the rightful owner, but there is a process of exchange, be it in lieu of money or anything else. But this goes against the idea of Locke that property is all internal & proves that the relationship between a person and property is wholly reliant upon one's relationship with others too.

## Locke vs Hegel

Though Locke & Hegel are both agreed upon the idea that property has an integral relation to a person, they differ with the kind of relationship they have with a person.

Locke constitutes the belief that we already have property in our own bodies such that they are *pre-social* and we are not dependent on anyone else for our property meaning that the property is within our bodies even before we come across any external thing/person because our appropriation just occurs naturally in the state of nature and is justified by the labour we put into a retrieving a thing from the commons. For Hegel on the other hand, a person & their property can only come through actualisation of oneself that one can recognise themselves, others are able to recognise you & you are also able to recognise others. This makes property *post-social*. You need an attachment with others to have your property to be recognised. Hegel basically believes that a person & their property is only fully constituted through their relationships with others; it needs external actualisation to be deemed as whole.

This is suggestive of Hegel's belief that a person needs property in order to be respected as a person. Though a person does not need an unlimited amount of property, but just enough to ensure that they are able to flourish. This is because property is interrelated with personhood; a person's dignity & well-being as well as their ability to identify themselves with their own property. The way you decorate your house, the way you keep your garden, the car you drive, all have a say about your personality & allows you to engage in self-actualisation & to be able to recognise yourself.

## Recognition

Property is very fiercely linked with the struggles for freedom. This is because as mentioned above, people from minorities were refused the title of being complete human beings. In fact, in Article 1, Section 2 of the Constitution of the US 1787, a slave was deemed as 3/5ths of a human being. The problems with not having freedom were many, including:

- In slavery, you were the subject of ownership – as an individual, forget Locke's idea of having property in yourself, as a slave, you were wholly someone else's property.
- Freedom was imperative in achieving the status of an equal human being

This too was the case in the United Kingdom, where prior to the Married Women's Property Act 1882, when a woman owned any property, upon marriage, it would be combined and subsequently belong to her husband, as she would be required to surrender her rights to that property. This is because, her legal identity submerged into her husbands, such that it would be declared to cease in existence. This was epitomised by the lack of rights afforded to women in relation to inheritance laws, such that women, more often than not, were unable to receive significant wealth through such dispositions. This was evident such that women were very unlikely to ever be the beneficiaries of real property in their inheritance from their fathers such as land but would more often than not be limited to receiving some form of personal property by way of chattels like clothing, jewellery or something similar.

Radin argues in the modern context that people are in need of property to actually be respected as a person. This can be seen in today's day & age; if someone doesn't have a house, they're homeless & we all know of the pathetic conditions in which they live in. Likewise, if you don't have property of the new phones, nice cars, branded clothes etc., then your rank as a recognised individual are much lower than a person who has the latest phones, beautiful cars & the most expensive branded clothes. Radin says that a person doesn't need unlimited property to be recognised as such, but merely those things which are needed to support a person to flourish. This again links in with my example of a homeless person; they do not have the basics in order to flourish & thus they aren't seen as a whole person in a way.

## The Foundations of Property Law

### Bentham's views on property

Bentham viewed property as an extremely powerful tool which if not kept within certain constraints & boundaries, runs the ultimate risk of causing problems & havoc in society. He states the 'property and law are born and die together' which implies that he believes in the notion that property is an absolute construct of the law. He completely disagrees with Locke's beliefs of property being within oneself & declares natural rights property to be 'nonsense on stilts' and rather property is but a critical element of our legal system such that the legal system would not work without property & likewise, property would not work without our legal system; they go hand in hand because they are born and they die together.

For Bentham, security is one of, if not the most vital concept of property & property rights. Owning property must be deemed to be secure & safe by the state, for it to hold any weight because if something you own has no security or safety, it instantly holds no value, as you cannot tie it down & keep a control of it such that it can wholly be declared yours, otherwise you live with a constant fear of dispossession particularly with potential for anarchy.

With regards to having an absolute right to property, Bentham uses the example of a sword. He explains that owning a sword is fine and you can do anything you want to do with it, up until you're about to cause some harm to someone else – this links in with the Harm Principle which is covered in Public Law and the idea/political concept of Liberalism. Likewise, you can own a car, but there are limits on where you can drive it, the speed at which you can drive, the manner in which you drive etc. Similarly, you can own a house, but there's limits on what you can do with it; planning regulations/permissions etc. This correlates with his notion that there is, quite simply, no such thing as absolute property.

The Foundations of Property Law

# Introduction to Personal Property

I. Is Property Law Land Law?
II. Contract Law to Property Law

Is Property Law Land Law?

Property can be either real or personal:

I. Real property = Associated with Land; property associated with land and all the interests associated with it.
II. Personal Property = interests that are associated with a piece of land which are personal to the interest holder such as mortgages which are a form of debt attached to a person to a piece of property. Equitable property interests usually fall under this category.

Personalty property are movable chattels, anything that is not land as such whereas a personal right is what you have against another individual; if contract is breached, one has a personal right to sue. A trust is a personalty; you have a right to sue against not only one person, but against the world.

So, the distinction between a personal and property right is that a personal right can be both contractual and tortious; if I get injured as I walk around SOAS, I have a personal right to sue in tort for negligence and contractual breach too. The rights here are between the two individuals who are involved – either the two people between whom the contract is made, the person injured and the one who created the dangerous situation, or the person injured & subsequently also breached a duty of care for instance.

Contract Law to Property Law

Some rights can move from their contractual basis to a proprietary right. Last year, we looked at a contract which became a property right; a lease. At its heart, is a contract between two parties which then gets elevated into a proprietary right. This move is important because of the element of a privity of contract; a 3rd party to a contract cannot sue or be sued in relation to any breaches within a contract. This was the case in *Tweedle v Atkinson* which I'm sure you've looked at in Contract Law (we don't talk about that topic out here) which was a valid contract where two fathers had contracted to give their son/son-in-law to be a sum of £300 in exchange for marrying. The son then tried to enforce this promise, but could not, as he was a 3rd party to the contract & him not receiving the money, albeit he was meant to be the beneficiary of that contract, amounts to nothing in Contract Law due to the notion of Privity of Contract.

If this, however, was done as a proprietary right, then, what we look at in detail in this topic, is the idea that actually the 3rd party can actually sue in this. In a proprietary right, not only can the benefit of a contract be passed, so can the burden. In contract Law, benefit of a contract can be passed; this is proven in those situations where bailiffs will buy a debt of for instance £1,000 for a sum of £800 from the person/group who is owed that money. They will then enforce their new right to that sum of £1,000 and ensure that they receive their money, thus the benefit of the money is now in their possession having been passed to them in return for them to keep £200 extra.

However, in contract, the burden cannot be passed. The burden in property law, however, can also be passed. This means, that there is now a fundamental change in the whole process of the relationship between the contracting parties; the landlord and the tenant, the lessor and the lessee. In Tweedle v Atkinson, the benefit could have passed if the correct formalities had been adhered to. What this is trying to illustrate is that rather than the actual contract laws being a problem, it was a problem of the formalities and how complicated they are to be adhered to properly. There are so many rules to be complied with if benefit is to be passed; who is owed that beneficial interest in that property – the beneficiary principle which we looked at last year.

So, the advantage of a property right is that the contract between A and B is a right in actions, a shows in action. The benefit of that chose in action can pass; that benefit can be sold/passed on to another party in both contract and property. Burden, however, cannot pass in contract & so we come to this easy breakdown:

## The Foundations of Property Law

I. Benefit can pass in contract/law
II. Benefit can pass in property/equity
III. Burden **cannot** pass in contract
IV. Burden can pass in property

The reason for this differentiation comes a lot down to the fact that property, unlike contract, has the ability to be perpetual; that it will never change hands but the people/persons responsible will change because land outlives human life. Contracts are typically renewed and there may indeed be a series of contracts, but there are often situations where original contracting parties in a property contract no longer exist and therefore there must be a range of rules to accommodate for this.

### What is different about Property Law?

Property is a generic term, whereas a lease is a contract at heart, but has been turned into a unique thing which is held under both contractual and proprietary requirements. Property is all about the relationship between people & though it may not be objectively valuable anymore, the incentives to create property rights, which are economic, require there to be laws to govern property rights now. Though property and property rights may not be tangible, there are situations where property rights actually are not protected by the state anymore.

The two cases which prove this are that of:

I. *National Provincial Bank v Ainsworth* – property right to stay in martial home was not protected as it was determined that Mrs Ainsworth did not have a proprietary interest in the land which was capable of amounting to an overriding interest. Her right to remain in the house was a mere personal right as against her husband. It did not confer on her any equitable estate or interest in the house and thus her personal right was not upheld by the state. This was in the time where women were really not given many rights at all & slowly as they got more rights, women's occupations can now be protected by registration and have their rights officially recognised; an overriding interest which again is not a proprietary right as such.

II. *Hunter v Canary Wharf* – The property right claimed was said to be their right to television signals; the signals were disturbed by the building of Canary Wharf, but the court said nah mate, these aren't a property right, sit back down! Courts are constantly being asked to create property rights but more often than not, they really don't change their stance.

# Communal, Private & State Property – Property & Ownership

   I.   Relationship between property & ownership
   II.  Private, communal & state ownership
   III. Honore's incidents of ownership
   IV.  Possession as a right in rem v right to possess in rem
   V.   Determinate, determinable & indeterminate interests
   VI.  Milirrpum v Nabalco

Relationship between property & ownership

These two terms are ones which we use together; property is owned & what you own is your property. So, is there really a difference? Ownership of a thing brings about the idea that a person owns the rights of that property, whereas property is an abstract term which widely commonly refers to the rights held in a thing.

Private, communal & state ownership

According to Cohen, Private property is defined by the right to exclude the rest of the world from your property.

Communal property on the other hand is that property which can be enjoyed by any individual who is a member of any community, such that their right is to not be exclude from that property. This is the difference between communal property & no-property; the idea that an individual who is a member of the community has not only the privilege to use the thing, but also a right to not be excluded from using that thing/property which obliges others to ensure they do not interfere with their access to that property, because they are members of that community & thus they are entitled wholly to use it.

On the outset, it looks as though the difference between private & communal property is the difference between the right to exclude & the right to not be excluded, but upon further analysis you see that it actually goes beyond this.

## The Foundations of Property Law

With regards to private property, let us say that both you & I own a property. It cost £100,000 so we both put in £50,000 – we are co-owners of the property. Now as we're both owners, we both have the right to exclude the rest of the world from our property; from annoying aunties to dodgy neighbours as is the case with all private property. But neither of us have the right to exclude the other from the property at any time, because we're both owners of that property. So, in effect, we both also hold the right to **not** be excluded from that piece of private property which is a quality of communal property! So, in effect, co-ownership (which we look at in more detail during the term gives an owner the right to exclude but also the right to not be excluded by their co-owner.

Likewise, if there's a communal piece of property such as a park, which is for members of the community in Edgware Road, even though all members of that community have the right to not be excluded from that property, they also have the right to exclude members who are not a part of that community from enjoying the benefits of that property. So here it comes to ground that even with communal property, there's the notions of both the right to exclude & the right to not be excluded.

So now it looks as though both private & communal property shares the same rights. However, in property law, the primary right for both is different in the sense that the primary right for private property is the right to exclude & the primary right for communal property is the right to not be excluded. Likewise, the way the rights are derived for that property differ too. For private property, rights are derived by being the owner of the rights of the property whist for communal property, they are derived by simply being a member of the associated community.

State property is the idea that all property is owned by one entity; the state and the primary right, like private property, is the right of the state to exclude others from that property. For example, as much as I would love to, I can't just turn up to Number 10 Downing Street & claim I have a right to enter because I am a voting citizen of the UK & thus have a right to not be excluded from that property like communal property. The only difference in this regard between state & private property is that the state owns the property rather than an individual(s) or organisation.

## The Foundations of Property Law

And the example of me going into Number 10 is the sole reason for distinguishing between state & communal property because if you think about it, as a voting citizen, I am a member of the state & have an indirect control over who gets to reside in Number 10 & thus in a distant way, I exercise some of my property rights on Number 10.

Think of it like this – private & communal property are 2 forms of extreme property rights, whereas state property sits in between both such that it has aspects of both public & private properties.

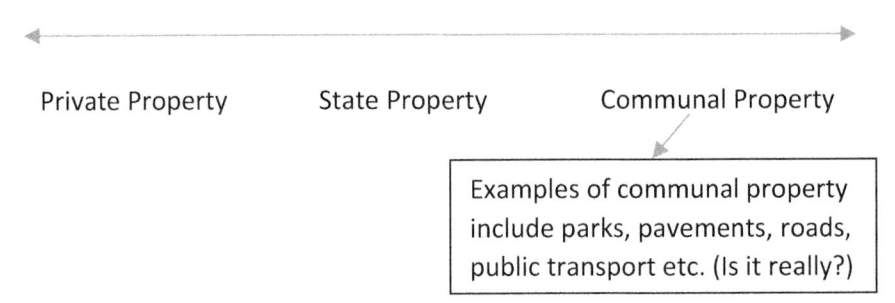

⟵──────────────────────────────────────⟶

Private Property          State Property          Communal Property

> Examples of communal property include parks, pavements, roads, public transport etc. (Is it really?)

With regards to these 3 forms of property, Aristotle suggests that it is impossible to conceive a society which does not have all 3 branches within it. The reality is that it is impossible to not have all 3; there will always be all 3. Communal property is always there; roads, pavements etc. All states have some sort of official offices & these are deemed state property. And private property may not always be in the form of homes or buildings such as is the case in communist countries & Cohen's suggestion that there is no such thing as private property in communist states. But in this regard, you'd consider the clothes a person wears, the food on their plate to be a form of private property. Yes, it is a smaller idea of private property which can be deemed inadequate but nonetheless, it relates directly with the notion of private property.

Outside the realm of all 3 comes the notion of no-property. This is the idea that there are some things in respect of which no one has property rights. In essence, each of us has a privilege to use such things (we are free to use them, and the rest of the world has the correlative no-right to object to us doing so), but none of us has the right not to have our use interfered with by others, nor the duty to abstain from interfering with anyone else's use.

## The Foundations of Property Law

To put it in terms of exclusion, none of us has the right to exclude others from such things, nor do we ourselves have the right not to be excluded from use. This came to light in the *Hunter v Canary Wharf [1997]* case where there was an argument from Hunter that the television signals were interrupted by the buildings of Canary Wharf, but the House of Lords decided that terrestrial television signals come within the category of no-property. It was held that, although everyone has a privilege to receive them, no one has a right to do so. Consequently, residents in the Isle of Dogs were held not to be entitled to complain when Canary Wharf Ltd built Canary Wharf Tower which, because of its size and construction, interfered with their television reception by preventing television signals reaching buildings which fell within its 'electromagnetic shadow'.

### Honore's Incidents of Ownership

Honore has 11 standard incidents of ownership on which he published an essay in 1969 through which he sets out a substantive analysis which tackles the understanding of what constitutes ownership & I want to look at them first:

I. Right to possess - to have exclusive physical control of a thing, or to have such control as the nature of the thing admits, is the foundation on which the whole superstructure of ownership rests.
II. Right to use - refers to the owner's personal use and enjoyment of the thing owned
III. Right to manage - right to decide how and by whom the thing owned shall be used.
IV. Right to income - Income in the more ordinary sense (fruits, rents, profits) may be thought of as a surrogate of use, a benefit derived from forgoing the personal use of a thing and allowing others to use it for reward; as a reward for work done in exploiting the thing; or as the brute product of a thing, made by nature or by others.
V. Right to capital - consists in the power to alienate the thing and the liberty to consume, waste, or destroy the whole or part of it.
VI. Right to security - An important aspect of the owner's position is that he should be able to look forward to remaining owner indefinitely if he so chooses and if he remains solvent. Legally, this

|       | is in effect an immunity from expropriation, based on rules which provide that, apart from bankruptcy and execution for debt, the transmission of ownership is consensual. Incident of transmissibility |
|-------|---|
| VII.  | Transmissibility - What is called unlimited duration comprises at least two elements: |
|       | a. that the interest can be transmitted to the holder's successors, and so on ad infinitum |
|       | b. that it is not certain to determine at a future date. |
| VIII. | Absence of term - The rules of a legal system usually provide for determinate, indeterminate, and determinable interests which are wholly discussed below |
| IX.   | Duty to prevent harm - An owner's liberty to use and manage the thing owned as he chooses is subject to the condition that not only may he not use it to harm others, but he must prevent others using the thing to harm other members of society |
| X.    | Liability to execution - Of a somewhat similar character is the liability of the owner's interest to be taken away from him for debt, either by execution for a judgment debt or on insolvency. |
| XI.   | Ownership & lesser interests – Residuary character |

He says with regards to his incidents right from the offset, *"The standard incidents of ownership . . . may be regarded as necessary elements in the notion of ownership, in the following sense. If a system did not admit them and did not provide for them to be united in a single person, we would conclude that it did not know the liberal concept of ownership, though it might have a modified version of ownership, either primitive or sophisticated. But the listed incidents, though they may be together sufficient, are not individually necessary conditions for the person of inherence to be designated owner of a particular thing for the use of 'owner' will extend to cases in which not all the listed incidents are present."*

With regards to these, Honore suggest that these are "necessary ingredients" but not "individually necessary. What he means by this is that any society that embraces the notions of private property & private ownership takes on all 11 incidents. They are necessary in the abstract & ideal notion of ownership but for the actual genuine ownership of property, all 11 incidents are not needed. For example, if I own a piece of land & I give a lease or even a licence to you, even though I do not necessarily now have all 11 property incidents over that property, as I am the owner, I still ultimately can claim ownership of that land even without the right to use etc. Honore is explicitly not attempting to provide a litmus test of ownership whereby any particular link between a person and a thing can be analysed to see if such-and-such a person is the owner. For his interest lies not with particular person–thing relationships but in the system where such relationships exist.

So, what Honore is saying is that you can no doubt be the owner of something, but still not have all 11 incidents of ownership. He is in essence, providing a template in which he lists those incidents with which any system claiming to embrace a liberal notion of ownership must correspond. Penner in response to this is that he suggests that Honore's purpose for these incidents is to define the provision of "criteria for the correct application of the term owner in English Law." But he is wrong in this suggestion; he is basically saying that Honore is attempting to use these incidents as a checklist to decide who an owner is, but this is wholly against what Honore was trying to do.

A good way to understand this is the case of a lessor & a lessee and deciding who actually owns the property. Is it the lessor who has ultimate possession of the land, or is it the lessee during the tenancy period at least, as he has numerous rights to that land particularly the right to exclude the rest of the world including the lessor too? Or maybe it is completely pathetic & a waste of time to try & find a single owner of the property because in this case there will always be two owners because both will have some of the rights from the 11 incidents set out by Honore; neither one will have all & there's no point trying to see which one has more of the incidents because each holds a different weighting in importance. So, trying to find the single owner would quite simply be foolish.

As a rule of thumb, Honore declares that when trying to find out who the owner of a piece of land is you first identify the rights & then determine who owns those rights. Honore says that if you want to see who actually owns a piece of land in a lease, you see who will end up with the property at the end of time; the lessor. But then there is an argument that if the lessor has no heirs, then the land returns to the state & this fuels the argument that ultimately, the state owns all the land.

In the case of *Burton v London & Quadrant Housing [1999]* the council gave a licence to a housing association who then gave a licence to an individual who stated that they had a tenant in the house who under the Landlord & Tenant Act should be responsible for certain repairs. But looking at this case, surely it seems illogical for the tenant to be held under the Landlord & Tenant Act because how can the anyone claim that they have property rights over that property except the housing association who actually gave out leases & not licences. However, in the judgement of this case, the House of Lords declared that as there was a certainty of term & the right to exclude existed for the tenant, all the required criteria to fulfil a lease were met & thus regardless that there was no $3^{rd}$ party binding agreement, this was a lease & therefore it falls under the act requiring the tenant to do those repairs. Contrast this with *M'cr Airport v Dutton* from the previous topic & then treat both judgements with suspicion!

Possession as a right in rem v right to possess in rem

**Right in rem refers to the right in the thing & with regards to property, it'll always refer to property rights.**

In order to try & differentiate between possession as a right in the property & the right to possess in rights of the property, and this can be understood by way of an example.

It was coming to the end of December in the Matthew household & Christmas was approaching. The family decided that this year, for Christmas presents the family would not declare who's present was for who. Whoever got any present, it would be theirs. So, if you picked it up, you would have to protect it in order to keep it. Here, there are no property rights.

Now it's December of the next year & we say that nah this time, there will be the right to possess in rem; meaning that everyone will get one sheep, but you have to find it. Once you've found any sheep & you've picked it up, that's yours & you can't do anything about it; meaning attempt to take someone else's healthier meatier sheep.

We then complete another year & December is almost over & it's Christmas of the following year again & this time the Matthew household decides to allocate presents with every child's name on it. This is then their possession as a right in rem because it has their name on it, it will belong to them & no one can take it off them; it has been declared as their property.

Once you are in possession of something, then you are protected by property rights, be that possession by lease, licence or even illegally. You are protected up until someone can claim a better title/right to that property than you & this claim must be legally judged.

Determinate, determinable & indeterminate interests

**Determinate = Will definitely happen**

**Determinable = Not certain to happen but can happen if...**

**Indeterminable = Will never happen**

Look at the example of *Berrisford & Mexfield [2011]* from the topic on Leases & Licenses below. The determinate interest was there, Ms Berrisford would definitely die eventually & the changing of the lease to 90 years instead of end of life did nothing because it remained a determinate interest both ways.

Milirrpum v Nabalco

In 1968, the Government of Australia granted Nabalco Pty Ltd a forty-two-year mineral lease of land in the Gove Peninsula in the Northern Territory of Australia to enable it to mine the rich fields of bauxite that had been discovered in the area, and to establish a township there. Representatives from several different Aboriginal clans brought this action against Nabalco and the government, claiming that they had property rights in the land in question that would be infringed by Nabalco's activities. They argued that these rights had been in existence before the land became vested in the Crown in 1788, that they were property rights that survived that event and continued in existence unless and until validly terminated by the Crown, that they never had been terminated, and that, consequently, they were still in existence and enforceable against Nabalco.

In this case, there were two questions that needed to be answered in order for there to be a valid case to be held for the Aboriginals & those questions were:

I. Did Australian/English common law recognise the communal native title?
II. If yes, was the aboriginal use of the land a proprietary use of the land – do we recognise pre-existing property rights?

There are 3 ways in which land can be acquired in a foreign country:

I. Conquest – meaning through war or some other form, taking the land by force;
II. Seeding it – meaning to contractually give land from one state to another
III. Terra Nullius – land that was previously unoccupied & you are the first residents of that land; in this case, there are no pre-existing property rights that need to be respected because there is no property which means that the state can go in & do whatsoever, they want.

And in the case above, it was deemed that the land taken by the aboriginal people was terra nullius because the aboriginals were so low class that their ownership was not deemed sufficient for a land to be owned. This means that the first question was answered in negative & thus there couldn't even be a case. The action was heard by Blackburn J in the Supreme Court of the Northern Territory. He held that, as a matter of law, any rights of native inhabitants were automatically extinguished when land in Australia was acquired by the Crown. Consequently, the second question – whether these particular clans had had property rights in the land at that time – did not arise.

But the court did consider the 2nd question too & Blackburn in the judgement basically rejected all the claims of the government that they had no boundaries, no system of law & that they were not a community which would suggest that maybe the 2nd question could've been answered in affirmative. But Blackburn defined property in a very narrow way; "Right to use, exclude & alienate." Honore in his definitions was talking about private property & Blackburn was talking about communal property which enhances just how limited his definition was.

One of the biggest weaknesses of Blackburn's reasoning in regard to property was how he defined the use of land by both the clans & the bands. The clans in the Milirrpum case are those who are said to have access to the land because of their religious attachment to it whilst the bands claimed title to the land for their togetherness through hunting & their working together for a common goal.

A second factor which influenced Blackburn J in coming to this conclusion was something that also troubled Dawson J in his dissenting judgment in Mabo (No. 2). It is generally accepted that it is within the power of a sovereign state to extinguish pre-existing property rights, provided that, in doing so, it is acting lawfully according to the rules of its own system (or according to the rules of international law if it is taking over new territory). It is also generally (although not so universally) accepted that, when colonising a new territory, whether inhabited or not, the Crown could lawfully extinguish pre-existing rights without specific legislation provided it made its intentions plain. It seems clear that this is what the Crown thought it had done in Australia. From the outset, the Crown assumed that the land was its own, to use or dispose of absolutely as it saw fit, with no legal constraints imposed by any pre-existing rights of indigenous inhabitants, and it acted on this basis. If the law as it was perceived to be at the time was that the Crown was legally entitled to absolute beneficial ownership of Australia, and that any claims of Aboriginal tribes had been extinguished by colonisation, is it now open to the courts to say that this was wrong in law?

In this case, it was deemed that the bands had the economic use of the land but no geographic link, whereas the clans had a geographic link but no economic link & thus neither one party completed both tests to be deemed instantly as the owner of the property rights for that land.

There is a question over Blackburn's refusal to just turn around & say to both the clans & the bands that they should come together to live together & make use of the land collectively, because if you think about it, if they used it together, they would eventually suffice both the economic & geographic links respectively.

Blackburn's very narrow definition of property was of 3 things, which he then used to back up his conclusion that the clans had not made proper use of the land which we however critique:

I. Use - The land use of the clans wasn't deemed a sufficient land use for it to be deemed proper; imagine telling that to a religious group of people that their use of a land isn't legitimate because it's solely for religious reasons.

II. Exclude – Blackburn says that the clans did not exclude others from their property. He is right, but there was quite simply no need for the clans to exclude others from their land, because there was a long-standing tradition & acceptance that due to the mutual respect between the clans & all the other neighbouring groups, there was quite simply no need to build fences etc., because their land boundaries were known and just mutually accepted

III. Alienate – as in for them to pass the title of their land on. They didn't need to do this either because the land was solely for religious purposes

With this, we can conclude that Blackburn's judgement is wrong for 3 different reasons. His definition of property is wrong & insufficient for communal property. It is also wrong & insufficient for private property. And on top of that, even if we accept his definition, in this case, 2 of the criterion he stated are actually met whilst the 3rd is wholly irrelevant.

In the case of *Mabo v Queensland,* the Aboriginals who brought the claims in Mabo (No. 2), the Meriam Indians who inhabited the Murray Islands, used their land in a very different way from the Gove Peninsula Indians. They lived mostly in settled villages rather than nomadically and lived primarily by cultivating gardens rather than by hunting and gathering. Also, they inhabited a part of Australia that had been annexed to the Crown at a different time and by a different process. The High Court of Australia could therefore technically have allowed the Aboriginals' claim in Mabo (No. 2) without overruling Milirrpum, confining the effect of Milirrpum to the claims of Aboriginal tribes of a culturally similar type who inhabited that locality.

There was a rejection of the terra nullius concept which was used to define the aboriginal title initially. With the rejection, the court state that they rejected this rather racist idea that the land which had been occupied by the aboriginal people would be unaccepted because their culture & being was seen to be so low their use of land was seen as non-existent. Yes, this judgement gets rid of this unfair view and the common law begins to accept the native title, but the case is actually not as radical as it first seems.

The actual detail of the judgement allows us to see that a Bentham approach of property is taken; property is not a natural right, but rather something that quite simply is born & dies with the law. The state could effectively turn around and wholly take away the rights of the land, even of the aboriginal people & this is an idea which is backed up by ex-Tory Minister, Michael Howard, who when introducing legislation with regards to limiting the rights of the landlord, said that it is impossible to legislate on property without in one way or another, affecting property rights which suggests that even private property is not completely private.

In this case however, the judges had an array of opinions. Toohey was of the position that communal property does indeed have property rights and thus in this case, the aboriginal people, as a community, had property rights against the world, to the extent to be able to exclude the world from their property. Deane & Guardon suggested that the native title is not property but is rather personal & personal rights are recognised by the state, even for aboriginal people. So, if a 3$^{rd}$ party brought the land, the only thing the aboriginal people would be entitled to would be compensation from the state for an infringement on their personal rights; they have no property rights & thus they cannot claim anything for property rights. However, the majority of the judges, 4 in fact, believed that the aboriginals could actually lose their land & not be owed any compensation at all.

## The Foundations of Property Law

As you can see, this case has a wide range of different extremes & this case is indeed worth looking into a little bit more.

In essence, the principles which we can derive from these 2 Aboriginal cases are very simple. As there had long been a principle of international law that the law in force in a newly acquired territory depended on the circumstances of its acquisition. If it was acquired by conquest, then the inhabitants continued to be governed by their own private laws unless and until these laws were positively abrogated by the invading sovereign. However, a sovereign state could acquire new territory by occupation the territory was terra nullius – a territory belonging to no one. In a territory acquired by occupation the law of the settler became the law of the newly acquired territory and all property vested in the occupying state. Moreover, it had become accepted by the nineteenth century that terra nullius extended beyond territory that was genuinely uninhabited to territory that was 'practically uninhabited, without settled inhabitants or settled law' In other words, if a territory was occupied only by 'backward' people who could not be regarded as settled inhabitants or having a settled law, then their territory was regarded as terra nullius and so capable of being acquired by settlement or occupation rather than by conquest. When a sovereign state, such as the British Crown or another European colonial nation, acquired territory which was in this condition (i.e. occupied only by people who were taken to be 'backward' or 'barbarian' as was the case deemed in Milirrpum) this was treated in international law as an occupation or settlement of the territory, with the consequence that all indigenous inhabitants were not only treated as subject to the sovereignty of the acquiring state but also became governed solely by its laws – they were treated as having no pre-existing rights arising out of their own system of law.

# Property Economics

I. Externalities, Communal Property & externalities
II. Tragedy of the commons
III. Private Property & externalities
IV. Private Nuisance – who can sue? And who is protected?
V. Relevance of motive
VI. Market role in law of nuisance

Externalities & Communal property with externalities

An externality is an affect to a 3rd party which comes about as a result of an individual's actions. That individual doesn't feel the effects of his action but rather an external person feels them. Externalities can be both positive or negative; something I do can have both a positive or negative impact on a 3rd party. For example, if I light a fire in my garden, the neighbour, a 3rd party, will get the negative externality of the smoke affecting him which is a negative externality.

Demsetz has an argument that property is all about internalising externalities and by internalising them, we are able to consider them more & bring them further into the equation of understanding property. The way to internalise externalities was to make all property into that of private property. He explains this suggestion by highlighting that human nature is such that when we get benefit from something ourselves directly, we are much more likely to be concerned with everything relating to it, including that of externalities to the 3rd parties around us, be they positive or negative. Only as a private owner, does an individual really get the full impact of using a thing & be concerned with all aspects of his property.

The problem Demsetz finds is that with communal property, is that to get around negative externalities, the only real solution is to enter into negotiations. In the case of *Hunter v Canary Wharf* there was a suggestion that all homeowners who lost TV signals, should have initially entered into negotiations to get paid off by the contractors for the disturbance of their signal. The problem with this, is that negotiations are a very expensive & time-consuming activity, making it wholly inefficient to enter into negotiations for the negative externalities experienced in communal property. The problem specifically with this case, was also the idea that no one really knew what the externality on home owners would be up until they started working; the notion of imperfect information.

But really? Are negotiation costs really that deep? More often than not, there would actually be no reason to actually enter into negotiations, because certain principles are just widely accepted by humans, to respect the rights of the others, just like in the case of Milirrpum. There are quite simply, just some rights & obligations in communities which are just widely accepted & respected & an infringement is highly unlikely and thus negotiations are not required.

Communal property is deemed to be inefficient compared to private property because of the greater number of externalities involved with communal property.

Grunebaum goes on to talk about state property and the idea that by state sanction, there can be the overriding determination of how communal property should be used. The sole idea that state sanction can decide how communal property is used suggests that there is an acceptance even amongst the state, that communal property does indeed have more externalities than private property.

The problem about externalities, as far as economics is concerned, is that they tend to lead to misuse of resources, because the full costs and benefits of the use are not taken into account. The use of the resource may therefore be inefficient, in the sense that a different use or use in a different way might yield a higher aggregate value (i.e. the aggregate benefit to all minus the aggregate costs of all would be higher).

Tragedy of the commons

This leads to the debate of the tragedy of the commons which quintessentially involves a piece of common/communal land. Hardin, the developer of this tragedy, gives the example that on this piece of land, there are 10 farmers, each with 10 cattle. The optimum number of cattle on the land, is 100 cattle; meaning that in the current situation, the land is being used most efficiently. Any less or any more cattle would make the use of the land wholly inefficient & eventually lead to the complete destruction of the land.

The tragedy of the commons adopts the perception that one farmer, being a naturally greedy human being, will want to increase his wealth & thus works to increase his cattle, albeit by one. He, a rationally thinking man, thinks that with an increase in his cattle, he'll receive 10% more profit, whilst the 1% extra cattle on the land which results from him, will be a cost shared by all the farmers and not borne solely by him; so in a purely economic sense for him it makes sense for him to do that. But what he doesn't see is that every single other farmer would probably want to then do the same which would obviously mean that eventually, the whole land would be completely destroyed & KO'd! This is what Kohler connotes as "Schizophrenic herdsmen" – they can see that by wanting more cattle, they can increase their profit, but they cannot seem to see that every single other farmer would want to do the exact same thing. If they wanted to be rational humans, they would bring in rules to put things right in the first place & make sure that nothing can go wrong at all anyways because the rules will form a law if you like of what can & cannot be done with that piece of land.

But is this whole notion of the tragedy of the commons entirely correct?

If you look at Hardin's perception, what he's effectively saying is that it's quite impossible for communal land to survive, because of this tragedy. But if you begin to think historically, for centuries, if not millenniums, communal land has not only existed, but has worked so effectively. So surely Hardin must be exaggerating just a tiny bit. Furthermore, Hardin is writing at a time just prior to which farmers in America, on their private land, erected great dust balls; meaning they used land so much that it simply just became infertile & gave up. This was a private piece of land which was run into the ground; it was not communal property that was the cause of this collapse in the land. Additionally, if you look carefully, you'll see that in the tragedy of commons, Hardin is trying to prove his point that communal property is the problem. But if you look carefully at the example he gives, you can see he doesn't actually achieve what he sets out to do. If his analysis is accepted,

## The Foundations of Property Law

he is suggesting that the cattle being increased is the problem; but surely the cattle is privately owned & not communally owned. So, in this regard, private property is the problem, not communal property.

A community has communal property rights. And all communal property rights will show that there will always be rules to make sure that these things do not actually occur. Rules such as limited access rules are all communal resources have rules from the community or directly from the state to limit what can & cannot be done with that communal property. You do not have unlimited exclusive rights over the communal property rights even if you are a member of that community.

So in essence, Hardin's suggestion only works if there are no rules/norms/expectations set in the community & also there are no property rights in that land; so effectively you can do whatsoever you want to do with it, linking to the "no property regime" as explained by Cohen.

If looking back at Locke now, we see that Locke effectively considers the idea of how we move from communal property into private property because of his provisos; the sufficiency & spoliation provisos & it's clear that he isn't actually talking about land which is under the circumstance of 'no-property.' No property is the idea if how on a piece of land, we can do whatsoever we want with the resources which we are given. There is often the idea of no-property being linked to something which is infinity, such as was previously suggested for water & air which now have communal property rights rather than no property rights, which can be understood by seeing rules on pollution etc.

Private Property & externalities and The Law of Nuisance

Let's start with an example. I own a house & you own a house next door to me. I decide to be an absolute idiot & build a salt-mill in my back garden because I want to produce salt at home & sell it. I'm happy, I'm making salt, selling it & making a lot of money. But you as my neighbour, you're being hugely impacted. The noise, the smell, the left-over salt is all affecting your quality of life in your own home & you're getting really frustrated with me. You've asked me many times to stop, but I'm making way too much money to stop just for you. So, you now take me to court.

## The Foundations of Property Law

English law deals with this idea of infringement of rights with the Tort law of nuisance which we will indeed do in more detail during Tort Law but must understand briefly for Land law too. This law is all about ascertaining property rights in order to define what you can & cannot do with your property. The law of nuisance particularly deals with private nuisance even though historically, it did also deal with public nuisance too.

Public nuisance was a doctrine where detriment occurred to the public by large & so the common law would intervene to set things straight. This is no longer important as such, or rather relevant, because now days, with the increasing presence of a state legislature, they now tend to step in & legislate against large public nuisances to ensure a cohesive society.

The law of private nuisance is concerned with nuisances between land owners, under 3 key branches:

I. Encroachment - This is that idea where my something from my property merely goes into your property. For example, the roots or branches from the tree in my back garden, make their way into your garden

II. Damage – This is when something from my property not only goes into your land, but also does damage to your land/property. For example, a cricket ball from my property comes into your property & breaks a window. Or sticking with the tree example, the trees branches from my garden stretch over into your property & start damaging the tiles on your roof, or the roots of the tree start damaging the soil and ground in your garden. Something from my property is now causing real damage to your property/land.

III. Interference – This is where you make the life of your neighbour that much more difficult for them to live. They may refer to you as 'a bloody pain in the arse!' For example, with the salt-mill example from above, the noise and smell is interfering with their life & making their lives that much more difficult to live.

And a common feature with all 3 nuisances, is that they arise because of land ownership. If we own land, we will always do something which affects our neighbours, but not always us. And what the law of nuisance does, is

## The Foundations of Property Law

forces owners of private property to internalise the externalities because they're wholly aware of the fines and charges which one would be faced with if they are forced to be the subject of a court case.

So, who can actually sue in private nuisance?

There is a question which arises with regards to who can actually have the right to sue under the notion of private nuisance? Is it limited to someone who has property rights (a lease/freeholder) or could it extend to someone who has a licence too? Because surely both are affected in the same way in the sense that their freedoms are impacted on in an equal way.

In the *Hunter v Canary Wharf* [1997] case which I briefly described above, the judge said that the right to sue should extend to those beyond property owners & to licensees too because you suffer harm regardless of who you are. Markesinis & Deakin attacked Lord Goff by saying his decision was wrong, because if you consider what property rights actually are, only if you're a lease/freeholder of a property, can you have the right to bind 3rd parties and thus it's clear that licensees do not actually have the right to bind 3rd parties and thus the right to sue as such should not be applicable to them.

And so surely, as discussed above, is the argument of whether or not the best solution to such a problem would be to enter into negotiations where the 3rd party would simply give the property right holders a fee in order to compensate them for the interference in their lives. But the debate for this was done above.

So, who is protected under the law of nuisance?

*Bradford Corporation v Pickles* [1895] is a case concerned a landowner called Mr Pickles. Water flowing underneath his land would eventually find its way into reservoirs run by the Bradford Corporation, which supplied the town of Bradford with water. Pickles intercepted the water flowing underneath his land and stopped it flowing into the Bradford Corporation's waters. It is not clear why he did this (but I guess he did it for the banter ☺). Either he wanted to sell his land and he thought that cutting off the water flowing into the reservoirs would give the Bradford Corporation an incentive to buy his land or rather he wanted to get the Bradford Corporation to pay him a yearly fee for allowing water to flow under his land and into its reservoirs to act as ab easy bit of money for him. Either way, Pickles was hardly acting in a very public-spirited way when he did what he did. Bradford Corporation sued Pickles in tort. Their claim failed. Lord Ashbourne observed, 'Bradford Corporation have no case unless they can show that they are entitled to the flow of water in question...' Now, at the time Bradford Corporation v Pickles was decided the law on water rights said that if water flows in undefined channels underneath A's land and flows from there onto B's land, B has no right to receive any part of that water. As the water that flowed under Pickles' land flowed in undefined channels, Bradford Corporation had no right to receive any of the water flowing under Pickles' land. So, Pickles did not violate Bradford Corporation's rights when he intercepting the water flowing under his land. He therefore committed no tort in relation to Bradford Corporation by acting as he did. There is the suggestion that if the water had been taken from a defined stream, the common law would have instantly recognised that land as a piece of communal property such as they recognise riverbanks etc. And therefore, the water in the different channels would have been subject to communal property interests/regimes, which would've changed the judgement of the case.

Likewise, the same laws would not have applied for percolated water but as you can see in the *Stephens v Anglian Water Authority* [1987] case that it can indeed cause damage to a neighbour and the fact that it can cause damage is that one can be stopped from engaging in such an activity which involves damageable percolated water.

What is the role of motive in the Law of nuisance?

In the case of *Christie v Davey* [1893] there were 2 neighbours who lived next door to each other in terraced housing in Brixton. Now anyone who has lived in Brixton would know that the Victorian terraced housing in Brixton has extremely thin wells which means that Christie could hear the Davey's doing their music practical recitals & practice much more often that he wanted to; it was effectively all day & most problematic was that it'd be

## The Foundations of Property Law

at unsociable times too. Christie got a bit cheesed off so decided that he would start banging trays on his walls to annoy them too.

The case ended up in court & the courts looked at the motive of the 2 parties – the motive of Christie was to simply annoy them & make as much noise as he possibly could which thus led to the court determining it as actionable nuisance. On the other hand, the Davey's were not doing it on purpose; they were simply enjoying the freedoms of their house to enjoy the pleasures of their music which led to the courts being much more sympathetic towards them. Yes, they did place limits on how long they could practice, 11pm, but they were allowed to play whilst Christie was told to stop completely. Here, it is obvious & clear for all to see that it was surely motive which was the differentiating factor between the 2 parties.

In the *Hollywood Silver Fox Farm v Emmet* [1936] case, Emmet was annoyed that the fox cubs were coming onto his land and thus decided to start firing shotguns in order to make the foxes panic. It is a known fact that when they are disturbed, foxes tend to eat their young cubs & the Fox Farm filed for nuisance; Emmet had no intention to kill the cubs, but effectively knew that by shooting at them, they'd be forced to disperse.

These 2 cases, however, are different from the Canary Wharf case. Lord Cooke is said to be wrong in in his judgement to bring parallels of the cases. In these 2 case, both are asserting their existing property rights, such as that to not be disturbed by excessive noise disturbance. In Canary Wharf & Bradford, there are actually no property rights to be violated because no property rights had existed.

The market also plays a significant role in the law of nuisance. Coase has a theory which he explains using the example of 2 neighbours.

One neighbour has a small piece of land where he grows crops (a farmer) & the other has a large land where he raises cattle (a rancher.) With no fence, the cattle go onto the farmer's land & destroys the crops, causing damages of £1,500. Let's say that to build a fence around the small farm, would cost the farmer £500 whereas the building of the fence for the ranches, would cost £1,000. So, who should build the fence?

A rationale big farm owner would give £750 to the small farm owner to build a fence around his farm. This would mean he'd save £250 whilst the farmer would gain £250 for building the fence. But this is based on the presumption that the rancher is liable for damage caused by his cattle. If there is, however, no liability on the rancher, the farmer will simply have to build the fence for himself because if he does not, he stands to lose £1,500 worth of crops. The £500 spent, will be recovered because it becomes worth his while to spend that money to build the fence.

In both situations, the same person builds the fence. The first instance, the rancher pays the farmer to build it. An in the second, the law says that the farmer will suffer damage & thus he pays for the fence. This denotes that the building of the fence will be the burden of whom is more economically viable to do so; who economically is more in need of the fence being built. But legal entitlement also is viable but requires negotiations & agreements to be drawn up for the first instance & thus, as a whole, the second instance is the most efficient to do so.

However, one must also take into consideration the idea of distributional preferences. This is the idea that society as a whole may want to spend that money on other things that they would suggest would be beneficial for the community as a whole. Additionally, though economic & legal efficiency should be looked at, there should also be a consideration of what we think is morally correct; for example, the farmer paid for the fence, but morally most would agree that the rancher should've paid for the fence/built it.

# Property Economics Hypothetical

Hypothetical Example

Robbie owned a farm that was overrun by rats that came onto his land from a public canal via an adjoining field. In 2002, after years of unsuccessfully trying to exterminate the rats, he decided to open a rat hunting business in which members of the public were charged to come onto his land to hunt and shoot rats. The business was a great success and within months Robbie decided to abandon farming and devote all his energies to the new enterprise. In 2004 Elton bought the adjoining land as he was 'tired of metropolitan life' and 'craved the quiet of the country', building a mansion which, on completion, blocked Robbie's view of the canal. Because he was disturbed by the sound of shotguns and was a keen animal rights campaigner Elton built a barrier in his garden that prevented the rats 18 crossing onto Robbie's land. To save his business, Robbie installed a clay pigeon shoot providing his customers with an alternative target via clay pigeons that were fired into the air. Although no shots were ever fired over Elton's land, a clay pigeon did sometimes land on his land, occasionally hitting his mansion, whilst the sound of shooting disturbed Elton's afternoon siesta. In retaliation, and because he was concerned at the prospect of being hit by a wayward clay pigeon, Elton used a high-pressure water hose to intercept the clay pigeons on Robbie's land the moment they were fired into the air. In response, and because he still harboured a grudge after the value of his land was reduced when his view of the canal was obliterated, Robbie allowed a local newspaper photographer onto his land to take photos over the fence when Elton held a garden party attended by many of his famous friends from the metropolis.

The different rules

A Property Rule is the idea that you can get injunctions & get people to stop because this is built within the property itself; the right to exclude etc.

A Liability rule is the idea that you can get a certain amount of money (compensation) for the invasion based on liability!

Public nuisance is that nuisance that affects a class of people/a whole group of people. So, let's say for example that if I own a property, if buses going past my house affected the foundations of all houses in my road but particularly mine is a public nuisance

Private nuisance is the idea that an individual's/groups actions are affecting my individual property rights

## Answer to hypothetical

There are 6 things for which both parties could potentially claim for/against:

I. Rat barrier - Elton does have the right to put up the barrier with the right to exclude. Property rights are not absolute because if you did have it, you could then infringe on the rights of your neighbours etc. The rats are not actually a property right because Robbie does not own them as such. If Robbie wants those rats into his land, then he must negotiate with Elton on free market to take down that fence; the market will regulate. This assumes that there will be endless resources in the sense that we can value something but not actually have the financial backing to actually back it up or protect our rights accordingly.

II. Photographer (Privacy) - Taking of pictures of his property is an invasion of privacy in the sense that there was no consent given from Elton to Robbie to take pics, let alone allow photographers to take pictures! The camera itself may be taking pictures from over the fence in the sense that the camera may end up in the property of Elton.

Intention of Elton is to have a party, but intention of Robbie is to actually infringe on his privacy & to indirectly disturb the property rights of Elton.

Property right is to exclude the world & by Robbie allowing photographers to infringe on Elton's privacy, violates his basic property right.

Could also argue nuisance in the sense that they have, by taking pictures even once, made the lives of the Elton's that much more

## The Foundations of Property Law

        difficult on a mental level because privacy has been infringed on & they fear another invasion as such!

        But ultimately the onus of ensuring privacy, is the idea that it'll be Elton's requirement to build the fence is down to him because Robbie can do whatever he wants on his property in that way. It should be Elton who values his privacy to build a fence. Privacy is not a property right! So, if I was sat in my garden stark naked & my neighbour started taking pictures of me, the onus would be on me to build a higher fence to make it impossible for them to take pictures. If I don't value my privacy enough, I won't build a fence but if I do, I'll go to any cost to make sure I do albeit with negotiating with he who infringes on my privacy!

III.    Hose - Private nuisance & damage! Damages are liability rule, not a property Rule!

IV.    Noise - not infringement on property right

V.    Pigeons falling - draw parallels to Miller v Jackson in terms of the pigeons are basically the equivalent to the cricket balls; Elton has right to stop Robbie doing it & if he does not, then he has the right to get damages.

        Who gets the priority in terms of what is more important - should Elton be given priority to not be hit or should Robbie be given preference because of his economic link to the land? This would tie in with Locke & the economic link giving preference to Robbie then

VI.    View - British common law actually has no right to a view: you cannot claim if someone blocks your view! Everyone has a right to build but if I value it enough, I can pay someone enough money to stop then ppm building. My value of that view will be so high, I will be happy to pay x amount. But then I have to have those infinite resources to be able to then externalise that value in the sense that I can financially make sure my value is upheld.

Put simply, the economic theory is all about the idea of how much you value your right; if it is a property right, then even if you don't value it much, you'll still have it upheld. If it's a liability right/rule, then your value will determine whether or not it'll be infringed upon or not. If you value it so highly, you will go to any cost to ensure that your right is upheld but there'll reach a stage where your economic position is such that it is no longer viable for you to attempt to uphold your rights & you will give in. But before giving in, you will negotiate with the person infringing on your rights to claim liability for the damage they are causing you.

If you get a nuisance question in exam, then it is quite simply down to the economic theory - the rules etc. If you know the rules, then it is quite simple to answer!

# Property & Common Law

   I. Ambit of Private Property
   II. Classification of Property Interests
   III. Definition of land 3 dimensions
   IV. Doctrine of estates – 4$^{th}$ dimension
   V. Rules against perpetuities

The Ambit of Private Property

Private property is split between two key rights:

   I. Rights in Rem – these are those rights which an individual has in a thing; i.e., in the case of property, as an owner, the main right you have in a thing is the right to exclude the rest of the world from your property. Rights against the world, however, are not limited to just talking about the exclusion of everyone else from your land. Rather, it also includes your rights against the world to not suffer at anyone's hands; human rights are in essence a right in rem.
   II. Rights in Personam – This is the rights you have against an individual, i.e., contractual rights which you have. For instance, if I employ you to clean my shoes (no that's a bit rude lemme change it....) If I employ you to type my notes for me, I have a right to ensure that you complete your contractual obligation & type my notes for me. Basically, they are rights which were enforceable against certain categories of person, because it was considered to be fair or equitable that they should take subject to them. There are 2 types of contractual rights which are:
      a. Benefit of contract – This is a type of contract for which the right can be transferred. The rights in personam can be transferred from one individual/company to another. This is commonly seen in cases where mobile phone operators such as EE, Vodafone, O2 etc. when owed large amounts of money by a customer, can transfer their contract of being owed money to a professional debt collector. The reason they do this, is because it is more cost effective for them to do so because a debt collector is much more sophisticated

& thus likely to get the money from you! Effectively, the operator will sell the debt to the company for a lower price than the debt actually is who will then start to chase you up for their money!

b. Burden of contract – This is those contracts for which the burden cannot be transferred. So, for example, if I owe you £10,000, I might attempt to sell my debt/transfer my debt to a drunk man (or woman, no sexism here) under a bridge. So, I would sell it to them for something far less significant, like a crate of Alcohol or something & he'll take the burden on because he knows that no one will sue him. This isn't allowed because quite simply, it'll lead to a violation of the whole law of contracts & the burdens of contract & thus transfers are not allowed.

That being said however, there are some further limitations on private property that go beyond just the not existence of transfers in burdens of contract.

The most obvious & common of limitations on private property is that of the state; the state will always limit what we are able to do with our private property. For instance, when you own a car, even though it's your private property, the state imposes limits on how fast you can drive that car, where you can drive that car, how many people you can seat in your car, the manner in which you drive that car etc. Likewise, you can own a house which is the essence of private property, but the state can impose limits on what you can build on your land such as the problems with planning permissions etc.

The Law of perpetuities is essentially concerned with placing limits on what we can do with our property once we are dead. With the laws of land, we often see a conversation arise between generations. For instance, the land owned by the monarch is passed down every single generation such that a monarch will always be the owner of that land! The rule works such that if there is any possibility of gift vesting outside a perpetuity period, that gift becomes void. The period is 21 years; means that any gift which in the worst-case scenario can extend to beyond 21 years, will be deemed as void.

For example, if Professor Heller leaves behind black acre (imaginary piece of land) for any one of his 4 daughters who becomes a barrister, this would most likely be valid. However, let us assume that all 4 of his daughters pass away but his wife gives birth to another daughter who is born after the gift was made, If Professor Kohler dies but the daughter still becomes a barrister, the fact of the matter is that it'll be beyond the 21-year period which the gift would've been valid & thus the gift would indeed be void.

However, if this gift was made in his will by Professor Gangat, then it would've been valid regardless of the 21-year period; this is known as a post-mortem gift. This has been exempted since 2010 due to the *Perpetuities & Accumulation Act 2009.* The Inter-vivos gift which was described above is subject to the law of perpetuities, but post-mortem gifts are not.

As a result of the Perpetuities & Accumulation Act 2009, the 21-year period is no longer valid. Rather now, any agreement made after the 6th of April 2010, will be the subject of a 125-year period whilst any made before that date will have the benefit of a slightly shorter 100-year period.

Classification of property interests

Real property = land

This is then of two further types:

I. Corporeal hereditaments – This is tangible rights such as buildings on land, the land itself, crops growing on a piece of land etc.
II. Incorporeal hereditaments – This is intangible rights one has on a piece of land, such as the right of way, issuing covenants to that land, mortgages etc. Debt is also attached to land such that if someone buys a piece of land, they buy the benefits & harms of that land too meaning you buy the rights & obligations of a land when purchasing it. Trusts are the biggest type of incorporeal hereditaments which we look at later on in the term.

Personal property = non-land

This is also of two further types:

# The Foundations of Property Law

I. Chattels Real – This is leases one has over a piece of land. Historically, this category wasn't included in the real property category, because the definition of real property was where land could actually be seized & leases did not incorporate that.

II. Chattels Personal has two main factors:
   a. Choses in possession – These are tangible things; this is linked in with the right to take something/possess something so that you can sue someone using it.
   b. Choses in Action – These are intangible things such as the benefits of a contract etc.

There are a number of problems which come about as a result of these classifications. The most obvious one that stands out instantly is the idea that property, by definition, is the right to exclude the world, is an intangible thing in essence, but in the laws of land, it is deemed as a tangible thing.

As mentioned above too, leases are in the wrong category too.

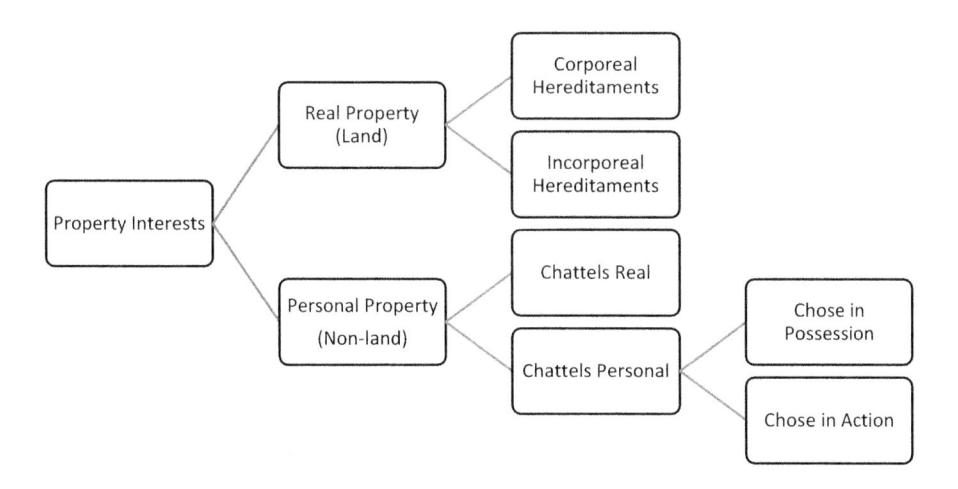

```
Property Interests
├── Real Property (Land)
│   ├── Corporeal Hereditaments
│   └── Incorporeal Hereditaments
└── Personal Property (Non-land)
    ├── Chattels Real
    └── Chattels Personal
        ├── Chose in Possession
        └── Chose in Action
```

## The Foundations of Property Law

### Doctrine of lands 3 dimensions

Land is deemed to have 3 dimensions (or is it???), which are:

I. 1st Dimension – Boundaries are not taken as correct; they are there to indicate the size of plots but not there to conclusively define/determine land registry. To actually work out the real boundaries, one must use other evidence such as topography etc. Basically, the notion of Height x Width x Depth of land

II. 2nd Dimension – Alluvion & Delvion is in essence the idea that land can be different from what it initially used to be meaning that land area increases & decreases from initial markings

III. 3rd dimension – This is the idea that we do not own the space above or below our property; you do not, as a property owner, own the land to heaven not to hell. This was signified by the *Bernstein v Skyviews [1978]* case where the owner objected to a plane flying over his land & taking pictures of his land. He in essence, has no right to stop planes flying over his land, because you do not own the airspace above your land so the objection to the flying is pointless. If you could own the airspace above your property it'd be ridiculous!

### Doctrine of the 4th dimension – Estates

Einstein's (I promise this is property, not science) 4th dimension is time. And this is very relevant in regard to land ownership because if you consider it carefully, though the land may change a crazy amount over time, the land in itself is indestructible because the land itself will always be on the face of the Earth in one shape or another.

And estates allow us to carve the future use of the land; it is an abstract concept whereby we can carve out how the land will be used in the future. This becomes possible in line with the Statutory definition of land as per the Land & Property Act 1925 s.205 (4), *"Land' includes land of any tenure, and mines and minerals, whether or not held apart from the surface, buildings or parts of buildings (whether the division is horizontal, vertical or made in any other way) and other corporeal hereditaments; also a manor, an advowson, and a rent and other incorporeal hereditaments, and an easement, right, privilege, or benefit in, over, or derived from land;... and "mines and minerals" include any strata or seam of minerals or substances in or under any land, and powers of working and getting the same . . .; and "manor" includes a lordship, and reputed manor or lordship; and "hereditament" means any real property which on an intestacy occurring before the commencement of this Act might have devolved upon an heir."*

What this in essence is saying is what we discussed in limitations to property & what we discussed when we spoke about how the Crown/State is the ultimate owner of all land. William the Conqueror in 1066 stated that all land is owned by the state & that pieces of land were passed down to lords etc. and let out to subjects on various types of holding ('tenures') which required the holder to perform services for the Crown in exchange for enjoyment of the land, each type of tenure requiring a different type of service. A holder of a tenure from the Crown could then 'subinfeudate' (in effect, sublet, although modern lease terminology is best avoided here). This would mean that the right to enjoy the land would be sub-contracted to someone else, for a different (or even the same) type of tenure, in return for services to be performed by the sub-holder to the original holder, and the sub-holder could then himself sub-subinfeudate to someone else. Consequently, a pyramid of tenures could build up, so that, in respect of any given piece of land, there would be one person who held directly from the Crown, delivering the appropriate services, and then a chain of sub- and sub-sub-holders, each sub-contracting rights of enjoyment in exchange for services, down to the person who actually had physical use of the land.

The pyramid that forms as a result brings about the doctrine of tenure. The fact of the matter is that all land is indeed ultimately owned by the state; this is the old cliché in English law that all land is owned by the crown & no one else can be the ultimate owner of a piece of land.

<u>System of Estates</u>

An estate is described as an 'interposed abstraction' which suggests that the state is lie an intangible being which stands between a tangible owner & a tangible piece of land. There are 2 main forms of estates which we will consider & remember, estates are linked with the 4th dimension of land; time.

    I.    Fee-simple estate – the is the idea that the right over a piece of land lasts with the owner forever & can only come to an end when an individual no longer has any heirs & as a result, the land is returned to the state.

    II.    Leases are also an estate because it adheres to the doctrine of fixed tenures/terms as discussed previously. Because it is concerned with time & that the period for which land is owned is defined, makes it an estate!

# Property Title & Possession

  I.   Title
 II.   Possession as a root of title
III.   The Law of Finding
 IV.   Law of Fixtures

Title

When attempting to understand the meaning of title, it is important to first be able to distinguish between title & interest because they constitute rather confusing terminology.

An interest in a thing is the quantum rights one must have in a thing, such as an estate or fee-simple which are effectively the rights to possess the land (forever). This links in with what we did the previous topic when we looked at estates how they are basically interests in land. Some of these can be lessor interests or interests which are for the rest of the world, such as right of way etc. which incorporate a 3$^{rd}$ party's interests on someone else's land. Some of the examples which we covered the previous topic whilst looking at incorporeal hereditaments such as covenants, mortgages etc. So effectively, in a broad sense, an interest is a quantum amount of rights we can have in a piece of land.

So why is there a need to differentiate between land & non-land in all ideas of title & interest? The basic & simple answer is that land will not perish as such; it is a permanent fixture of the Earth & as a result of its durability, it makes land a very complex issue to resolve. And there is actually a need for land to be a complex issue. This is because land is immobile and limited in the sense that it is a complex array of interests/estates whereby we can make use of the land efficiently. Without this array of interests, we cannot have used the land efficiently. For example, my land is on one end & the route to the main road is via your land. This means, that I have to go through your land in order to get to the main road to allow me to go about my business. I have an interest in your land by means of right of way & I am in need of land law to allow me to use your land in this way lawfully. Land is

## The Foundations of Property Law

fixed in its place & rights such as right of way allow me to go from one place to another to go about my business.

Title, however, refers to the strength of your interest; the idea that 2 or more people may have title to the same interest; ownership & possessing/possessory titles as is the case in a lessor/lessee agreement. 2 or more people may have title to the same interest in both land & non-land.

So how do you acquire title? There are 2 main ways in which title can be derived:

I. Derivative Acquisition:
   a. Disposition of an entire interest – This is when you buy a title/interest from a person who already has title to that land. This can be through means of purchasing that interest/title from them or they can merely transfer it to you by way of a gift
   b. Grant of a lesser interest – This can be through either a lease, sub-lease, life estate, easement, mortgage; meaning an owner of a piece of estate/land can turn around & give up some of their rights to you & thus you would have

II. Original Acquisition:
   a. Become first private owner – In the case we looked at a couple of topics ago & also in the case of *Bradford Corporation V Pickles* was the idea that no one actually owned the water as such & then the Corporation then claimed title to that water which allowed them to use the water as they willed. Effectively, what they did, was be the first owners of a piece of land. This can actually not only be limited to private property, but also to certain circumstances of communal property too. This can be explained with the idea that we as members of a community can take a communal resource & upon taking that resource, it becomes private property. For example, allowing your cattle to graze in the alpine meadows is you taking from a communal resource in order to help sustain your private sustenance & thus you're taking it into your

private property. This ties in very well with the ideas of Locke which we covered all the way back at the beginning of the book, where we considered adding labour to anything in nature makes it yours.

You are also the first private owner of your intellectual property which we don't really look at much at all in this course, but simply, when you copyright, patent or trademark your intellectual property, you become the first owner of it.

b. Exceptions to nemo Dat – The basic rule of Nemo Date says that you cannot give a better title than the one which you have. For example, if I steal a car & I sell it to you, the basic rule states that you cannot get a 'good' title from me because I don't have/possess a good title to transfer to you. This is what we looked at when we considered the case of *Bruten v London Quadrant Housing* [1999] who granted a sub-licence but was deemed by the courts to actually be a lease which means that London Quadrant Housing, who had a licence themselves could not grant a lease because they didn't have the good title themselves to give it. But then, there are exceptions to this basic rule & all of this will be deemed to be cases of original acquisition.

    i. Even though it is now abolished, there used to be an exception Market Overt. This is the idea that money could be earn from markets, wherein it was allowed for the sale of goods to get a good title even though the seller may not have had a good title because they had stolen the good, they were selling. But because as a buyer, you were acting in good faith, you could be deemed as the rightful owner of that good which was sold to you.

    ii. The Sale of Goods Act 1979 under Section 21 & sub-sections 23-26 build on this and suggest that a good faith purchaser can acquire title from someone with apparent authority to sell even though in

## The Foundations of Property Law

        reality, they may not actually have that good title to sell in the first place.

    iii.  Money is also an exception to the Nemo Dat rule which was established after the *Miller v Race [1758]* case where if you give value in return for money, you would get a good title in that money so long as you as the seller were acting in good faith. For example, if I was selling my car, which I value and you choose to buy my car with money that was stolen, as long as I acted in good faith & didn't know that the money was stolen, then I would get title to that money. This is because money is critical to the functioning of our society & the fear that engaging in excruciating checks on the legality & honesty of money would lead to inefficiency. The fact is that the checking of the provenance of money would be really difficult & also waste a lot of time.

    iv.  Equity's darling – we look at this in the coming chapters.

  c.  Taking Possession of an owned thing; take possession of something that someone already has possession of – this is the concept of Adverse Possession which is looked at in the following chapter.

### The Law of Finding

This is the idea of who has a better title to claim a property when an owner cannot be found. Usually, this constitutes a battle between a finder of a piece of property/land & an owner, however, in the case of *Parker v British Airways Board [1982]* this was in fact a battle between which arose between a finder of a piece of property which belonged neither to Parker nor British Airways, but to a 3$^{rd}$ party, yet the court case was wholly concerned with, as is the case in the UK Common Law system, the owner of the better, not best, title. What happened in this case, was that British Airways were the leasing a piece of land in an Airport Terminal. In this terminal space, Parker found a very valuable Golden bracelet which he then returned to a British

# The Foundations of Property Law

Airways member of staff saying that "listen mate, this is my name, this is where I live & so, if no one comes forward to claim this as their own property, I want you to send it to my yard for me please. Cheers mate." However, when no one claimed the bracelet, British Airways sold it on for £850 (around at least £5,000 worth today) but Parker was like yooooo, I staked a claim to it first, it's mine!

In order to find out who did have the better title, the court in the Parker case (the Court of Appeal) came up with 2 tests which they incited to determine the title holder based on the fixture of the property to the land:

I. If it is attached to or is inside the land, the property belongs to the occupier – lead judge of the Parker Case suggests that if something is on the land, it belongs to the occupier of that land. However, this observation/test is highly controversial and simplistic. Consider what we looked at the previous topic & how complex the law on fixtures is – how do you actually define as someone being inside the land/being fixed to the land. Furthermore, this is wrong because fair enough in the case of Parker the actual owner was not present, but if the owner was present, regardless of how fixed something becomes to a land, if the owner returns to claim it, it'll be their property regardless (with time constraints considered of course!)

II. If it is merely on the land, it belongs to the finder unless the owner manifests an intent to control it first – this is the notion which comes about from the bracelet in Parker, where the finder has a better title (not the best title) than the owner of the land so long as the owner did not actually manifest an intention to control the premises as such. This comes about from both arguing the idea that they were in possession first & to this, Donaldson says that when something is not attached to the land as a fixture is attached, it is the property of the finder.

Plus, in the judgement, there is no clear distinction on how to decipher between a lease holder & a licence holder alongside a tenant; if something is found on a piece of land whilst in the possession of a lease/licence holder, who owns it? Would it be them or the actual ultimate property owner? And what if an external finder finds something on a property under lease or licence; who would own it then? Finder, tenant or landlord? These are all potential disputes which could arise due to incomplete nature of the Parker case judgement & the tests which I feel are rather inadequately simplistic.

Law of fixtures

This is the notion of a chattel/a piece of personal property becomes attached to the land & as a result of the attachment, it becomes an actual part of the land. The *Holland v Hodgson [1872]* case & Blackburn J's judgement suggests that there come 2 tests for us to determine fixture & see if something has become a fixture:

I. The degree of annexation – This is when you consider how attached something is to a piece of land – primary test.
II. The purpose of annexation – You here see why something became attached to the piece of land & this is the doctrine which is deemed to be more important because the reason for which something becomes attached to the land is more important when determining if something is a fixture or not – secondary test.

Quite simply, the presumption is that if something is not fixed adequately to the land, it is quite simply not a fixture! But if the purpose is argued of wat was on the land such as architectural setting or determining how that piece of land was set out. If it can be proven that something is a fixture, then it can be deemed a fixture so long as it can be proven to be fixed.

# Adverse Possession

I. What is Adverse Possession?
II. Limitations of Action – Unregistered Land
III. Limitations of Action – Registered Land
IV. Establishing Adverse Possession

What is Adverse Possession?

Adverse Possession is concerned with the taking of possession of a piece of property without the permission of the owner/rightful and legal possessor; you have taken possession of the property adversely to the permission of the owner. When adversely possession, you are effectively there illegally, but the owner has not initiated any proceedings to try & remove you from their property.

In the case of *Manchester Airport v Dutton* [1999], the licensee was deemed that they did not have possession and thus they could not assert 3rd party binding, but if they had been in possession of a lease, then they would have been able to fight against a 3rd party. However, English Law protects possession. So, for instance, if I pick up your phone, my possession means that I'm protected against the rest of the wold except the rightful owner, who is the only person to have a better title than me. The reason possession is protected, is because quite simply, if it was not protected, there would constantly be a state of anarchy where the strongest would prevail (look back at my Christmas presents example) which would look to chaos & the whole notion of ownership would be in disarray. Therefore, if you are in possession of something, the law will respect you for being in possession; there will be someone who has a stronger title than you & only they have the right to take back possession from you (looked at in a bit more detail below.)

English Law focuses on who has the better title between A & B rather than who has the best title in the whole world. This is because, the civil law, as our judges are not involved in the actual investigation and thus they are simply deciding who has a better title between A & B; there may be a person C who has a better title than both in reality, but as they may not be in court, the judges may not be aware of this 3rd person & thus cannot declare who has the best title but rather only who has the better title between A & B. So therefore, possession is actually a good root to title; not the best route to a title but most certainly one that works very well. If someone can prove a better title, they will get possession such as an owner, or even previous owner, but they must do so in a specified time frame.

Limitations of Actions – Unregistered Land

For possessions, you only have a certain amount of time to claim your title – if you sleep on your rights, your rights can be lost as per the Limitations Act 1980. It is **vital** to remember that all this applies to only unregistered land & not registered land which we look at below.

The time period for one to claim title is:

I. Land = 12 years (stated in Section 15 in the Limitations Act 1980) which begins that the period begins the moment the adverse possessor starts possessing & it is stated in Section 17 that rights disappear after this 12-year period such that this previous owner becomes nothing more than a 'paper owner.'

II. Non-land = 6 years which means that the period starts once the possessor is liable for conversion (a tort) which basically means that you start using the thing when it is not actually yours. For both, with regards to a thief, time does not start at all; title will never be extinguished.

The reason we have these time limits is because of the underlying fact that evidence deteriorates over time. Some of the evidence that might be lost can form to be the factual evidence needed to prove one's ownership & the loss of evidence over time can be the evidence because of which the case can be won or lost. Adverse possession may well appear to connote title by theft or robbery; a primitive method of acquiring land without actually paying for it.

But ultimately, the fact of the matter is that any flaw in one's title will eventually come back to haunt you. And without statutory limitations, such as adverse possession protections, your title is protected for a period of time. This is best signified by the example of squatters & deciding who has a legal title:

- Squatter 1 dispossesses Owner in 2001
- Squatter 2 dispossesses Squatter 1 in 2003
- Squatter 3 dispossesses Squatter 2 in 2005

With this, the outcomes are as follows:

- Owner has no legal title because 15 years have passed since they were displaced & this is more than the 12-year period
- S1 also has no legal title either because 13 years have passed with no claim being made
- S2 does have legal title because only 11 years have passed
- S3 also has a legal title BUT S2 has a bigger/better legal title than S3 because S2 has had a title for a longer period than S3 & thus as they are the 'older' owner, they have a bigger right to the land than S3. His cause of action is still valid.

<u>Limitations of Actions – Registered Land</u>

In unregistered land, for adverse possession, the conditions which had to be fulfilled for adverse possession to be claimed were:

I. An intent to possess
II. Factual possession
III. Possession must be adverse
IV. 12-year adverse possession period

If land is registered under the LRA 1925, then the exact same 12-year rules apply as with unregistered land. However, the limitation for these old rules is that the period ought to have expired before the 13th of October 2003 because the rules of the game changed after this as per the Land Registration Act 2002.

Under the LRA 2002, the fundamental 3 points mentioned above remain the same. However, the time period differs. This roots from **Schedule 6 of the LRA 2002** which states the rules as of today. An Adverse Possessor who has been in adverse possession for 10 years has to make an application to the registrar asking to make him the legal title holder/owner of the property. So first the registrar will check to validate that he has indeed been an adverse possessor for 10 years as per all the criterion above & if he passes these tests, the owner is given 65 days (yeah idk why it's so specifically 65 days either I'm ngl to you) but if he fails to reply in these 65 days, then the adverse possessor will get the legal title. If he responds & is okay for the adverse possessor to have title, then he will get that title.

However, in the majority of cases, he will respond with an objection & thus he will then have a period of 2 years to recover possession of his registered property. If the Adverse possessor doesn't come under any of the categories mentioned in **Para 5 of Schedule 6 of the LRA 2002** then the owner will have 2 years to commence proceedings to get possession back. If after 2 years the owner hasn't commenced proceedings, then the adverse possessor will have to go to the registrar again to get title & this time he will indeed be given title.

Establishing Adverse Possession

I. Factual Possession – this is the idea that you must be possessing land in a way that the owner will be expected to own that land. This was noted by Lord Slade LJ in the *Powell v McFarlane [1979]* case, where he stated, *"Factual possession signifies an appropriate degree of physical control. It must be a single and [exclusive] possession, though there can be a single possession exercised by or on behalf of several persons jointly. Thus, an owner of land and a person intruding on that land without his consent cannot both be in possession of the land at the same time. The question of what acts constitute a sufficient degree of exclusive physical control must depend on the circumstances, in particular the nature of the land and the manner in which land of that nature is commonly used or enjoyed.[...] Everything must depend on the particular circumstances, but broadly, I think what must be shown as constituting factual possession is that the alleged possessor has been dealing with the land in question as an occupying owner might have been expected to deal with it and that no-one else has done so."* Effectively, possession must be open, adverse but if there is an acceptance/willingness from the squatter/adverse possessor to take a lease/licence, then even if the owner refuses to give it, the willingness cannot constitute to make the adverse possession invalid.

II. Intent to Possess land (not own) – Therefore, it is not fatal to claim that you acknowledge that you are the owner & acknowledge that owner has a better title but if your possession is adverse over the owner, such as is the case with the lease, the clock will stop working. This was cited in the case of *Pye v Graham [2003]* "*Intention, in one's own name and on one's own behalf, to exclude the world at large, including the owner with the paper title if he be not himself the possessor, so far as is reasonably practicable and so far as the processes of the law will allow.*"

III. Possession must be adverse – This means that you must possess contrary to the owner's (the to-be paper owners) permission. However, this can also be implied & not always explicit. If the owner comes along & was happy to see you at his land, then you can suggest that fact is, he has given you a licence (to squatter) – nothing was said but just by not saying anything, it implies that the owner isn't against your being there; thus adverse possession title was not existent.

Possession can be gained in 2 ways:

I. Dispossession – Your forced them out & took possession of that property
II. Discontinuance – They stopped owning that property

Just as a side note, it is very important to know with regards to this, that in English Common Law, there is no such thing as implied consent. This means that you cannot turn around & having been dispossessed, say that you had implied your consent for the adverse possessor to be there which in essence is you trying to say that they were there legitimately & not illegally/adversely.

# Leases and Licences

   I. The Importance of Leaseholds
   II. The requirements of a Lease
   III. Distinction between Leases & Licences

The Importance of Leaseholds

According to Section 1(1) of the Law of Property Act 1925, which is the most significant piece of legislation historically for the development of Land Law, as of the 1st of January 1926, legal estates in land can only exist in one of two ways:

   I. The fee simple in absolute possession – this is what is more commonly known as a Freehold interest in the land.
   II. The terms of years absolute – this is what is more commonly known as a Leasehold interest in the land.

This clearly means, that in order to receive proper legal protections for any estate in land which you own, you are required to have either a freehold or leasehold. Without either of them, you may struggle to protect your legal rights, which would... bind the world! But put simply, your leasehold serves as a very good form of protection for a property interest, which you may not be able to purchase the freehold for, because you can't afford to buy it outright.

The Requirements of a lease

There are 2 requirements (not 3!) for a lease:

   I. Exclusive Possession – this is a legal term which embodies the idea that if you have a lease, you have the right to exclude the whole world from your property, and most significantly, the landlord too. You can allow entrance to anyone you wish, but at the same time, also refuse entry to anyone who you wish to refuse entry to.
   II. Certainty of term – A lease must have a certain duration for it to last, be it a certain number of days, months; there is absolutely no limit on how long or short a lease must be – this can be a period

which is continuous or discontinuous meaning that the term can be set for days on end or for days at a time. This comes to light from the *Smallwood v Sheppards [1895]* case where the lease of a fairground sites for three successive bank holidays in a year was deemed to be valid by the Queens Benches whilst in the *Cottage Holiday Associates Ltd. V Customs & Excise [1983]* case the agreement for the occupant to have a lease possession of a holiday cottage on a time-share agreement whereby in Cornwall they took possession of a property for one week a year for 80 years was declared as being a valid lease; this you have to remember is discontinuous such that it is a lease of a single week comprised of 80 discontinuous weeks. In the case we refer to time and again *Prudential Assurance Co. Ltd v LRB [1992]*, the House of Lords held that a certainty of term/duration means that both parties must know from the very outset the earliest date on which the commitment on the side of either party can be brought to an end. The end date must be known.

The 3rd requirement which many mistakes to be a requirement, but actually isn't is rent. It is often indicative of a lease but there is no legal requirement for a lease to entail rent for it to be legitimate. This can be taken directly from the Law of Property Act 1925 in Section 205, where it is explicitly stated that there can be a lease without rent, *"Term of years absolute' means a term of years (taking effect either in possession or in reversion whether or not at a rent)."* This is also exemplified by the *Ashburn Anstalt v Arnold [1989]* case where LJ Fox held that rent was not necessary to create a tenancy and that the occupation agreement was certain enough to deem the agreement as a lease, and it was thus an overriding interest, as they were in actual occupation of the property.

However, that being said, it is the law which is responsible in determining what kind of an agreement two parties have entered into. This is because of the *Street V Mountford [1985]* case where there were attempts by landlords at this time to create agreements which would not be deemed as leases in an attempt to remove exclusive possession and to thus not make the agreement liable to the Rent Act 1977 which protects leaseholders from evictions. So, for instance, there would be stipulations thrown in such as sending in cleaners once or twice a week from the landlord; this removes exclusive possession because the landlord, not the tenant is stipulating who can & can't come into the house. In this case, Mr Street granted to Miss Mountford a right to occupy rooms. The parties entered into a written agreement which described the arrangement throughout as a 'licence' and called the agreed payment a 'licence fee.' Mr Street also reserved the right to enter at any time for any reasonable purpose. The House of Lords held that this was *in substance* a tenancy, rather than a licence. Lord Templeman said that Mr Street's express reservation of a right to enter only served to emphasise the fact that Miss Mountford was entitled to exclusive possession and was therefore a tenant.

Therefore, in order to determine what kind of an agreement it is (lease or licence), Wilberforce suggests that 3 things must be looked into when considering this:

I. The Terms – what clauses were inserted & were those clauses actually carried out?
II. Purpose – Why was that clause inserted? And for what reasons was the agreement reached
III. Circumstance – Was it a business transaction, a family agreement or one based on friendship

The reasons for this, is because in a lease, the leaseholder has exclusive possession, but in a licence, the licensee is not granted exclusive possession, as in the right to exclude the world from your property. However, in the case of *Manchester Airport v Dutton [2000]* the House of Lords said that the licensee does not have the right to sue a 3$^{rd}$ party because the purpose of a licence is that it cannot bind a 3$^{rd}$ party; that's the simple definition of a licence! Being able to sue a 3$^{rd}$ party would mean that it' have to be a lease!

However, exclusive possession can be granted in return for rent, which is known as a Periodic Tenancy, of which the 2 requirements for a periodic tenancy are exclusive possession & rent. So, for a short period of time, there is a continuous rent which has to be paid. These are not a series of separate leases each period that a rent is due, but rather it is a lease which is slowly elongated over time. The notice period to leave that agreement/periodic tenancy is one period, such that a weekly tenancy periods notice is a week, a monthly period is a month but in a yearly tenancy period, the notice is 6 months. Periodic tenancies were not recognised by the courts until 1702 by which time it had become quite common in practice to give out periodic tenancies as a means of giving tenants a lesser interest than a tenancy under a proper lease.

The way a periodic tenancy comes about is through 2 ways & can be brought to an end by either the tenant or the landlord:

I. Expressly – one expresses clearly that they intend to enter into that kind of an agreement
II. Inference – this is when in a period of failed attempts to create a lease due to, for example, the lack of a certainty of term. So for example, in the case of *Lace v Chantler [1944]* where the agreement was that the lease would be valid to the end of the war, the courts struck down the lease as void & the way to get around it was to simply enter into a periodic tenancy that would simply end when the war came to an end. Parliament actually legislated through the Validation of War Time Leases Act 1944 to say that all leases of this type were converted into 10-year leases which could be ended early.

This is because there is a condition of leases that there must be a certainty of term, but this is merely a technical requirement that any half decent lawyer can get around! And this then raises the question that why on earth do we actually need the certainty of term?

One suggestion is that parties need to know the maximum commitment of their agreement, but this raises the question that what actually is the difference between a lease of a million years & the end of the war. Both make clear the maximum period, albeit the end of the war agreement cannot be pinpointed as an exact time as such. This has been pointed out in the *Prudential v LRB [1992]* case where even though the decision of the court was to uphold the importance of certainty of term, 4 of the 5 judges sat on the case where sceptical with the decision they made; they all agreed

The Foundations of Property Law

with the one judge such that the House of Lords held that it means that both parties must know from the outset the earliest date on which their commitment under the lease can be brought to an end – or, as the House of Lords put it, the maximum duration of their liability under the lease.

The case is in regard to an individual who owned a piece of land & the council wanted to expand a road, for which they needed to buy the land from the owner. The council brought the land & then leased it back to the previous owner, with the stipulation 'until the land is needed back to expand the road.' This is an agreement which makes sense for both parties because the council has the land for whenever they need it & the tenant still gets to use his land for a period of time & to reap benefit from it. The lease was however, deemed void because of uncertainty of the term. This is because the judge which all the remaining judges followed, Templeman, was assured that the lease was void due to uncertainty of term. Yes, he did agree that there was a periodic tenancy, but the lease was a void one.

The reason for his adamant stance is because as a QC, he lost a case 20 years previously as a result of the uncertainty of term principle. This haunted him! So, he decided to now after 20 years get his own back at losing the case (Midland Railway case) This judgement in particular seemed to uphold the law as per *Lace v Chantler [1944]* in which it was held that an agreement for a lease for the duration of the war was an uncertain one and thus did not create a good leasehold interest.

It is clear & obvious to all that the majority in the House of Lords in Prudential expressed distaste for the complex rule and opted for it only in order to avoid upsetting long-established property relationships. The minority gave it more positive support. Part of their motivation appears to have been a desire to produce a formulation of the rule that accommodates not only fixed-term leases but also periodic tenancies, tenancies at will and tenancies at sufferance. The complex rule achieves this, although it is not wholly clear why such uniformity is thought necessary. In addition to this, however, those positively in favour of the rigid, complex rule also clearly considered that the general, flexible rule was inherently objectionable.

## The Foundations of Property Law

However, the Supreme Court under the *Berrisford v Mexfield [2011]* case determined a way to overturn the ruling from Prudential to act as an escape route. They embraced a trick in order to get around the prudential decision. The Supreme Court established 2 legal fictions which allowed for this trick to be applied.

I. Common Law fiction – this is the notion that prior to 1926, leases for uncertain terms
II. Statutory fiction was such that leases for life, were granted such that in 1925, these leases were automatically reverted into 90-year leases.

Put these 2 fictions together & you come to a suggestion that Mrs Berrisford's void lease can actually be turned into a 90-year lease.

The problem with this is exactly what the benefit of it is; it's drawn from 2 fictions. And this also raises two problems:

I. If the tenant is a company rather than a human being, the lease for life approach cannot work, because a company can & usually does outlast a human life
II. This only works if rent is being paid

Distinction between leases & licences

A couple of key terms to keep in mind when discussing leases:

- The lease giver = Landlord or Lessor. They are in possession of the freehold.
- The lease taker = Tennant or Lessee. They are in possession of the leasehold.

Both have property rights over the single piece of land!

Put very simply, in very simple and basic terms, a lease is a legal right to enjoy a piece of property as the exclusive possessor. During this period, it is as though you are the owner of the land and no one, not even your landlord, has the right to displace you from it.

## The Foundations of Property Law

A licence on the other hand, is a short-term permission which allows you to be on a piece of property for a period of time. During this period, you are basically a guest on the property of the landlord/owner.

A significant point to understand is that a lease is something that is binding on 3$^{rd}$ parties. What this means, is that if as a Landlord, I sign a lease with you for 50 years. But in Year 26 of the lease, I decide to sell that piece of land to a 3$^{rd}$ party/person. In selling that land, even though the 3$^{rd}$ party now becomes the Landlord/Lessor, they are still bound by our lease agreement until the end of the lease of 50 years; they cannot just kick you out because they are the new holders of the freehold. Specifically, if the Landlord, the fee simple owner of land, grants the Tenant the right to possession of the land for a limited period of time, then Tenant acquires a lease of the land. One of the rights that Tenant enjoys by virtue of having possession as a tenant is the right to exclusive occupation of the land during the lease which basically is the right to occupy that property to such an extent that they have the ability to exclude the Landlord or any third party from their property. In this context, then, 'possession' includes, but means something more than, exclusive occupation.

A licence on the other hand is something by which someone may go onto a piece of land and not be found guilty of trespass. For example, when owning a house, one implicitly gives a licence to (gives permission to) 3$^{rd}$ parties to come up to your front door, be it to ring the doorbell to deliver a parcel, to speak to you, to post something through your letter box etc. You cannot find the postman guilty of trespass unless you explicitly refuse them entry to your front door through erecting a gate or something else which would require them to request your permission before entering your property. This is a personal licence.

- **Lease = Property Interest received**
- **Licence = Personal Right received**

There are some contractual licences, such as when you go to a train station, you are only permitted entrance beyond the barriers once you have paid for a valid ticket/Oyster card. Likewise, at a theatre, you are only permitted beyond the ticket booths once you have purchased a valid ticket to one of the shows.

Similarly, other licences are gratuitous like the example of a shopping centre or a shop. You are invited into a shop/shopping centre, but you do not actually have to buy anything to be able to go inside. It's a grateful invitation being extended to you in the hope that you will go in & buy something, leading to business for the shop. In both circumstances, you have no property rights, but rather all you have is a licence to enter that property.

The key difference however between a lease & a licence is that a licence has no binding on a 3$^{rd}$ party. The best way to highlight this is through the understanding of living in a hotel room. When you book a hotel room for a night, you are signing a contractual licence which gives you the right to stay the night. If in the night/day that you're staying there, the owner of the hotel decides to sell the hotel to a 3$^{rd}$ party, the new owner is not bound to honour your licence with the previous owner. They have every right to kick you out & order you out of their premises. In remedy of this, there are 2 things which an individual can do:

    I. Sue the previous owner for a breach of contract
    II. Create a new contract or to negotiate with them

Another way to highlight the difference between a lease & a licence is by citing the example of having to change a lightbulb in a hotel room vs changing the bulb in a house you're living in under leasehold. At a hotel room, one would instantly call room service & request them to come up & change the bulb. In a house under leasehold, you wouldn't call up your landlord to fix it, but rather you would go out, buy a lightbulb & change it yourself. In a hotel, you wouldn't go out & buy a lightbulb for the room!

Another reason why it is so important to distinguish between a lease & a licence (many more will be built on as we go through the course) is in order to understand that statutory protection for occupiers (whether residential, business or agricultural) has traditionally been available only for tenants (people with leases), not licensees (people with a licence). In the case of residential premises in particular, landowners have sought to disguise leases as licences in order to avoid giving occupiers the rent control, security of tenure and protection against unlawful eviction conferred on tenants by the Rent Acts (seen in a case below). This reason is less pressing than it once was. This is partly because a dramatic decrease in statutory protection for residential occupiers has made the issue less important from the landlord's point of view, and partly because some of the more recent statutory protection has been drafted so as to cover those who occupy residential premises as licensees as well as tenants. However, there continue to be important statutory rights which are available only to tenants and not to licensees – see, for example, the enfranchisement rights conferred on tenants by statutes from the Leasehold Reform Act 1967 to the Leasehold Reform, Housing and Urban Development Act 1993, and the statutory covenants for structural and exterior repair implied into residential tenancies by the Landlord and Tenant Act 1985 as amended.

How is this relevant to Bentham?

A lease is a full bundle of rights which suggests that there are obligations & rights which come about as a result of a lease. A lease is a construct of the law, which in turn gives both involved parties' expectations from the property; the lessor has expectations as does the lessee such as rent being paid, peaceful uninterrupted living, security of tenure etc.

# **Co-Ownership**

I. Significance of the difference between legal & equitable interests
II. What is co-ownership?
III. Joint Tenancy
IV. Tenants in Common
V. Owning land legally and in equity
VI. Severing joint tenancies

The significance of the difference between legal & equitable interests

Equitable interests were originally those property interests that were recognised by the Chancery courts but not by the common law courts. There were several circumstances in which the Chancery courts would regard someone other than the legal title holder as having a proprietary interest in a thing. For example, if I want to grant you a ten-year lease of my house, I must do so by executing a deed: if I do not use a deed, you will not get a legal lease even if you move in and pay the agreed rent and we both act throughout the ten years as if you had the lease which I have purported to grant you. However, the Chancery courts were more flexible, and in certain circumstances they would regard you as having a lease even though all the requirements for creating a valid legal lease had not been observed. You would then quite simply be deemed to have an equitable lease rather than a legal lease. The major differences between legal and equitable interests are that the formalities necessary for their creation and transfer are different, and, in general, legal interests are enforceable against a wider range of third parties than equitable interests.

Legal rights are seen to be rights in rem whilst equitable rights are only rights in personam. Basically, it's like the idea of a lease & a licence – a lease is a right in rem & thus you bind the whole world to your rights. A licence is a right in personam and thus you can only bind certain people using the rights you have in that property and thus 'equitable rights bind the world with the exception of the bona fide purchaser of a legal estate for value without notice', often referred to as equity's darling. And this is indeed the key exception – equitable interests are susceptible to encroachment from equity's darling whereas legal title/interests cannot be affected even by equity's darling at all.

Co-ownership

This is a concept that is concerned with the notion surrounding 2 or more people having a simultaneous interest in a piece of land at the same time; this can be either a freehold or leasehold interest in a land. This means that this is not concerned with the notion of successive interests in land and the idea of owning one after the other, but rather the idea that a piece of land is co-owned by two or more parties at the same time.

The rules of co-ownership have been significantly simplified and made easier to understand post the Law of Property Act 1925 and thus as a result, we look at the two methods of co-ownership which have been stipulated post this act and are the only viable options for co-owning property as of 1st January 1926 and they are:

I. Joint Tenancy (JT)
II. Tenancy in Common (TiC)

Before looking at these two in more detail, we must consider 4 key terms & revise the meanings of these, to fully be able to comprehend the meaning of both a joint tenancy as well as tenancy in common:

I. Lease – A proprietary interest which adheres to the conditions of exclusive possession and being binding on 3rd parties such that it binds the whole world including the landlord himself, as well as the idea of having a certainty of term.
II. Licence – This is a personal right which allows someone a right to a piece of land without being sued for trespass for a stipulated period of time.
III. Equitable Interests – This is an interest that can bind the world & works in parallel with legal interests that always bind the world. In essence, legal rules are those which are very firm and equity rules are those which come and fill in the gaps such as to build bridges between the two

## The Foundations of Property Law

IV. Trusts - A trust is simply a division of ownership between the legal title holder and an equitable interest holder. In a trust agreement, the two parties are the trustee and the beneficiary. The trustee will be the legal owner of the property whilst the beneficiary will be the equitable owner of that property. This is a distinction which must be understood!

### Joint Tenancy

A Joint Tenancy is where two or more people have an interest in the entity, typically land, where both/all parties have a 100% interest in the land meaning that there are no distinct shares amongst the land joint tenants; they each have 100% of the land which means that each has an equal right to the land under one formal title jointly owned by all the tenants. This is imperative to understand – in a joint tenancy, each of the tenants is deemed to have a 100% control of the land; there is no division of the land in anyway.

For owners under a joint tenancy, there is an understanding that they must possess 4 unities in order for a joint tenancy to be valid. If ANY of the 4 unities is not present, then the agreement between the parties will not be a joint tenancy, but rather a Tenancy in common. These 4 unities are:

I. Possession – this is very similar to the concept of exclusive possession discussed in leases and the idea that the joint tenants have the right to equally bind the whole world & refuse possession to the world except to their fellow tenants. All tenants have an exclusive possession of the whole property.

> Acronym for the 4 unities are PITT – so just remember Brad Pitt!

II. Interest – This is the idea that all of the owners should have identical interests in the property with regards to the nature of their interest, duration of their interest etc.
III. Time – Their interests must all arise from the exact same time
IV. Title - Their title, interests and time must all arise from the same deed

The Foundations of Property Law

A joint tenancy has a right of survivorship for which all joint tenants are liable to. This is simply the idea that is best explained by way of an example. If 4 individuals are in a joint tenancy and have a 100% interest in the property each, and suddenly one dies, the right to survivorship states that nothing will happen in the sense that the 100% interest in the property will merely be absorbed by the remaining 3 tenants; there will be no transfer of tenant to an heir or the state as such in a joint tenancy so long as there is another tenant that is alive.

In the case of *AG Securities v Vaughan* [1990] were two House of Lords cases which were decided with the same ruling and thus titled together.

In the first case, AG Securities, an unlimited company, had a long lease of 25 Linden Mansions, Hornsey Lane, London, with four bedrooms and communal areas. It rented to Nigel Vaughan and three others. Each moved in at different times from 1982, signing independent agreements. In May 1985 AG Securities terminated the agreements. They claimed they jointly held the lease and therefore had statutory protection. The judge held there was no lease. The Court of Appeal held the occupiers had a lease, but Sir George Waller dissented.

In *Antoniades v. Villiers [1988]* case, an unmarried couple occupied a flat which comprised kitchen, bathroom, bedroom and sitting room. Each occupier had entered into a separate agreement with the plaintiff. Among the many terms which purported to negative the grant of exclusive possession, clause 16 provided that the plaintiff was "entitled at any time to use the rooms together with the licensee and permit other persons to use all of the rooms together with the licensee." When the plaintiff gave the occupiers four weeks' notice to quit, they resisted, claiming Rent Act protection.

The House of Lords & Lord Templeman held that Mr Vaughan with his co-tenants were licensees only and not tenants, because none had exclusive possession and their rights could not be amalgamated to give a joint lease, while Mr Villiers and Ms Bridger did have exclusive possession of their room - albeit jointly - and therefore did have a lease, despite the wording of their agreements which identified them as having only a license to occupy. All the members of the House of Lords agreed that clause 16 was a sham and concluded that the occupiers were joint tenants. However, Lord Templeman took the view that even if clause 16 had been genuine the occupiers would still have been protected by the Rent Act 1977.

In discussing these cases, Lord Templeman observed that tenants could be described as those people entitled to be protected with security of tenure and maximum rents since the Rent Act 1915, up to the Rent Act 1977. People could not contract out of such laws, which were intended to protect the vulnerable from harm and to prevent consent to substandard treatment by means of coercion, nor could they be avoided by choosing words that did not match the reality. If that were possible, then sham wordings would merely become the norm, and the protective intent of the law would be unachieved. Templeman says, *"Clause 16, if genuine, was a reservation by a landlord of a power at some time during the currency of the tenancy to share occupation with the tenant. The exclusive occupation of the tenant coupled with the payment of rent created a tenancy which at common law could be terminated and converted into a licence as soon as the landlord exercised his power to share occupation. But under the Rent Acts, if a contractual tenancy is terminated, the Acts protect the occupiers from eviction."* However, it need hardly be said that this analysis is unorthodox. Indeed, Lord Templeman makes a fundamental mistake. If the court had found that clause 16 was genuine the occupiers would have been licensees. Although the occupiers would have had immediate exclusive occupation by virtue of the landlord's failure to exercise his right to share the accommodation, they would not have been tenants because they would not have had a right to exclusive possession.

Tenants in Common:

This is the idea that two or more people have an undivided share in an entity, usually a property, such that each will have a specific interest in that property. Although you cannot literally draw your share into the property as such, you own a share in relation to the ownership of that property. This is basically the idea that, for example, if me & you decide to buy a house together as tenants in common & I pay for 30% of its & you pay for 70% of

## The Foundations of Property Law

it (because you're rich ☺) your share of the property will be 70% whilst I will only own 30% of the property.

With regards to the PITT unities mentioned above, it is likely that a unity of possession will exist but is unlikely that any other unity will be present be that interest, title or time.

Additionally, unlike in a Joint Tenancy, in a Tenancy in Common, there is no right to survivorship. What this means, is that unlike in a joint tenancy where the share is simply absorbed by the remaining tenant(s), in a Tenancy in Common, the share is received by an heir of the deceased tenant, or the state if no heir is found.

<u>Owning land legally & in equity</u>

Since the enactment of the Law of Property Act 1925 as of the 1<sup>st</sup> of January 1926, there were a number of steps taken to introduce our modern regime of co-ownership as how we understand it today.

I. The first step was to reduce all the types of co-ownership to two types discussed above:
    a. Joint Tenancy
    b. Tenants in Common

It was here made impossible to legally create a Tenancy in Common and the idea that a legal title of Tenants in Common quite simply cannot exist became law. What this means, is that the only possible legal title for co-ownership is that of a joint tenancy.

II. There was a development of a statutory trust and the idea that the persons to whom the legal title is conveyed are the trustees of the legal title of the land under the statutorily imposed trust on the land. The legal title of the land will be held by the Joint Tenants trust on the land. This means that the legal owners, those in a joint tenancy, are trustees for themselves as well as all the other legal owners; their fellow tenants.

III. Even though legal titles can only be held by Joint Tenants, an equitable title can be held by either a Joint Tenant or even a Tenant in Common.

The rule here, however, is that equity will follow the law; if legally you have a Joint Tenancy, it'll be presumed that even in equity, you have a Joint Tenancy. If any of the unities are missing, then & only then, will you have a Tenancy in Common which is only possible as an equitable title. This means that the words in the conveyance must be wholly conclusive and specified in order for the tenancy in common to be stipulated; the norm will be to assume a joint tenancy, however, if a tenancy in common is clearly stipulated, then a tenancy in common will be assumed.

Additionally, if there is an indication that there will be a severance of the interests in the property, then a Tenancy in Common will be assumed because as soon as the notion of shares in a property are introduced, it can no longer be a Joint Tenancy, as there are no shares in a Joint tenancy; in it there will always only be 100% ownership of the land for each of the tenants.

There are of course a couple of situations where the afore mentioned presumptions not be upheld & they are:

I. In a business agreement, there is naturally the implication that there is a profit v loss situation and there is no intention between the parties to be in joint possession as such; there will not be an intention to have a unity of interest & thus a tenancy in common will always be assumed.

II. Where purchasers provide money unequally when purchasing something, it'll be assumed that there'll be a tenancy in common. Again, in the example of me & you buying a house, let's say its £100,000 for which I pay £30,000 & you pay £70,000, naturally it'll be assumed that I have a 30% share of the property & you have a 70% share. This was considered in 3 cases;
   a. Bull v Bull [1955]
   b. Stack v Dowden [2007] should be noted
   c. Jones v Kernott [2011]

The House of Lords clearly states (with the express exception of Lord Neuberger) that in the context of 'domestic' properties (i.e. family homes), the presumption of tenancy in common arising from unequal purchase contributions will not apply unless one of the parties can provide evidence to the contrary. The Supreme Court took the opportunity to confirm this approach in the case of *Jones v Kernott* [2011] that where a 'home' is to be held in joint names, equitable title would also be presumed to be held as joint tenants, even if contributions to the purchase price were unequal. This presumption would only be displaced if the parties' common intention could justify it in the light of their whole course of conduct.

Remember this statement – Equity follows the law!

Severance

With regards to a legal title, meaning a Joint Tenancy, it can never be severed; you can't break away from it as such. In equity however, you can break away from a joint tenancy & when doing so, you will receive an equal share from the property. For example, with 4 owners, you'll receive 25% & upon you leaving, the remaining 3 tenants will return to having 100% ownership of the property each. You will always receive an equal share irrespective of your initial input into the property/entity.

A severance can occur through:

I. A statutory notice as per Section 36(2) in the Law of Property Act 1925 under which the notice must be a unilateral act, in writing that is a clear, final and irrevocable intention to sever the joint tenancy.
II. By selling your shares & thus your stake in the property be it to a fellow tenant or to a 3rd party.
III. Through mutual agreement – decide with the other tenants for them to buy you out as such to sever the Joint Tenancy

This was considered in the case of *Kinch v Bullard* [1998] where notice of severance was sent by registered post from one joint tenant to the other and was delivered at the latter's address. The noticee never saw it, because he died prior to opening it. The sender, then realising that all of a sudden, with the death of her joint tenant she would be entitled to absorb 100% of the property, sought to destroy the letter, because if it was found, she would only be entitled to 50% of the property, not all of it! She thought she was smart & could finesse the system, but... You can finesse the system, but the system will always find a way to finesse you back ☺

# Leasehold Covenants

I. What are Leasehold Covenants?
II. A worked example

What are Leasehold Covenants?

This is looking at the agreements which are explicitly mentioned between the landlord and the tenant and are included in the contractual lease agreement between the parties.

Contracts in relation to land must be in writing as per the requirements of Section 2 of the LP(MP)A 1989 which we looked at last year and specifies the following requirements for a contract of land:

I. Must be in writing – unless of course it is a lease of less than 3 years in which case it can be made orally which we look later on. However, don't get it twisted – even though the lease agreement does not need to be in writing as such, the contract does need to be in writing specifying what the terms of the contract are, what the consideration etc. is.
II. The contract must incorporate all the terms
III. The contract must be signed by both/all parties

And remember (this is covered later under formalities), all leases which 3 years are over must all be by deed, which have the following requirements:

I. Must be in writing
II. Must be clear that it is intended to be a deed as per Section 1(2)(a) of LP(MP)A 1989
III. Signed as per Section 1(2)(a) of LP(MP)A 1989
IV. Need witnesses to prove signature as per Section 1(3) of LP(MP)A
V. Delivery to show that parties are actually bound by the contract as per Section 1(3) LP(MP)A

The fact of the matter is that leases can last more than one generation especially because leases can be assigned (given), inherited (left behind for an inheritor/next of kin) or even sold – thought the original contracting parties may no longer be alive/around or affiliated with the contacting parties, the leases will still be valid which is why we have to look at how 3rd parties to the original contract can protect their rights.

## Worked Example

- I enter into an agreement with Katie to rent my house to her for 100 years
- A covenant in that agreement is that I will repair the roof as long as Katie promises to pay the rent
- 10 years later, I sell my freehold in the house to Nabeel
- Katie after a few years then decides to sub-lease/transfer her lease to Maryam

Now, Maryam needs the roof to be repaired, but has not paid rent (probably still walking to the post office to post her cheque) but the question would be, can Maryam get the repairs done & can Nabeel get the rent paid to them, despite the contractual obligations originally being between him & Katie.

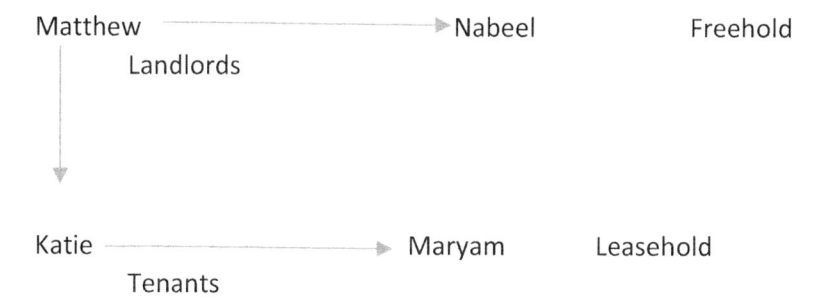

```
Matthew ─────────────► Nabeel         Freehold
   │       Landlords
   │
   ▼
Katie   ─────────────► Maryam         Leasehold
           Tenants
```

Remember: receiving rent = benefit whereas repairing the roof = burden. Paying rent is also a burden whereas receiving a fixed roof = benefit.

Now, under contract law, it would be that Katie cannot force Nabeel to repair the roof because burden cannot be transferred in a contract. But in Property Law, there is a remedy available for Katie to enforce that promise.

So, the question will be, if Maryam hasn't paid the rent, can she get Nabeel to repair the roof under proprietary rules under property law.

The Foundations of Property Law

According to Section 136 of the LPA 1925, the benefit of a contract can be assigned, sold, or transferred to another person as in this is done through one's own personal choice; it is a right in action which has been passed on – the benefit can be passed. It is literally a document showcasing the transfer of the benefit of the contract.

**Privity of Contract** denotes the relationship between landlord & tenant that exists as a result of the contractual agreement. Each party is entitled to enforce covenants, due to the contract between them. It's concerned with the actual contract. Burden cannot pass under contract.

**Privity of estate** on the other hand is the legal relationship that exists between parties where the estate constitutes one in law; it exists where two or more parties have an interest in the same real property. It's concerned with the estate & the title holders.

The case of *Spencer* from 1583 allows for both the benefit & the burden to be passed on from the tenant to a successor too if 3 criteria are met:

I. The covenant touches the land – the promise is attached directly to the land itself to a personal right. Here it is important to understand that historically, land was seen as a mechanism/a tool to gain wealth & it is this wealth which is attached directly to the land – the benefit of land is to gain wealth from it; this is a property right, not a personal one. This is further epitomised when considering that once I've sold my freehold to Nabeel, I am no longer going to be the one who'll claim the rent from Katie; the benefit of that rent isn't associated with me therefore it isn't a personal right, but rather because it is associated/attached with the land, it'll be deemed a property/proprietary right.

II. There is a privity of estate between the contracting parties; there are two estates that can estate in land as derived from Section 1(1) of the LPA 1925:
    a. Freehold
    b. Leasehold

The Foundations of Property Law

III.  There has been a legal assignment of a legal lease by way of deed and all other formalities required to legally uphold a lease agreement.

So, can Nabeel get his due rent?

Between Matthew and Katie, there was a privity of contract. Between Katie & Nabeel however, not only is there a privity of contract, there is also a privity of estate too.

The benefit of the covenant, which is to get their rent, will be transferred to Nabeel from me through Section 141 of the LPA which is essentially what was derived in *Spencer's* case. Therefore, if Maryam doesn't pay the rent, Katie is still liable for the rent, therefore, if Nabeel doesn't sue Maryam, he could always sue Katie to recover the rent from her too as per Section 79 of the LPA but the burden of having to pay rent, as it's touching and concerning the land, under Spencer's case, it can transfer to Maryam & she will be under a burden to pay rent = A privity of estate.

It must be noted, that leases create after January 1st, 1996, there are different rules under the Landlord & Tenant (Covenants Act 1995.) Spencer's case no longer applies for leases after 1996 and before then, only applies for tenants.

Therefore, Nabeel can get his rent!

So, can Maryam get her repairs done?

This is a different one because though she can sue both Katie and Matthew (snake) there's actually no point in her doing so, because the only remedy she'll get from suing either of them, is money & if she actually wants something repaired, money isn't actually the remedy she's after as such. Therefore, under Section 142 of the LPA, the burden of the covenant was also transferred from me to Nabeel when I sold him my freehold which means that Maryam can sue Nabeel to get the repairs done to the roof; he is liable to get them repaired due to the privity of estate between them.

To break this down:

I. Nabeel has taken both benefit (Section 141 of LPA) & burden (Section 142 of LPA) of the land from Matthew & thus if he does not receive rent, can sue:
   a. Maryam for not paying rent
   b. Katie for not paying rent
      i. Katie can sue Maryam for not paying rent
II. Maryam can sue:
   a. Katie for not repairing the roof – she'll only get damages, money. Katie can actually still sue Matthew too for a breach of contract; he broke the promise of their agreement.
   b. Nabeel for not repairing the roof & he will actually have to repair the roof because he took the burden of the contract from Matthew under Section 142 of the LPA.
   c. Matthew for not repairing the roof all so long as she's paying her rent & here too, she'll only get damages, money.

Put simply, remember these rules:

I. Benefit of landlord can pass under S141 of the LPA
II. Burden of landlord can pass under S142 of the LPA
III. Burden of tenant can pass under S136 of the LPA
IV. Burden of Tenant can pass under *Spencer* [1583] or what is now Section 3 of the Landlord & Tenant Covenants Act 1995.

# Non-Leasehold Covenants

I. Non-Leasehold Covenants
II. Original Parties & Successors
III. Tulk v Moxhay
IV. Types of Covenants
V. Enforcing Covenants
VI. Benefit at Common Law
VII. Burden at Common Law
VIII. Benefit in Equity
IX. Burden in Equity
X. Examples
XI. Discharge from Covenants
XII. Summary

Non-Leasehold Covenants

These are also known as incorporeal hereditaments which give the owner of one property, rights over the land belonging to someone else. So, for instance, it could potentially give Susan, my next door neighbour, property rights to my land. They work to allow one party to restrict (usually) the use of the land which belongs to someone else. In essence, they are simply promises made by deed between freeholders where one party promises to do (positive) or to not do (negative) things on their own land for the benefit of the other person's land.

Negative covenants are often termed restrictive covenants, and this is what many textbooks will refer to when they're talking about non-leasehold covenants. Me, well it depends what I feel like calling it I'm ngl!

Right from the offset, it is important for us to make a note of the fact that the original contracting parties will always be bound by the initial contractual obligations that they have upon themselves; they may not necessarily be continued in property, but they are very often continued in contract.

Covenants are enforced by a deed; so long as there is a deed, it will be enforced because a deed is effectively the 'badge of enforceability' of the covenant; in essence you could call it the consideration. This whole notion of covenants in this light were developed in the 19$^{th}$ century to protect the interest of the rising middle class against growing development and property ownership. There was an effort to protect values of homes which led to the insertions of many covenants to restrict the building of property in or around their area. This was to protect the rich in the west & centre of London (in particular) at the time of increasing urban populations from having to live next to what they quite simply described as slums for the low-income, poor people. This was permitted because initially there was no element of governmental control; these things were solely subjected to the law of nuisance and that was it. The control for these covenants and the restrictions surrounding them came directly from the people themselves and it was created by those for those who could access the legal system. The cycle that was born was simple; power was derived from covenants, which led to the formation of enclaves, which led to the creation of racial and class divisions in society.

Just a note to add on from the concept of privity of contract from the previous topic, it is important to note that these are only rights which are enforceable in personam; they are personal rights. Therefore, in order to have these rights upheld in a property sense, they must be moved from person rights into property rights and be inherently attached to the land rather than in a contract only.

Original Parties and successors

It is important to note that between the original parties, rights and obligations will always be enforceable by way of contract law. This means, taking a look back at my example from the previous topic, both myself & Katie as the original contracting landlord and tenant, will always be held under the original obligations. The question, however, is that in the same way as leaseholds, for covenants, can the benefit and burden both be passed to the successors.

One thing to keep in mind always is that benefit can pass to another under contract law through Section 136 of the LPA 1925 as we looked at the previous topic. Under common law, Section 56 of the LPA states that it is possible to say that the contract was actually made with the 3$^{rd}$ party; this party was part of the actual bi-lateral agreement and thus at the time of contracting, it must be said that the parties who are successors were in existence right from the offset.

Section 136 also states that you can assign the right to the covenantor in writing which will serve as a notice to them. The Contract (Rights of Third Parties) Act 1999 only has prospective application from May 2000 and replaces Section 56 of the LPA but always remember that at common law, burden **cannot** pass.

I. Benefit of landlord can pass under S141 of the LPA
II. Burden of landlord can pass under S142 of the LPA
III. Burden of tenant can pass under S136 of the LPA
IV. Burden of Tenant can pass under *Spencer* [1583] or what is now Section 3 of the Landlord & Tenant Covenants Act 1995.

Tulk v Moxhay

In 1807 Charles Augustus Tulk was settled with the Leicester square gardens and some properties adjoining it. He covenanted with this father that he would "at all times hereafter keep... the piece or parcel of ground in Leicester Square now used as a garden... In its present form and in an open state uncovered by any buildings upon the same and shall and will keep ... the said piece or parcel of ground now used as a Garden in neat and ornamental order." Effectively, there were two covenants which were drawn up by Tulk which were:

I. The land shall not be built on
II. It shall be kept in neat/ornamental order

The land then went through a bit of a selling craze such that it ended up in the hands of Moxhay; the path it took was the following:

I. In 1808, Tulk sold it to Elms with the same clauses
II. Elms died and left the garden to Barren

III. Barren sold it to Inderwick with the same covenants
IV. It was then brought by Hyams at an auction.
V. Hyams assigned it to Moxhay who was a builder, a clever one at that but brought it subject to the covenants.

He thought that hold up, there's a huge piece of land here in the middle of London which I can build on and sell for a lot of money. His argument was effectively that I wasn't entered into the original contract between Tulk and his father therefore I will not be privy to the original covenants as a result of which I can pay Hyam £120 to be released from the covenants – he treated it like it was a contractual matter when rather it went far beyond this and into the realms of property law.

Moxhay described the garden as *"a most unsightly object and a disgrace and reproach to the neighbourhood."* He was clearly upset with the state of the garden and thought he could do a much better job which is fair enough. The reason I agree with him, is that in an economic sense, the land would be better served with him as the owner, rather than how it was now. He would make more of an economic impact on the land and make it even more valuable than it was, but still, the covenants were a problem for him.

Through his frustration, Moxhay decided that he was going to just pay £120 to Hyam, release himself from the contractual obligations and started to cut down the tress in the garden in preparation for building works. Tulk came about & said yoo what you doing fam & went to the courts to seek an order to prevent this nonsense from Moxhay. The neighbours all thought that their land had much more value if Leicester Square was kept as an open garden rather than being built on.

The question the courts had to answer was really simple; did the burden, or did it not pass to the covenantor (the person with the burden of the covenant) when sold in the chain from Tulk down to Moxhay?

Well the courts held that action could be brought against Moxhay because he was bound by the covenants. If he wasn't bound, then the courts said, *"If that were so, it would be impossible for an owner of land to sell part of it without incurring the risk of rendering what he retains worthless."* What they were effectively saying, was that it's just not fair to just not abide by the covenants as per your own wishes! In essence, the courts determined that Moxhay was indeed bound by the covenants because there was a protection for the original owner. I personally do not agree with this; the original owner has sold the land, freed himself from the covenants & actually benefitted from the sale of the land so much so that he made money from it. Why on Earth should his interests be protected? Well... He was a rich man who had access to the courts & the rest is all about protecting the interests of the White Upper Class!

The courts went on to state the following, *"Can there, then, be anything more inequitable or contrary to good conscience, than that a party who takes property at a less price because it is subject to a restriction should receive the full value from a third party and that such third party should then hold it unfettered by the restriction under which it was granted?...you will not be permitted to hand over that property, and give to your assignee or your vendee a higher title with regard to the interests as between yourself and your vendor, than you yourself possess."* What the courts are saying, is that there is a step by step process that was undertaken with these covenants:

I. It gets converted from a contractual right into a proprietary right
II. It moves from being a right in personam to a right in rem
III. The equity is now attached to the land and is burdened without that promise – it cannot be sold without that promise and thus it has to be sold with the land much like a fixture annexed to the land; it inherently becomes a part of the identity of the land. The land is wholly burdened with that promise.

Some keywords to be kept in mind when discussing non-leasehold covenants:

- The Servient land is the land which is being burdened by the covenant – the servient tenement
- The Dominant land is the one who stops doing something to it; the beneficiary land if you like – the dominant tenement
- The Covenantor is the one who is burdened by the covenant – the servient

The Foundations of Property Law

- The Covenantee is the maker of the covenant – the dominant

Types of Covenants

There are mainly two different types of covenants:

I. Freehold v Leasehold Covenants
II. Positive v negative/restrictive Covenants

Enforcing Covenants

There are also a number of requirements attached to the enforcing of covenant as a proprietary right which are:

I. The covenantor's land bears the burden of the covenant
II. The covenantee's land bears the benefit of the covenant
III. There is a duality of benefit & burden; both the benefit of the covenant has to run to the claimant and the burden has to run to the defendant

So, between the original covenantor and the original covenantee, the obligations are enforceable as a matter of contract in that both positive and negative covenants can be enforced solely for being the original contracting parties. Now, what we will do, is break it down into 4 further categories; whether burden and benefit respectively can pass in common law & in equity.

Common Law – Benefit

The benefit **can** pass at common law & can do so through a number of possible ways:

I. Express assignment through S136 of the LPA
II. Implied assignment through S56 of the LPA – this looks at the case of *P & A Swift Investment v Combined English Stores* [1989] requires that there will be an initial assignment from noting whether or not it touches or concerns the dominant land. If it is seen to touch or concern the dominant land, it will pass to the successor automatically through implied assignment which means that there is no need for an express assignment if:

> > a. It touches or concerns the land – must benefit the current owner only whilst they own the land
> > b. The covenantor and the covenantee both have legal title
> > c. There must be an intention for the covenant to pass – if it benefits the land, then the automatic assumption will be that the covenant was indeed intended to pass
> > d. The successors to the land have a legal title
> III. Express of Statutory annexation – this is the idea that the covenant becomes a part of the land like a fixture. This was explored in the case of *Rogers v Housegood* [1900] where it was stated that it was 'for the benefit of the dominant land.' Once something touches & concerns the land, there will be an automatic assumption that there was an intention for the land to be benefitted & thus it will pass automatically.
>
> In the case of *Federated Homes v Mill Lodge* [1980] reference was made to S78 of the LPA which allows for the benefit of a covenant to be passed to successors in title. Up until this case, this had to be done expressly but this section allows for any form of written intention to prove that successors were to be bound, will suffice. The case of *Roake v Chada* exemplifies the current rule; the obligations will be automatically transferred unless it is otherwise specifically stated that it is not intended to be transferred. You must expressly say no, otherwise it will automatically transfer.

From here derives an interesting case of *Smith & Snipes Hall v River Douglas Catchment Board* [1949] where the board agreed with the landowners to maintain the riverbanks; they took the burden on themselves. A successor to the land sued for breach of contract when the banks of the river burst and flooded the land (Loooool shame fam that's what you get for being extra haha) & the courts agreed insofar to say that the covenant had run alongside S78 of the LPA as if the covenant had been annexed to the land itself.

The Foundations of Property Law

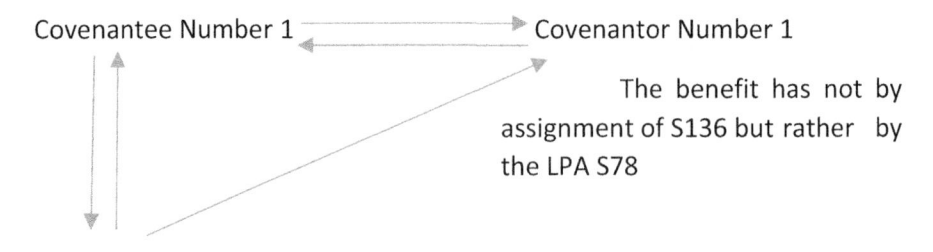

Covenantee Number 1 ⟷ Covenantor Number 1

The benefit has not by assignment of S136 but rather by the LPA S78

Covenantee Number 1

The question is raised that if S78 can be read by the judges in this way to allow for S78 to automatically transfer the burden, then S79 should be allowed to be read in the same light to allow for burden to be passed like that too!

Actually, Denning LJ goes so far to say that no, this is incorrect, it should be brought back to being passed at S56 of the LPA because reading of laws in this way of S78 will lead to the question being raised about S79 too.

Common Law – Burden

This roots from the case of *Rhone v Stephens* [1994] where it is stated that quite simply, burden **cannot** pass at common law – this is the very opposite to leaseholds; a major difference. The courts in this case said, *"Equity cannot compel an owner to comply with a positive covenant entered into by his predecessors...without flatly contradicting the common law rule that a person cannot be liable upon a contract unless he was a party to it. Enforcement of a positive covenant lies in contract; a negative covenant lies in property."* This epitomised the fact that a negative covenant cannot require the burderned party to have to engage in anything except passive acceptance; just letting the dominant party use it, is enough!

There are two ways it can be done so indirectly:

I. Chain of indemnity; this is the concept that:
   a. A sells to B and the grant has a covenant to do
   b. B sells to C and the grant has a covenant to do
   c. C sells to D and the grant has a covenant to do

d.  D sells to E and so on....

The problem with this is that it is quite unreliable in that there is no guarantee that this chain will always carry on; someone may sell their contractual obligation on/be brought out so there is a weak point of the chain. There is a requirement for an active inclusion in the agreement of these covenants, in order to ensure that the covenant actually remains valid.

II.  The case of *Halsall v Brizell* [1957] is where for example Matthew covenants with Katie to pay for the upkeep of the drive which they both use to access their properties. The covenant is that if Matthew wants to use the drive (so to benefit from the drive) then Matthew must contribute financially to the upkeep of the drive (so I must have some burden of the covenant too.) If I don't pay for the upkeep, then Katie (wasteman wow) can get an injunction issued to prevent me from using the path which I need to use to access my property because this in essence forms a kind of trespass. This concept known as the *Halsall v Brizell* concept is that for benefit, a burden must be had too. If you want, you must give too.

## Equity – the benefit

This is pretty much the same as what we looked at above with regards to the common law with the difference being that there is no need to be a purchaser of a legal estate as such. Rather you could be the beneficiary of a trust or something similar to that and still be able to obtain the benefit of a covenant.

## Equity – the burden

Now this the way in which the case of *Tulk v Moxhay* [1848] was determined by the courts. There are a few requirements to allow for the burden to pass in equity and they are:

I.  The covenant must be negative in nature – it must be a restrictive covenant, not a positive one. It should stop someone from doing something in a sense. It must be negative in nature in that it just requires the servient to allow the dominant to use; there is nothing that the servient needs to actually do.

II. It must benefit the dominant tenement – it must touch or concern the land. This is the idea that the covenant must also be identifiable & proximate – there must be some sort of correlation between the direct benefit to one's own land.

III. It must be intended to pass – this is automatic under Section 79 of the LPA unless there is a clear contrary intention which explicitly allows for it to not be passed. There is no specific requirement that it is exclusively for negative covenants, but it seems to be used only for negative ones

IV. The successor to the covenant must have notice of the covenant which can be given based on the following statues below. It must be noted that mere knowledge is not enough, it must be registered under:
   a. Registered land notice will be given under Section 32 of the LRA 2002
   b. Unregistered land notice will be given due to the LCA 1972, Section 2 as these fall under Class D (ii)

Section 79 talks about burden, however, does not explicitly mention that it only applies to negative covenants. This is of course how it has been interpreted, but in terms of what it actually says, it really doesn't specify that it only relates to negative covenants.

The principle derived from Tulk v Moxhay can be shown as below using the same example as the previous topic:

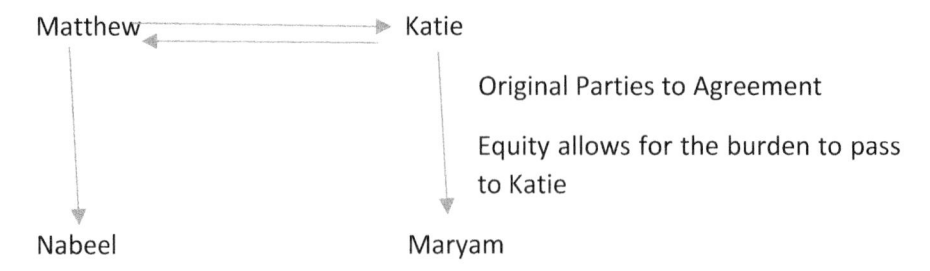

Matthew ⟷ Katie

Original Parties to Agreement

Equity allows for the burden to pass to Katie

Nabeel         Maryam

Contract allows for benefit to be passed

Contract does not allow for burden to transfer.

But if burden passes in equity than so must the benefit!

Restrictive v Positive Covenants

The following are examples of what could be restrictive or positive covenants:

I. "Shall maintain to the reasonable satisfaction of the purchasers and successors in title such part of the roof as lies above the property conveyed, in wind and water-tight condition." – Maintaining the roof is a positive covenant requiring work to be done, which means it cannot pass in equity whereas in common law, it may have a remedy. This is the covenant from *Rhone v Stevons.*
II. "Shall ensure that the land is kept free from any buildings." – Negative Covenant which can only be passed in equity.
III. "Shall not allow the hedge separating the properties to grow above 5 feet in height." – Could be either, depending on what kind of hedges they are; it depends on if they're growing ones or if they're ones that just don't grow.

An Exemplar Problem

Marcell divides his property in two portions: Camberwell House and Brixton House. He retains Camberwell House and sells Brixton House to John with the following covenants:

I. The owner of Brixton house shall allow free flow of the stream that flows from Brixton House to Camberwell House. **This is a negative covenant**
II. The owner of Brixton House shall ensure that hedges on the boundary shall not be allowed to grow beyond 5 feet. **This is a positive covenant based on the kind of hedges they are**
III. The owner of Brixton House shall contribute to the upkeep of the shared drive. **This is a positive covenant but one which is like the case above; if you want benefit, take the burden too.**

## The Foundations of Property Law

In these kind of questions, the following steps need to be taken:

I. Determine who is the covenantor and who is the covenantee
II. Which is the burdened land, and which is the dominant land
III. Are the covenants positive or negative?
IV. If A does not abide by the stipulations in the covenants, what can B do about it?

### Scenario 1

John sells Brixton House to Laura (successor covenantor) and Laura does not abide by the stipulations. Marcell still owns Camberwell House.

I. The burden cannot pass at law. Hence Marcell can only sue in equity.
II. Only the restrictive covenant can be directly enforced
III. So, which are the restrictive covenants? This is done by determining which of the covenants are positive and which ones are negative.
IV. Can the burden pass indirectly?
V. What will be the remedy?
   a. Damages are available at common law
   b. Injunctions are available in equity

### Discharge from covenants

This can be done through S84 of the LPA which states:

I. Apply to the Land Tribunal for discharge or alteration of covenants if
II. The covenant is obsolete by reason of changes in the property or the neighbourhood.
III. The continuance of the covenant could obstruct the reasonable use of the land for private or public purposes.
IV. Person entitled to the benefit has agreed to the discharge/modification
V. Person entitled to the benefit would not come to loss by the discharge/modification.

The Foundations of Property Law

Summary

The golden rules are this for each of the following and this is all that needs to be remembered in all honesty (thank me later xo):

I. Benefit at Common Law can pass through:
   a. S56 of the LPA or through the CR(TP)A 1999 – made with the 3rd party
   b. Expressly assigned as per S136 of the LPA
   c. Annexed to the land:
      i. Touches and concerns the land
      ii. Is a legal estate
   d. There is an intention as per S78 of the LPA even though this is determined as always being there unless expressly denied
II. Benefit at equity can pass but:
   a. There is no need for a legal estate
III. Burden at Common Law cannot pass – this is the very opposite to that in leaseholds which roots from Rhone v Stephens case but can pass indirectly in two ways:
   a. Chain of Indemnity
   b. Backed up by Halsall v Brizell which requires that for a benefit to be enjoyed, a burden must also pass; this is the benefit in lieu of a burden concept
IV. Burden at equity can pass:
   a. Roots from case of Tulk v Moxhay and thus must have the following:
      i. Be a negative covenant in substance
      ii. Must touch & concern the land
      iii. Intention must be present as per S79; this will be there unless expressly mentioned otherwise
   b. There must be notice given to the successors of the covenant being transferred
      i. S32 of the LRA 2002 for Registered Land
      ii. S72 of the LCA 1972 under Class D(ii)

# Easements

I. What is an easement?
II. What an easement is not
III. Creating a valid easement
IV. Wheeldon v Burrows
V. Section 62 of the LPA
VI. Worked Example
VII. Prescription
VIII. Termination of an Easement

What is an easement?

An easement is an intangible property right which gives a right to do something to another person's land. What it does, is give the dominant tenement rights over the servient tenement. In essence, what it must do is offer a significant benefit on the dominant land as to be distinct from merely offering some sort of personal advantage or facility to the dominant owner. An easement, it can be summarised is something that makes the dominant land more beneficial or commodious in a way. It must be a benefit for the land, rather than a personal one.

There are certain requirements for an easement which are derived from the case of *Re Ellenborough Park* [1956] and they are as follows:

I. There must be an identified Dominant and Servient Tenement – this is the requirement that at the time of creation of the easement & when it comes into existence, you must specifically be able to point to a dominant and servient tenement. This was proven in the case of *Hawkins v Rutter* where a man claimed an easement for his large barge yet the problem with this case was that there was no dominant tenement that could be identified because the barge of land cannot be determined as a plot of land as such.

II. Must Accommodate the dominant tenement – the Dominant tenement must receive the benefit. This was considered in the case of *Hill v Tupper* wherein a man had a right to run a boat hiring service across the canal. When another company was given these

The Foundations of Property Law

      rights too having set up in competition to him, the man held that he had an easement which allowed him to be able to run the service himself & not face competition. This was disregarded by the courts because it was only a personal contractual right that he had and not a property right, therefore you could hold that the canal owner was in breach of contract, but there was no easement that was breached.

III.    This was also looked at in the case of *Moodle v Steggles* [1879] where there was an advertisement/sign on the main road which showed the direction to a public house/pub that was away in a small side street/alleyway. A new owner of the main road tore down the sign, however, the courts held that no, the use of the sign had become an intrinsic part of benefitting from the land and was a benefit to the land, therefore, the sign was to remain on the land & not be torn down; it was a property right for the dominant tenement (the pub/public house) over the servient tenement (the main road.)

IV.    There must be a diversity of ownership meaning that there must be rights of one estate over another – this is what was considered in the case of *Roe v Siddons* [1888] where it was held that the diversity of ownership must be such that it must be somebody else's land that you are claiming against; the dominant tenement must belong to one entity/person

V.    and the servient tenement to another entity. One cannot have an easement over ones own property!

VI.    Must be capable of being the subject matter of a grant such as a lease – these are the typically established easements such as a right of way, use of drainage etc. which will usually be clearly defined – a drainage runs through an established channel whereas a right to way is defined by way of established paths too. In the case of *Re Aldred's* [1610] (yes, that really said 1610, 500 year old cases are judging us still!) it was held that a right to a view was not an established easement because a view is a subjective, imprecise definition and can differ in definition from person to person, therefore cannot be valid. This too was the case, in the case of *Hunter v Canary Whar* [1997].

An easy acronym to remember this by is:

**D**ominant

**A**ccommodate

**D**iversity

**DADS**

**S**ubject Matter

<u>What an Easement is not!</u>

An easement is not three things:

I. An easement cannot have exclusive possession – if there was exclusive possession, then remember that this would be a lease as we looked at earlier in the book The purpose of an easement is to effectively create an infusion of two lands, such that they can both benefit from a common piece of ground. It is in essence the co-existence of two property rights where two landowners have rights to use their respective properties in appropriate ways. This was proven in the parking case of *Batchelor v Marlow* [2001] where there was an agreement that a party would have car parking spaces from 8:30 till 6pm Monday to Friday & if anyone else parked in these spaces, they could be evicted from the spaces. This makes it look a lot like exclusive possession – I have it & if anyone else tries to take it, I can remove them from it. If you can eject the owner of the servient tenement from the land, then you are taking away the property rights that they have of that land & for an easement, this is not allowed. In this case what was done, was that it was said to the servient tenement that you do not have the right to be here during these hours & this of course inevitably amounts to exclusive possession due to the loss of the reasonable use & enjoyment of the land for the servient tenement during that time. This is an invalid easement!

This was also considered in the case of *Miller v Emcer* [1955] where a right to use a toilet does not come under exclusive possession and can be determined as an easement in that light. Yes, fair enough when you're in the toilet you can be said to be in exclusive possession of it, however, you're not going to spend all day in there (I hope!!), so it can't really be said to be constantly in exclusive possession so a public/shared toilet can be used as an easement. One is said to be in exclusive use of the toilet!

Likewise, in the case of *Wright v Macadam* [1949] it was held that the whole of the servient land must be looked at when determining if an easement can be passed to a successor, not just the part of the land which is specified by the easement. Fair enough the shed could not be used, but the rest of the land was actually usable & was not limited in one's possession of that land.

II. An easement cannot infer the servient tenement to have to incur a cost/spend in order to maintain it. An easement is a negative burden on the servient tenement which means that you simply just have to let someone use it and do not have to actively do anything in order for them to benefit from using it. This was epitomised in the case of *Regis Property v Redman* [1956] where it was held by the courts than a benefit to use a swimming pool cannot be a covenant if active steps need to be taken in order to spend to maintain the swimming pool.

III. An easement in a right, not a permission. This differentiation was made clear in the case of *Green v Ashco* [1966] where a gate had to be asked to be opened to a path & was determined as being an easement. The courts said no, this isn't an easement because this is requesting permission; you should be allowed to open the gate & close it whenever & however you wish, permission should not need to be sought. Seeking permission can make it seem like it isn't a right as such, but rather a permission which is wrong! A property right is a right to do something, including access land whenever.

Creating a Valid Easement

There are a number of requirement for the creation of a valid easement:

I. Express easement – to expressly give permission
   a. Must be by deed if it is to be a legal easement as per S52 of the LPA 1925
   b. It needs to be registered as per S27 of the LRA 2002
   c. Must be equal to an estate in land as per S1(2)a) of the LPA 1925 – must be for a defined period
II. Express equitable easement can also be created:
   a. Expressly by stating for it to be an equitable easement
   b. Where there is a failure to comply with the formalities mentioned above for a legal easement
   c. Must adhere to Section 2 of the LP(MP)A 1989 which says that it must be in writing, incorporate all the terms etc.
III. Implied legal easements – these are those legal easements which concern a legal estate where only a part of the land has been sold. This is what we focus a lot on & exam questions too will be focused on this element. There are two ways in which a legal easement can be implied:
   a. Sell the land and **grant** an easement – if the Dominant Tenement is that of the purchaser, then the easement will have been granted & has been retained by the Servient Tenement. This is where you grant a right.
   b. Sell the land and **reserve** an easement & this is where you then reserve a right/easement.

In essence, when selling the Dominant Tenement, one is granting a right/easement & when selling the Servient Tenement, one reserves the right/easement.

With regards to implied legal easements, there is an opportunity to suggest that there are two situations under which a legal easement can also be issued impliedly. The first is that under necessity; there was no other option but to ensure that there is an easement otherwise the land is pretty much useless & worthless. Drainage is not deemed a necessity because quite simply, you can find alternative ways to ensure drainage – use a bucket & then chuck it! This can be rooted to the case of *Manjang v Drammah* [1990] wherein it was held that there is no need for the right to the use of a footbridge to be an implied legal easement by way of necessity because there was a river & a boat which could be used to get to the other side; you didn't rely wholly on the footbridge alone to access the property, there was another way to the property which means that it wasn't useless & worthless without access to the footbridge. To be honest, I think that's too much of a limited view of necessity but hey, I ain't no judge so (although Judge Gangat sounds mad cool)...

The second way in which a legal easement can be issued impliedly is that of common intention. This is whereby way of allowing a contract or by taking certain steps in certain directions, you automatically imply that there is a legal easement. Where this roots from, is the case of *Wong v Beaumont* [1965] where a lease was granted to a Chinese restaurant which required for some pipes to pass through from the dominant tenement and the servient tenement too. The owner of the servient tenement decided to claim that no, there was no easement for these pipes to go through his land, but the courts held that no, if you make a lease agreement where there is a requirement for ventilation, then the steps needed to make that happen needs to be upheld too. Likewise, if you give someone a house with a toilet, sink, gutter etc. then you are impliedly allowing them, by way of common intention, to use the drainage; I don't need to ask for permission additionally to use the drainage even though both necessity & common intention through the case of *Nickerson v Barraclough* [1981] can be expressly excluded.

For the grant of an easement, which is where only the dominant tenement has been sold, there are two ways, it is important to look at the case of *Wheeldon v Burrows* or S62 of the LPA. *The* **grant** is where the person gives an easement over their land. So, for these two methods – if the dominant tenement has been sold. *A* **reservation** is where a person retains an easement over another person's land – So where the servient tenement has been sold.

Wheeldon v Burrows

An implied legal easement can be granted using this case and is often referred to as quasi easements. This is where the land is owned by one party, but then a part of the land is sold on. The owner of that sold part, continues to use the rights which the previous original owners would have over their retained land such as the use of the pathways, drainage etc.

So, let's say for instance, I own a piece of land (jheeezeee) & on it, there is a house & a cottage, with a path from the house to the cottage which also leads out to the main road. I decide to sell the cottage to Katie and keep the house for myself (and my kids!) There can be an implied legal easement that the path from the house to the cottage which leads out to the main road, can be used by Katie, so long as the following criterion are met:

I. The land was initially owned wholly by one person.
II. My use of the path is continuous and apparent in the sense that upon careful inspection, it can be told that that there was a usage of that piece of land but then there are some situations which you just know – the presence of a toilet means that the drainage use was continuous and apparent.
III. The use that is being claimed, must be for the reasonable enjoyment of the land. It does not need to be essential to the core purpose of the of the enjoyment of the land, but it should be reasonable to have it for the enjoyment of the lands purpose.
IV. The right must be used immediately before the grant, as in within months before, in that it is a requirement to not sleep on your rights & when you are given rights, to act on them, use them and exercise them or you risk losing them.
V. There must be no contrary intention in that it must not be intended for the property right to not pass – if it has been mentioned that the intention is there for it to not pass, then the implied legal easement would not work because it has been expressly categorically denied.

Section 62 of the LPA

This is also a word saving device like we looked at the previous topic for S78 & S79. For this to be used, there here are a number of requirements & formalities too:

I. Diversity of Occupation – it was noted by the courts in the *P&S Platt v Crouch* [2003] case by the Court of Appeal that there is no requirement for a diversity of occupation when relying on S62 of the LPA so long as the use of the land is continuous and apparent. However, the requirement for Diversity of Occupation was confirmed in *Sovemots Investment* [1979].
II. Permission to use the land has been granted by the servient tenement to use the land for any purpose
III. The dominant land is conveyed properly with the correct formalities of the dominant land meaning that it is conveyed by way of a Deed as per Section 205 of the LPA. This implies that all rights & benefits enjoyed by a piece of land, are intended to pass in the conveyance of a property, unless explicitly stated otherwise.

So, again, let's say that I own a piece of land and I grant a permission to my tenant Katie of the path. I then sell or lease the cottage on my land to Katie.

So, if there's the following, then Section 62 can be used:

I. There must be a conveyance of the property by way of a lease by instance for B/Katie in this instance
II. There must be rights which exist at the time of the creation of the conveyance as in, for instance, the permission to use the path to the road for Katie must exist at the time at which the land is conveyed to her.
III. Priori diversity of occupation – see above
IV. No contrary intention – see above

SO effectively, what we go through is the questions of:

I. Necessity
II. Common Intention
III. Wheeldon v Burrows
IV. Section 62 of the LPA

All 4 can be used for the granting of an easement, however, for a reservation, one can only use the first two. The key differences between Wheeldon v Burrows & Section 62 of the LPA are two:

I. Wheeldon v Burrows does not need diversity of occupation but Section 62 (arguably) does.
II. Wheeldon v Burrows needs necessary for reasonable enjoyment but Section 62 doesn't

<u>Worked example</u>

I am the owner of a large estate. I sell half of my estate to Katie & before I sold the land to Katie, I was using the driveway across the land which I sold to Katie. I want to however, continue to use the driveway. Can I reserve the right to use the driveway?

Yes, I can because potentially there is no other access to the land & therefore under necessity, I could say that I have to have access to the path to the road. This is the only way in which I can get my easement so, if there's another access point to the land, then I cannot get the easement.

I am the owner of a large estate. I sell half of my estate to Katie & before I sold the land to Katie, I was using the driveway across the land which I sold to Katie. Katie wants to however use the driveway. Can Katie reserve the right to use the driveway?

Well in this instance, you're now looking at a grant & the dominant landowner is now Katie & I'm the one with the servient land. Because of this, Wheeldon v Burrows will apply because it only applies to the grant of the easement & therefore, we'll go through the steps of Wheeldon v Burrows discussed above. Remember, Wheeldon v Burrows is automatically applied to the cases where there is a grant:

I. Was there continuous & apparent use? Yes, there was
II. Necessary for the reasonable enjoyment to the land? Yes, there is because access is a reasonable enjoyment to the land.
III. Right used immediately before grant? Yes, it was
IV. No contrary intention? No there isn't = Katie can use the driveway.

<u>Prescription</u>

There is a requirement that due to long use of a piece of land, as a result of the dint of time, one can acquire a property right if:

I.   It must be used as a right, not as a permission
II.  It must be used continuously
III. It must be between fee simple owners

You can claim under prescription under:

I.   Common Law by saying that you've used the land since immemorial which is 1189 which is when Henry II died which is basically for as long as anyone could ever remember & presumed by long use of the land
II.  Lost Modern Grant which roots from the case of *Orme v Lyons* [2012] which stated that where there was a deed that was lost, 20 years of uninterrupted use would prove that the land is actually yours.
III. Prescription Act which states that there must be 20 or 40 years of uninterrupted use before the date of action. 20 years of uninturrupted use can be rebutted by oral evidence whereas 40 years needs written evidence for it to be rebutted.

There is a very limited acceptance of the right to light as per the case of *Flight v Thomas*.

**Remember:** the question is whether or not it will bind a legal purchaser?

- For an implied easement, this forms an over-riding interest as per Schedule 3 Part 3 of the LRA 2002.
- Legal easements which are created before 2002 are binding on purchasers regardless.

Termination of an easement

An easement can be terminated in 3 ways:

I.  A merger which mean that the Dominant Tenement & the Servient Tenement are both owned by the same person in fee simple
II. Release by way of contractual obligation, however. Law Commission says that it should be reformed that if the easement is not used for 25 years, then it should be automatically released from however right now, it cannot automatically be released from.

The Foundations of Property Law

III. Change of Character - The easement is reasonable use – if this become unreasonable then the nature of the right has changed as per *Attwood v Bovis Homes* [2000].

So, the step by step process when answering a question on easements will be the following:

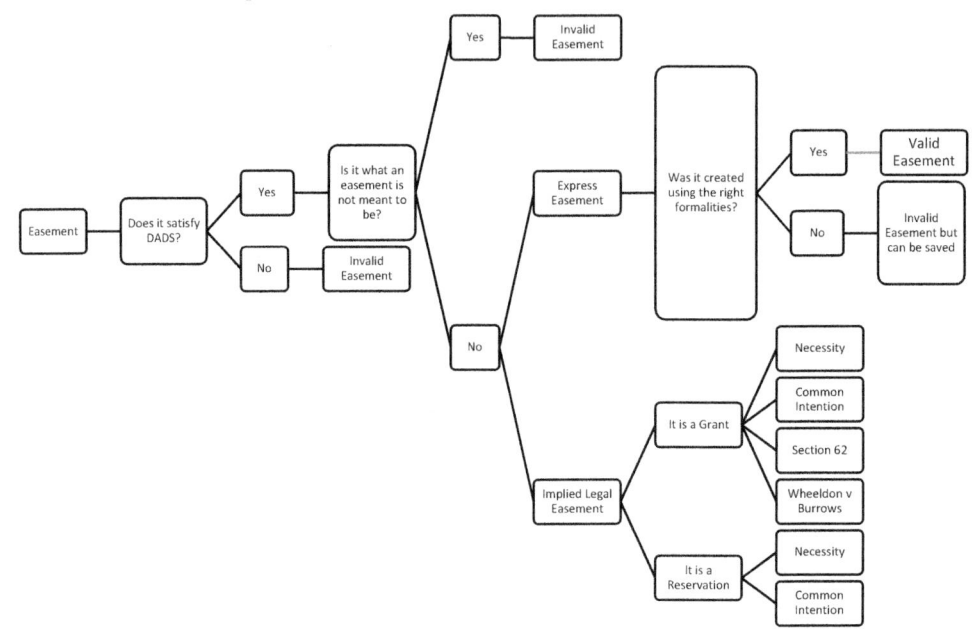

```
Easement → Does it satisfy DADS?
  Yes → Is it what an easement is not meant to be?
    Yes → Invalid Easement
    No → Express Easement
      Was it created using the right formalities?
        Yes → Valid Easement
        No → Invalid Easement but can be saved
      (No branch) → Implied Legal Easement
        It is a Grant → Necessity / Common Intention / Section 62
        It is a Reservation → Wheeldon v Burrows / Necessity / Common Intention
  No → Invalid Easement
```

**Top Tip:** draw out a tree-diagram for this to help understand which method needs to be used in which circumstance

# **Unregistered Interests in Land**

I. Registration of Land & the system for it
II. What is unregistered land?
III. Title in Unregistered Land
IV. Equitable Interests
V. Looking at the Land Charges Act 1972

Registration of land; a history & today's system for it

Okay long boring story cut short, the beginnings of land registration root back to the Passage of the statute of Frauds, 1677 which basically stated that there was a requirement of written evidence to be produced in order to enforce legal effect on promises that were made. These were applied to promises that rooted beyond simple estate transfers, but also engaged in marriages etc. This meant that in order to transfer an interest in land, there was a requirement of a deed & upon the transferring of that interest, the deed wold be transferred as well.

There was, however, an accepted notion of problems arising with the whole concept of deeds. The biggest problem was that it was a requirement that deeds had to be proven by chains. What this meant was that if I was selling you my house, I would have to show deeds from me to numerous previous owners to prove that I actually had a good title to sell that property; it was tedious & very messy. Additionally, deeds are such documents that they can be forged. In the case of Pilcher and Rawlins, it was a case where the deeds had been effectively forged & it was made to look there was no deed when in fact there a deed was, refer to the notes on the case above.

But the first mechanism for registration of land was that of the Merchant Shipping Act 1854 which was used as a registration system for ships coming into and out of the ports of England and Wales. Ships had to be registered in order to dock or sail from these ports and thus effectively, registration was compulsory.

In terms of land, the Royal Commission on Registration of Title 1857 was the first significant order to demand registration, however this was only ation. Compulsory land registration came about through [...]y Act 1862, but this was only for certain titles in certain [...] as London, Liverpool, Manchester, Birmingham etc. The [...]ct 1897 was the first form of wholesome compulsory registration as long as the local council did not say otherwise. So typically, London was the first area where title had to be registered. All of these acts are pretty much irrelevant & that's why I haven't gone into a lot of detail about them.

The big one is that of the Land Registration Act 1925. This was the first set of wholesome changes that were introduced and simply enforced registration of a piece of land upon certain trigger events. The reason thus was introduced was because of the importance attached to the certainty required for a purchaser when purchasing a piece of land in relation to ensure they are protected from any sort of nasty surprise having completed the purchase. They need to know that upon purchase, all interests in the land will exclusively belong to them & as a result, their rights will be protected.

Though it was envisaged that the LRA 1925 would mean that all titles would be registered within 30 years, it was striking that still around 20% of the land area & 15% of titles remain unregistered. This is mainly because land which falls in this category is typically that kind of land which is infrequent to any of the trigger events because they are pieces of land that usually live for generations & are never sold. Buildings such as churches, universities, town halls, courts etc. do not tend to be sold and purchased frequently and these historic buildings are the ones that are yet to be registered.

The process of registering title in the UK is significantly different to the process or importance to those jurisdictions that adopt the method of Torrens title. This is an Australian system of land registration which basically holds that there is no title until your land has been registered. In the UK, you can have title, but it won't be protected until registered. In that system, you won't even be seen as having a title. Both ultimately have the same underlying purpose; register in order for your title to be protected by the state.

The Foundations of Property Law

This was all simply an introduction to what's going to come over the next couple of topics so don't stress if you don't get it in a lot of detail (plus who cares about history when you're studying Law!); the rest of this is now important!

What is unregistered land?

This is weird because unregistered land in this context doesn't actually fully mean that it's wholly unregistered. What it means, is that title to the land is found in previously registered paper deeds proven by an unbroken chain but has not been registered on the register as per the requirements of the Land Registration Act 2002. We will look at it later, but there are some pieces of land which cannot be registered will be partially registered under the Land Charges Act 1972.

The ultimate question when we're considering land in this way, is whether or not 3rd party interest bind the purchaser of the land or not? We look at both legal interests as well as equitable interests.

Titles in Unregistered land

It is important that we determine, as we have determined in previous lectures, that legal estates that are capable of existing under the LPA 1925 are both fee simples (freehold estates) & those estates with a term of years absolute (leasehold estates.)

So, in order to want to sell any land, root title must be investigated. What this means, is that it must be investigated as to whether or not the proposed seller of the land actually has a title which means that they own the land. Can they prove that they are the legal owner of that land which then gives them the ability to turn around & subsequently sell it? In order to do this, their quality of ownership must be determined. Before 1970, there as a requirement that you'd have to go back 30 years & check the deeds for 30 years to see if there was an unbroken, continued chain which allowed for it to be declared that the proposed seller was indeed owner of good title. Today however, that has been cut down to 15 years; so if I wanted to buy a house from you today, I would have to go back to March 2002 & check all

## The Foundations of Property Law

the deeds from that point till today to make sure that for the last 15 years, you've got credit as being the good title holder of that piece of property.

Upon me buying it, even if the land was unregistered, because of the existence of the LRA 2002, this forms as a triggering event which enforces registration upon me; I will have to register my title instantly after thus purchase.

So, in essence, the way a purchase will work, is that you see my unregistered house on the market, you want to buy it. You make an offer; I accept it and thus we exchange contracts. (This is hugely oversimplified, trust me!) I will then need to give you the necessary documents for you to be able to determine whether or not, for the last 15 years, I've been in a position to hold good title to that piece of property. If I do, then you will now go to the Land Registry & register you buying my house so that you will be put down on the register as the legal owner of my old house. After this, completion will occur & I wish you all the best in your new home (and will probably send you flowers, a card & some chocolates cos I'm nice like that ☺)

But the underlying question still remains – what about 3rd party interests? Do they bind the purchaser? Let's think of it by way of an example. I own my house. My neighbour has a legal easement over that property. I sell the house to you. Does my neighbour's easement still exist after you've become the owner – meaning, does the right of my neighbour survive the sale & subsequently bind you?

In order to answer this question, you have to divide it into a question of, is the third-party interest a legal one or an equitable one?

The simple rule to remember is this – **Legal rights bind the world. All legal rights as far as we're concerned this year bind the world. Legal rights bind the whole wide world. Everyone is bound by a legal right. A legal right is something which binds the world. Got it? Legal rights bind the world!!!** I don't think you quite understood what I was saying – legal rights, they bind the world! ☺

Regardless of notice, or anything else – legal rights will always stand. They are never quashed & they will always stay. A prudent purchaser and a purchaser who knows what he's doing will always make himself aware of this & ensure that they act in accordance with this; they'll always be aware of what 3rd party legal interests are attached to that property. Legal leases, or any legal interest will be upheld regardless of notice, regardless of not knowing, regardless of not being able to determine that there was someone who had a legal interest – they'll always be upheld! Legal rights (except for puisne mortgages) bind the transferee whether or not he knew about them, and whether or not they were obvious form an inspection of the title deeds or land.

Equitable Interests

Equitable interests have a partial registration system as per the Land Charges Act 1972 & when an interest has been determined as being equitable, 3 key questions must be asked:

I. Is the interest registerable under the LCA?
II. If so, has it been registered & what's the effect of that registration?
III. If it is registerable, and it hasn't been registered, then what's the effect of this?

Now this is all going to get a bit technical so it might be worth making notes about how this is done & go through a couple of examples – ask what needs to be done.

First, in order to determine whether or not an interest can be registerable, we must look towards **Section 2 of the Land Charges Act 1972** which gives us a list of those interests which can be registerable. This section gives us 6 classes which can be registerable but for our purposes, we are concerned mainly with **Class C, D & F.**

I. Class A - statutory charges that are created on the application of a person under an Act of Parliament. Work undertaken by a public body, the cost of which is chargeable to the owner. The cost is secured by means of a Class A land charge
II. Class B – Statutory charges that arise automatically (unlike class A's, which arise upon application)

The Foundations of Property Law

III. Class C - for us, this is a really Important class. Interests that are adverse to the owner, i.e. restrict owner's rights over the land and/or detract from value
  i. Legal/puisne mortgage
  ii. Limited owner's charge – charge/mortgage that a limited owner (such as a life estate holder) may be entitled to levy against the land because of obligations discharged by him (e.g. Payment of inheritance tax) – very uncommon
  iii. General equitable charge (except for equitable co-ownership)
  iv. Estate contracts – enforceable agreements to convey legal state. This is particularly important for our exam. An estate contract is where contracts have been exchanged but legal title is held with the initial owner still much like in the case of *Walsh v Lonsdale,* we looked at the previous topic.

IV. Class D(:
  i. Inland Revenue Charge
  ii. Restrictive covenants that are not between lessor and lessee. A promises neighbour that he will not carry out any business on his land. The neighbour can register a class D(ii) land charge against A's name.
  iii. Equitable easements created after 1925.

V. Class E – annuities created before 1926 (yearly sums paid to specific persons)

VI. Class F – Spousal right to the matrimonial home.

**Class C(iv) – estate contract.**

**Class D(ii) – restrictive covenant.**

**Class D(iii) – equitable easement.**

THESE ARE IMPORTANT ONES FOR MOST EXAMS!!!

**Class F – spousal rights of occupation under the Family Law Act 1996**

So, what are the effects of registering?

Under the 1972 Land Charges Act, it is a requirement that the interest is registered under the name of the person for whom the interest belongs too;

the person who is the estate owner at the time this charge is created. This must be registered by the correct name because if the name is wrong, the register is wrong which can put your title at threat because it'll be against that which the title is registered/upheld. Additionally, if the name is incorrect, then if a 3rd party does investigations & find that the name is wrong, well then you cannot try to bind the interest because you're not the title holder according to the register.

If the land has been registered properly then according to the requirements under LCA 1972, then & only then will **Section 198 of the Law of Property Act 1925** step in & protect the land. This section states, *"The registration of any instrument or matter in any register kept under the Land Charges Act 1972 … shall be deemed to constitute actual notice of such instrument or matter, and of the fact of such registration, to all persons and for all purposes connected with the land affected, as from the date of registration or other prescribed date and so long as the registration continues in force."*

What this means, is that by registering in this way, you constitute actual notice of your interest/title in that land which as a result, will bind all future purchasers of that land. You can only alert the purchaser of your interest/title in that land as long as you have registered it & once this is done, they'll be bound by it as well.

However, it isn't the end of the world if you don't register it; well it depends on how you look at it. If I have an equitable interest that is not registered in a piece of land & you behind my back, go ahead & sell the property, though the purchaser will not be bound by my interest, I'll be able to sue you for breaching the trust/contract between us. You had the legal title; I still had a title in that property too so I have a right to at least the proceeds of the sale so I will sue you. But beyond that, it isn't necessary that I will always lose my interest, and this is dependent on two things:

I. The Nature of the charge; the interest in the property
II. The nature of the transferee

For class A, B, C(i), C(ii), C(iii) and F land charges, if the interest is not registered, then the interest will not bind a purchaser of any interest in land who gives 'valuable consideration' as per Section 4 & 17 of the LCA 1972.

## The Foundations of Property Law

This is because a purchaser who gives 'valuable consideration 'for any interest will obtain that interest free of unregistered charges and thus having actual knowledge of who the title/interest holders are is irrelevant because giving valuable consideration is enough.

If on the other hand however, no valuable consideration has been given, then the purchaser will still bound by the unregistered charge. Consideration, as is the maxim in English Contract law, need be sufficient but need not be adequate.

As for the class C(iv) and D charges, if the title/interest is not registered, then it will not bind a purchaser of a legal estate who gives 'money or money's worth'. A purchaser who gives 'money or money's worth' for a legal estate, will obtain the legal estate free of the charge. Though if money or money's worth is not given, then the purchaser can still be susceptible to an estate contract. A purchaser of equitable estate (e.g. A equitable lease) remains bound by any unregistered class C(iv) and D land charge. What money or money's worth does, is that it will get the land free of the unregistered charge; you are no longer bound by it.

All land charges even if it is unregistered, will bind the transferee who is not a purchaser; if someone is gifted a piece of land, will be bound by it. Similarly, a purchaser who has acted in fraud will be bound by it because of the maxim, 'fraud unravels everything.'

In the case of *Midland Bank v Green* [1981] Walter was a farmer who had a wife named Evelyn and a son named Geoffrey. This was a case wherein Walter gave him son Geoffrey an option to purchase the farm for a price of £75 an acre over a period of 10 years. It was accepted by Geoffrey and as a result, he instructed his solicitor to register the option under Class C (iv) as an estate contract under the LCA 1972. Now unfortunately for Geoffrey the lad, the solicitor the bloody idiot, didn't register it & Geoffrey had no idea this was the case.

So, you can see where this is going... When the family had a feud & the relationships broke down, Walter decided to sell the property which was worth £40,000 to his wife Evelyn for just £500. Evelyn when purchasing the property carried out her investigation & found that there was no option (conspiracy theory????) & so brought the house. She then went on to make a will leaving behind the farm equally for all of her 5 children & once she died, Geoffrey gave notice of the exercising of his option which had not been registered but he was unaware of this!

The question to the courts initially was simply, is Evelyn bound by the estate contract which was held by Geoffrey & in order to do so, the following questions must be asked:

i. Was the interest equitable or legal? An estate contract is an equitable interest
ii. Was the interest registerable? Yes, under Class C (iv) an estate contract is registerable
iii. Was it registered? Nope – but this was the solicitor's fault
iv. Was Evelyn a purchaser of money or money's worth? The trial court said that yes, she was. Lord Denning in the Court of Appeal however felt that nah, this was a fraud fam. The sale was not for money or money's worth – how could Walter be willing to take an L of £39,500 to sell it to Evelyn like that, He said that the protection of the LCA was unavailable to people who committed fraud and that *"dishonest dealing to deprive innocents of their rightful due."*

In the House of Lords, those fighting the case for Geoffrey say two things:

i. There was no good faith from Evelyn & Walter – they were not purchasers of good faith and this was deliberate from them
ii. Evelyn was not a purchaser for money or money's worth because £500 is nominal value & thus they should not have been protected by the LCA. However, the House of Lord said that £500 was money or money's worth did not need for it to be adequate but rather just sufficient

And finally, what about those unregisterable interests that can be overreached? Remember for an interest to be overreached you need 2 trustees or a trust corporation along with capital money or security that represents capital money (from previous lectures.) Overreachable equitable interests cannot be registered because of Section 2(4)(iii) of the

Land Charges act. If an interest is Overreachable and has been overreached, then the purchaser will take the land without the interest, simple as.

As for those interest that are not registerable and not subject to overreaching either? Well these interests will be subject to the concept of equity's darling; bona fide purchaser for value without notice.

So, in essence, to work out whether or not 3rd parties are bound by the interest we must work out:

I. What is the interest in the land?
II. Was the title legal or equitable? For this, look at Section 1 of the LPA – can it be legal? If not, then all others will be equitable. If legal, has it followed the right formalities to be determined a legal interest? **Formalities topic is VERY VERY important – if you don't get it, you will NOT be able to answer a question in the exam 100%**
III. Is that interest binding on the purchaser? Look here at the concepts of overreaching & the LCA 1972.

# Registered Interests in Land

I. Registered Land
II. Registration of title/estates
III. Protection of interests via Notices & Restrictions
IV. Overriding Interests
V. Overriding & Overreaching
VI. Adverse Possession in registered land

Land Registration

1925 was a year of immense reform in terms of land laws; we had the Law of Property Act, the Land Charges Act & the Land Registration Act too! Okay fair enough the Land Registration Act 1925 was replaced by the 2002 act which at this point you should be completely familiar with, the LRA 1925 & 2002 together govern the vast majority of land in the UK. The purpose of the LRA was to ensure that there was an ease attached to the transactions which are coincided with land. The purchasing of land should be a quick, efficient & inexpensive method which should bring ease with whoever wishes to engage in the purchase of land.

The argument for advancing ease ties in with calls made for e-conveyancing and allowing all of this to occur online through forms online, rather than rafting through tonnes of paperwork. The purpose for these calls is to adhere with the fundamental root of the calls to ensure that the maximum number of estates in land are registerable beyond the registered leaseholds, freeholds which can be registered at this moment, but go beyond to ensure registration is possible for all 3rd party interests which may be attached to a piece of land.

This is all done to ensure that the time, effort, money that is invested to investigating things such as root title or what the interests on the land are, is effort which can be avoided and usurped by simply checking the register & today pay a mere £3 for the title register which will tell you what titles are attached to the piece of land. This ensures that both parties are protected; the purchaser is protected because he is made aware of all the interests on the land & saves himself from any nasty surprises whilst the

## The Foundations of Property Law

seller and more importantly, 3rd parties are protected from having their interests ignored & lose their title without their knowledge.

Additionally, it provides for a mechanism to protect 3rd party interests through the doctrines of:

I. Overreaching
II. Overriding
III. The fact that interests that are registered will always be protected

How does it work?

So as of the 1st of December 1990, upon the occurrence, as we mentioned the previous topic, of some trigger event, registration will become compulsory on the title holder insofar that, as we will look at in detail below, if after a certain period of the transaction/trigger event registration does not occur, title will be lost. Upon registration, the land registrars will do their usual investigations with regards to the validity of the title by investigating root title, which will then lead them to issue each interest with a unique title number.

There are 4 trigger events of this kind which we are concerned with:

I. Conveyance of a freehold, whether that be the purchasing of that freehold or as a gift
II. Grant of a lease for more than 7 years
III. Transfer of a lease on which there is more than 7 years left
IV. Creation of a mortgage on a property

When we talk about registered land, we must remember the following three types of interests:

I. Registerable interests are the ones that are given their due title number
II. Protectable interests, or traditionally known as minor interests, are also given positions on the title register; these are notices & restrictions

III. Overriding interests which effectively do exactly that; they override the register & doing so, as a result, they do not actually appear on the register as such.

Registerable Interests & Estates

These are the interests which are capable of being registered under **Section 27** of the Land Registration Act 2002. These are those interests which are capable of existing at law and not equity, which will lead to them receiving their own special unique title number from the register upon registration & they are:

I. A legal estate in fee simple absolute in possession
II. A legal lease for a term more than 7 year
III. A legal mortgage
IV. A profit a prendre in gross – don't worry about this but for your information, this is a French term which means that you can take the profits of that land from certain resources which arise from that land
V. A legal easement
VI. A rentcharge
VII. A franchise and a manor – again don't worry too much about this one too.

The above 7 are known as major interests & though we are only really concerned with 4/5 of them, it is vital to know that for each of these, these must be registered in line with the qualifying trigger events & upon registration, they will each have their own unique title numbers.

The LRA likes to differentiate the difference between registering an interest for the first time & registering something as a subsequent/latter disposition.

For the first registration of a fee-simple, purchasing a piece of land is a trigger event which enforces registration immediately such that **Section 4** of the LRA specifies that within 2 months of completion, title must be registered from being unregistered. This could be purchasing a fee-simple through sale or through a gift or getting it as a mortgage. The way that

## The Foundations of Property Law

registration will occur is that the registrar will get all the necessary required documents and inspect them thoroughly once & for all. The inspection will inspect the deeds and other documents to determine root title whilst also conducting investigations to uncover potential minor interests & in doing so then moves to register these minor interests as notices or restrictions; the distinction between them will be discussed below. And the effect of this? Well the effect is the whole purpose of registration – the state will guarantee the protection of registered interests as per **Section 58** of the LRA; the registered property will be deemed to have been vested with legal estate regardless of fraud and mistake.

But if for some wonderful reason you fail to register your property within two months, then as well as being a fool, you'll lose your legal title to that property. What will happen, is that though you will keep a hold of the equitable title to that property, the legal title will return to the seller (the original owner.) So, what you now have to do, is take the L & go back & do one of two things:

I. You can go to the Chief Land Register and as per **Section 6(4) & (5)** ask them that look, I'm a bit slow with these things, I'm sorry but can you give me the legal title; here's all the proof that I'm meant to have that legal title.

II. OR you just gotta go back to the person you brought the land from & tell them that bro, I messed up man, I didn't register the damn thing so you're now the legal title holder again LOL. So, do me a favour innit; drop me the fee simple legal title again innit. And I'll pay you back. Effectively here, you've got an estate contract & you may remember the rules with regards to estate contracts from a couple of lectures ago. It is those rules which will be applied here.

Remember, **Section 27** states that, "If a disposition of a registered estate or registered charge is required to be completed by registration, it does not operate at law until the relevant registration requirements are met." Until you do not register your title, you do not have legal title; you're just an equitable title holder & thus as a result, as per **Section 29(1)** this interest you have cannot be enforceable against anyone who acquires subsequent

## The Foundations of Property Law

registerable interest in the land for valuable consideration. So, if you don't register it, you stand to lose it – simple.

So, for example, if you sell me a piece of land & in that time, I fail to register it in the 2-month period. So, after this, Katie comes along & purchases the house from you for valuable consideration. Does she now take the fee simple absolutely? Yes of course she does; I failed to register it & so her purchasing it for valuable consideration gives her the fee simple.

The same as above applies for leases which are longer than 7 years-long.

So, what about those interests that are not registerable, minor interests?

Well these interests because they're not registerable, doesn't mean that they cannot be protected. These minor interests can be protected by making an entry into the register through a notice or a restriction. These interests won't have their own unique title number, but substantive registration can protect these interests regardless. Some of the interests which can be protected in this way are:

I. Equitable easements
II. Restrictive covenants
III. Estate contracts
IV. Interests behind a trust of land

The one thing to bear in mind is that protection does not involve a guarantee in the same way that registered land provides a protection because it is not the duty of the Land Registry to guarantee the upholding of protecting these interests. Rather, the owner is required to prove that it does exist and proving that it exists acts like a way to protect against subsequent registered dispositions.

There are 2 ways to protect an interest in this way which I will consider below…

<u>Notice</u>

A valid notice will work to bind 3$^{rd}$ party purchasers and can be used to protect most things but not excluded by Section 33 of the LRA. Notices can be used for a number of interests including those like estate contracts, options, pre-emptions, restrictive covenants, easements, leases granted for 7 years or less etc. It's literally what you're doing in a notice is you're giving a notice on the title document that you have an equitable interest in the land; you have an interest that is registered on the title document & it makes the potential purchasers aware of your interest – it's on the document so it's impossible for them not to be aware of it!

Restrictions

These are actually the weakest form of protecting one's interest because restrictions do not actually bind a purchaser. What a restriction does, is that it alerts a potential purchaser of a piece of land of your title and of any further limitations there may be on the registered title holders' powers, but still does not make the interest enforceable against anyone nor does it validate the interest. So here, even though it'll be on the register, the register can be ignored & your interest will be ignored completely.

So, let us say for example that I am a beneficiary of a trust of land held by Katie and Susan. I want to make sure that a prospective buyer knows that both Katie AND Susan are required to sell the land. As a result, I can enter into a restriction on the register to this effect. However, a purchaser can still purchase from Katie & Susan for capital money and will not bound by my interest.

In another example, let us say that I have has an option to purchase Katie's land. As it's an option, I can enter a notice under Section 34(1) LRA. If I register a notice, then it binds a purchaser. If, however, I do not register a notice, I can choose to enter a restriction. The restriction may not bind the purchaser, but I will be alerted if Katie tries to snake the ting & sell it someone else.

Overriding Interests

Overriding interests are those proprietary interests in land which are not registered, nor are they protected by the notice or by restriction. The protection of overriding interests comes from **Schedule 3 in the LRA 2002** which allows for overriding interests to be protected. Remember, we covered overriding interests when we considered overreaching a few topics back. Overriding interests arise because well there are some interests which are just too small and have no worth being kept on the register; to maintain them on the register would be a tougher task than it would be to leave them off it. They are very easily discoverable & work to protect those who typically shouldn't need to register their interests/are unable to. So, for example, wives of husbands shouldn't need to register their interest in a marital home because well they have the overriding interest of actual occupation along with their property interest.

Schedule 3 sets out 3 ways in which interests can work to override interests in the register in 3 different paras & they are:

I. Legal leases of 7 years or less – what this para means is that legal leases under 7 years can work to be overriding interests. Remember that, leases which are for a period of more than 7 years must be registered in their own right. As for those under 7 years, there's 2 different rules
    a. For legal leases which are more than 3 years long but less than 7 years, they can be protected by means of a notice which we discussed above. You do not need to rely on an overriding interest to protect your interest in the land.
    b. For legal leases for a period of less than 3 years, well these can only rely on overriding interests to protect them.
II. Proprietary interests in the land (be it legal or equitable) of a person in actual and discoverable occupation at the time of the disposition – equitable leases will have to comply with this and this they will need the protection of a notice or overriding interests coupled with actual occupation. Para 2 protects interest & actual occupation. It must be noted that interest does not have to be connected to the occupation as per the case of *Webb v Pollmount* [1966]. This is a case where an option was given to a lessor who was in actual occupation of a piece of property but had a 7-year lease of that property. The option that the lessor had was, as we saw above,

protectable by a notice, but this had not been entered onto the register. The freehold of the building was sold to a 3$^{rd}$ party & the question for the court was to determine that whether the leasehold A had was protected or not. It was clear that this leasehold acted as an overriding interest as per Schedule 3 Para 1. And the option was binding on 3$^{rd}$ party because of Para 2; A's option was binding because he had both actual occupation and a proprietary interest in the option.

Actual occupation was defined in the case of *Chokar v Chokar* where the courts said that actual occupation basically means that there's a reasonableness attached to the appearance of the person; they are more than likely to be there or to return there.

III. Legal easements & profit a prendre that are known or discoverable upon reasonable inspection. Under the 2002 Act, there is still no requirement of a causal link between interest and occupation.

In the case of *City of London Building Society v Flegg* [1988] which we looked at in previous lectures, the wife's parents contributed to the purchase price of a house for which the couple were the registered owners of that property & the beneficial title was held by the parents; all parties occupied the house. On that house, the couple took out the several mortgages on the property but the final loan, from the Building Society could not be paid off. The Building Society claimed for repossession of the house.

The trial judge said that the parents had an overriding interest as they had an interest in the property as well as actual occupation. But the judge held that despite this, these interests were overreached because the couple are deemed as two trustees and they had created a legal charge for money and thus the trial judge ruled that the building society should be granted possession.

The Court of Appeal reversed the decision and said that no, based on the case of Boland, a tenant in common in actual occupation is incapable of having his interest overreached.

In the House of Lords, the parents argued that they had an overriding interest which as a result could not be overreached. Lord Templeman held that in order to claim an overriding interest you should have an interest in land & actual occupation. The problem in this case, was that the parents' interest in the and was overreached & thus they no longer had an interest in the land but rather they had an interest in the proceeds of the sale.

So, what interest takes precedence & gets priority? Registerable interests will always get priority because once they are registered, they will bind the world.

There are 3 ways to think of land registration:

I. Mirror Principle – the register is meant to reflect the actual ways in which land is actually occupied/land on the ground but remember that overriding interests and not at all reflected
II. Curtain Principle – this is the idea that you can see what is shown to you, but you cannot see what is hidden.
III. Insurance – Here the state guarantees whatever interests exist once they're registered & they will be protected – remember if there is a mistake in the register then you stand to lose your title.

So, in essence, what are the differences between registered & unregistered land?

Title – registered land has recorded title on the register with unique title numbers which are guaranteed to be protected by the state. As for unregistered land, it is not protected by the state

Rights over the land – well in registered land, 3rd party rights are protected through registration, notice or through overriding interests. In unregistered land, 3rd part rights are protected if there are legal rights that bind the world, the interest is registered on the LCA or through equity's darling.

The Foundations of Property Law

# Equity Law

**Property Equity**

**Trusts**

**Express Trusts**

**Implied Trusts**

**Trusts of the Family Home**

**Unincorporated Associations & Rules against perpetuity**

**Charities**

**Formalities & Proprietary Estoppel**

**Doctrine of Notice & Overreaching**

**Trustees Powers & Duties**

**Breach of Duty & Fiduciary Duties**

**Proprietary Remedies & Tracing**

**3rd Party Liability – Personal Claims**

# **Property Equity**

I. 5th & 6th Dimensions of English Property Law
II. Equity's Darling

Before delving into anything else, we must first wholly understand the history of the development of English Legal property law which then allows us to uncover the system properly. So initially in the UK, we had 2 systems of laws, the common law courts & the courts of Chancery. The Common Law Courts, which were also known as the Kings' Courts, operated a Writ System, whereby if a person had a claim against a court decision against them, so long as their claim was recognised & realised by the writ system, they would be in a position to pursue a remedy. This meant that the writ system was highly formalised in the sense that one could only claim against a decision if the claim fell within one of the recognised writs. This formal procedure & mechanism was in fact the only effective way of adhering to a justice legal system because of the time & era, making it highly difficult to predict/know the law beforehand. There was, however, a system which was in essence a pressure valve in order to mitigate the formalism; in this system, it would be possible to appeal directly to the monarch if justice was not gained from the common law courts system because the claim didn't actually fall into one of the recognised Writ. This was obviously a way out which was highly abused particularly by the monarchs themselves because they would give access to this equitable system to the powerful & influential people who were important to keep happy & pleasant in order to keep their state running smoothly & wholly in their power. But effectively, the common law system was a rigid formal one whilst the court of chancery through the Monarch via the Lord Chancellor was on which mas supposed to improve the common law system.

This comes to light with the example of a Knight's tale. Imagine a Knight going off to do battle in distant climes leaving a wife and family in a time when women are not permitted to own land. The knight conveys his estate to a trusted friend to manage the estate for the 'use' of his wife. The trusted friend turns out to be untrustworthy and conveys the estate to a third party without the permission/knowledge of the Knight (man's actually fully a

## The Foundations of Property Law

snake fam.) The wife here has clearly suffered an injustice but will get no remedy from the Kings Courts as, in the eyes of the common law, the trusted friend was the legal owner, and the third party is the legal owner now in such circumstances, where the Kings Courts (Common Law Courts) could not offer justice, petition could be made to the Monarch who delegated questions of justice to his leading prelate, the Lord Chancellor, who decided such matters on the basis of conscience. Equity is all about this; was or should the conscience of the guilty party, have been affected? If so, then they have acted against equity and the laws of equity will come in to save the day. This exercise of delegated power slowly developed into what became the rules of Equity, administered by what for a long while was a separate Court of Chancery. Equity is an incomplete system parasitic on the complete but imperfect common law system, smoothing off its rough edges.

A court of conscience would then offer the property back to the wife in a number of circumstances:

I. If the transferee of the legal estate acted in bad faith, the title would return to the Knight/Wife – this means that they (the trusted friend) knew what they were doing & did it on purpose, which betrays the principle of the law of equity.
II. If the transferee of the legal estate gave no consideration meaning that they gave it away for free, thus the same as above will apply.
III. If the transferee of the legal estate knew of the wife's interest & still decided to transfer the property, which proves that they most certainly acted in bad faith and will thus be returned.

So, this means, that if someone is acting in bad faith, or gives no consideration or knew of the wife's interests, would give rise to the title being given back to the wife/Knight. (This isn't strictly true – the wife still wouldn't be able to have possession because she's a woman, so most probably, according to my understanding, the courts would appoint another trustee on behalf of the wife, or the wife would potentially be allowed to choose a trustee for herself to have title to that property with regard to the wife's property interests.

The Foundations of Property Law

But what if they hadn't been doing any of the above? This gives rise to…

Equity's Darling!

This is the notion that someone who acquires the legal estate in the state that they are:

I. Acting in good faith; AND
II. Giving Value to the estate; AND
III. Having no notice

This is also known as "Bona fide purchaser of a legal estate for value without notice," which is another exception to Nemo Dat which we covered the previous topic. But briefly, it's the idea that Dat says that you cannot give a better title than the one which you have. For example, if I steal a car & I sell it to you, the basic rule states that you cannot get a 'good' title from me because I don't have/possess a good title to transfer to you. This is what we looked at when we considered the case of *Bruten v London Quadrant Housing* [1999] who granted a sub-licence but was deemed by the courts to actually be a lease which means that London Quadrant Housing, who had a licence themselves could not grant a lease because they didn't have the good title themselves to give it.

And so, this is where the 5$^{th}$ & 6$^{th}$ dimensions of land come in, with the previous 4 dimensions being covered in The Foundations of Land Law.

The 5$^{th}$ dimension of property rights are something that we have already covered and it's the idea that with a property right, you bind the whole world except someone with a better right than you. This makes the 5$^{th}$ dimension of property rights valid for possession too & the notion that possession is also protected in English Common Law in order to prevent a potential state of anarchy. However, the simple idea here is that the 5$^{th}$ dimension is merely a legal right which binds the world.

The 6h dimension is the idea of equitable property rights which effectively are the same as a legal property right, in the sense that they bind the world, but the exception is that they bind the world except… "Bona fide purchaser of a legal estate for value without notice," meaning Equity's darling!

So simply, legal rights bind the world whilst equitable rights do bind the world too with the exception of equity's darling.

# Trusts

I. What is a Trust?
II. Types of Trust

## What is a Trust?

A trust is simply a division of ownership between the legal title holder and an equitable interest holder; for example, if I as a land owner give you an equitable property lease which means that your rights will over me will be supreme in all circumstances of exclusive possession, except of Equity's darling meaning that someone acting in good faith, giving value & having no notice will not be bound by your lease agreement. The trustee is required to manage the property and cannot profit from her trusteeship (although she can be paid to carry out her tasks, if that is permitted under the trust deed). The beneficiary has the right to use, enjoy and profit from the property and has the valuable interest (unless he is holding the equitable title on a sub-trust as discussed later). The trustee holds the titular title, a legal shell surrounding the substantive equitable interest. The trustee owes the beneficiary a fiduciary duty (requiring total loyalty and utmost good faith) and must always put the beneficiary's interests first and must never put herself in a position where her duty and her (self-)interest conflict. As we have noted, these days, the term beneficiary is invariably used in preference to the traditional term, *Cestui Queue Trust*, although that is a little misleading as the beneficiary is not the only one in whom the beneficial use of the property might vest.

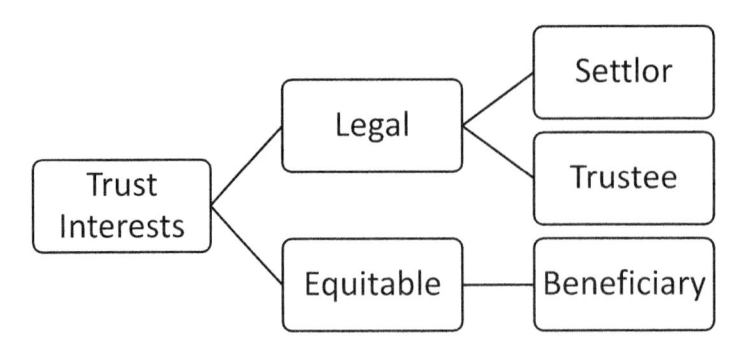

```
                    ┌─ Legal ─────┬─ Settlor
Trust Interests ────┤             └─ Trustee
                    └─ Equitable ──── Beneficiary
```

## Types of Trust

Before we begin, it's important to understand the actual concept of what a trust is. In essence, a trust is basically a confidence reposed from a trustee to a beneficiary. In essence, what this means, is that the legal owner(s) of a piece of property will be the trustee who can be a completely different party to the equitable owners who ae the beneficiaries of that property. Put simply, a trust is when one person(s) trust another party with their property; a trustee trusting a beneficiary with their property.

There are a range of different trusts which fall under two main categories both of which we look at throughout this book and they are:

I. Express Trusts – These are those trusts which we look at in first & it is basically where there is an explicit intention to create a trust. There are 2 types of express trust:
   a. Bare Trust – This is also known as a fixed, simple or naked trust which is the notion that a trustee must act in accordance with either the instrument by which the trust was created or as per the directions/orders of the beneficiary. The beneficiary is actually the person who receives all the benefit from the property. So, for example, if the instrument of that created the trust states that "The trustee must transfer a property of 500 shares to X." This is a very simple order; whoever the trustee is, needs to be the one who transfers 500 shares to the beneficiary, X. The trustee cannot do anything else with the property as for their own accord or their own benefit; they are merely the means by which the ends must be met. So, put simply, in a bare trust, the trustee basically has to do what the trust document/deed tells them to do or what the beneficiary directly asks them to do; they are compelled by their requirements.
   b. Special Trust – A special trust is simply any trust that isn't a bare trust; the trustee is given power to act with what they have been trusted with. One popular special trust is a discretionary trust; these are those trusts which are those

trusts which are trusts coupled with a power. This means that the trustee is given instructions as to what he must do but is given some discretion with regards to what he is and is not required to do. So, for example, if I say to you, that "I want to give you £2,000 to give to children in India as you wish to do so." What this means, is that I am giving you a trust of £2,000 to benefit the children in India with that money. But what you do with that money is down to you. You can feed the kids, you can buy them Eid gifts, buy them clothes, build a house, get toys etc. You have the discretion to use that £2,000 on the children as you see fit or as per the terms, as you wish to do so.

In this example, there are 3 terms which one needs to grasp:
  i. Settlor – the person who starts/sets the trust – in the example, I am the settlor
  ii. Trustee – the person who is entrusted with enacting the trust/the legal title holder of that property – in the example, you are the trustee
  iii. Beneficiary – the person who should benefit from the trust/the equitable title holder of that property – in the example, the children in India are the beneficiaries of the trust imposed on you by me, the settler.

II. Imputed/Implied Trusts – These are those trusts which are usually focused on domestic situations between a husband and a wife, who usually fall apart from each other & then there is a bit of an argument about who owns the house etc etc. Because there often is no express trust agreed between both parties, courts step in and look at the situation and determine if that there ever was an intention to create a trust between the parties & if merely the express term of intention was not observed. There are 2 types which we look at later in the term, but they are:
  a. Constructive
  b. Resulting

The Foundations of Property Law

This is a tree-diagram which will be built on as the topics go on, but this is the starting point of it – there are two kinds of trusts interests:

I. Express Trusts
II. Implied Trusts

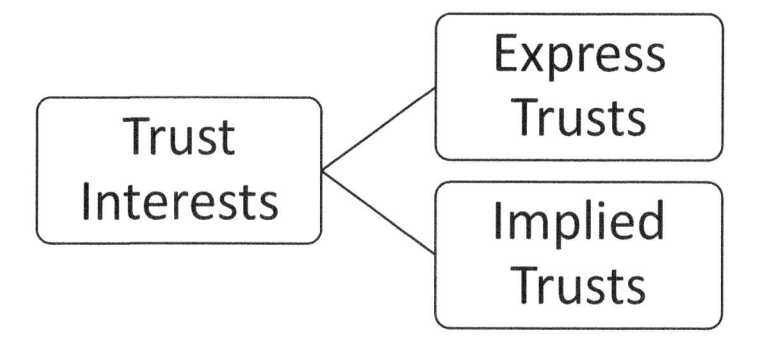

```
                    ┌─────────────┐
                    │   Express   │
                    │   Trusts    │
┌─────────────┐    └─────────────┘
│    Trust    │ <
│  Interests  │    ┌─────────────┐
└─────────────┘    │   Implied   │
                    │   Trusts    │
                    └─────────────┘
```

# **Express Trusts**

| | |
|---|---|
| I. | Types of Trust |
| II. | Express Trusts |
| III. | Certainty of Intention |
| IV. | Certainty of Subject Matter |
| V. | Certainty of Object Matter |
| VI. | List Certainty |
| VII. | A Power as a Trust |
| VIII. | The Evolution of the Law |
| IX. | The Law of Today |
| X. | Beneficiary Principle |
| XI. | Non-charitable purpose trusts |
| XII. | Anomalous Categories |

<u>Express Trust</u>

Building on what's been mentioned, there are a number of requirements for an express trust to be deemed as completely valid which we will look at below.

I. The settlor, the creator of the express trust, must have the capacity to create a trust. What this means, is the idea that they must be *Sui Juris* suggesting that they must be at least 18 years old & to not be mentally incapacitated. This is because with these two conditions met, then and only then do they have the required capacity to create the power to dispose of legal or equitable interests. A minor (someone under the age of 18) can create a trust of any property that they may own, but this will be repudiated (will be rejected & not accepted) when they reach the age of majority.

II. For a trust of a land, it is required that the property is in the hands of the trustee, meaning that they are the legal title holder of that property.

III. For the creation of a trust, it is a core requirement that there must be written evidence that a trust is being created. This can be through a will, a deed of a trust etc. But written evidence must be evident. The reason for this, is that the settlor and the trustee can, and most often is a different person and thus the settlor needs to convey legal title to the trustee because they are in essence transferring their property to the trustee; the trustee will have the legal title of the property. And as with selling any property, written evidence must be produced.

All of these are in order to ensure that the formalities are met so that the property can be completely constituted. Until the formalities are not complete, the property cannot be completely constituted. Completely constituted means that the property must wholly be in the hands of the trustee and non-other. That being said, there are 2 ways through which a trust can be created:

I. The person that is the absolute owner declares himself a trustee which in essence, can be seen that that settlor makes himself the trustee
II. The absolute owner, the settlor, transfers the property which should then be hold on trust for another person, the beneficiary. This is the kind of trust creation that was upheld in my above example of giving you £2,000 for the children of India; I must have completely constituted the property to you before it can be declared as being in a trust.

There is however, more to the creation of an express trust than this & this is the most important part to understand. There are 3 certainties which must be found in order for a trust to be valid cited from the case of *Knight v Knight* [1840] in dictum by Lord Langdale & they are:

I. Certainty of intention – must be a certainty that one intends to create an express trust; *"equity looks to intent rather than form."*
II. Certainty of subject matter - the idea that it must be known what property is being, and is not being subject to the trust
III. Certainty of object (we look at this in the next topic) – the idea that it must be known who the beneficiary actually is; they must be known.

It is worth noting & understanding from an early stage, that the three rules cannot be examined in isolation from each other & must be looked at as a collective whole, based on the notion suggested in *Mussoorie Bank v Raynor [1882]* where it was stated, *"Uncertainty in the subject matter of the gift has a reflex action, upon the previous words, and throws doubt upon the intention of the testator, and seems to show that he could not have possibly have intended his words of confidence, hope or whatever they may be – his appeal to the conscience of the first taker – to be imperative words."*

Certainty of Intention

For an express term to be deemed valid, it must be sure that there is an intention to create a trust obligation as such. You cannot deem a binding trust obligation to be created from a generalised intent to benefit but rather there must be a specific intent by the means of a trust. This can be done through any words (well any words which seem to suggest that you've made a promise & you intend to keep it) and it does not actually explicitly require the term 'trust' to be mentioned in the creation of the trust.

Courts choose to look specifically at the language used in establishing if an intention was there to create an express trust. They look at the language to see whether or not the agreement was conclusive and explicit & if the courts deem it to be so, then this shall suffice. If not however, they will use retrospective evidence to determine whether or not there was an intention to create an express trust. Basically, what this is, is the idea that they will look at the circumstances surrounding the agreement of the trust. If it is clear that there are signs that there was an intention for a trust to be created, then the trust will be deemed as valid. The issue for courts, much like in criminal law, is that courts are not God (as much as they often wish they were!) and thus, they can't exactly tell what someone's intention is, so in order to try & come to a fair judgement, they need to figure it out using the evidence which has been placed before them.

And when determining this, they take a keen interest in the expertise of the settlor. This comes to life in two particular cases:

I.  In the case of *Swain v Law Society [1982]* Swain left behind some money for the law society and the courts were attempting to determine whether or not this money was to be held as a trust. Swain was a lawyer & thus the courts clearly determined the fact that he would have the know-how of how to create a trust and would actually be able to do with some legal finesse too. And thus, if he wanted to create a trust, he would've explicitly done so because he has the ability/intelligence/expertise to do just that. Lord Brightman said, *"It would indeed be surprising if a society of lawyers, who above all might be expected to make their intention clear in a document they compose, should have failed to express the existence of a trust, if that is what they intended to create."* What they're trying to say here, is that it would be shocking if a lawyer didn't know that he needed to use more specific language in order to create a trust! (I mean he may have bunked most of his lectures, didn't study but spent all his time in law school partying & became a lawyer by mere luck, but that's probably unlikely!)

II. In the case of *Paul v Constance* [1976], Mr Constance's marriage broke down, and he moved in with Ms Paul (they were having an affair and cos men are trash, Mr Constance was cheating on his wife which ultimately meant he obviously got caught and his marriage subsequently broke down... hope it was worth it, idiot!) After a workplace accident he received £950 in damages, and following discussions with a bank manager, paid it into a new joint account. They were unmarried, so the account was just put in Mr Constance's sole name. He said repeatedly, 'the money is as much yours as mine'. They paid in joint bingo winnings too, and they made a £150 withdrawal, which they split to spend on Christmas presents and food. But 13 months after Mr Constance died without a will. Ms Paul claimed the account was hers. Mrs Constance reappeared and claimed the money was hers. The courts here determined that Mr Constance most definitely lacked the legal expertise as thus by the conduct of both him & Ms Paul, the account could be deemed to indeed be a trust between Mr Constance & Ms Paul – Mrs Constance had no trust in that account.

However, sometimes, there are a few grey areas, with particular reference to 3 concepts:

# The Foundations of Property Law

I. Precatory Words – these are those words which suggest some form of hope/wish that something will happen; meaning that you hope/pray/wish that the trust you leave behind will be used in a certain way. For example, I give you £2,000 for the people of India & I say to you, "Ah I wish you use it to feed them." In the 19th century, up until 1871, it was deemed that this would indeed be a valid trust, but the trust would be imposed such that you would not in any way be able to justify any spending of the £2,000 on anyone, including yourself, except for the expressed children of India.

In 1871, the case of *Lambe v Eames* [1871] came about wherein Lord Justice James determined a term, *"cruel kindness"* to explain the fact that the trust went from the being kind to Lambe's kids to being cruel to his wife because she was unable to spend any money on herself from that trust.

Thus, the modern approach to precatory words is significantly different. In the *Re Adams & Kensington Vestry* [1884] case, the Husband left property to his Wife in *"full confidence that she will do what is right between my children."* Here, it was determined by the courts and Lord Justice Cotton, that the wife actually takes absolute control of the property; she now has a choice of using the land howsoever she wishes; she can choose to act on the trust and do what was right between his children or ignore it and use it how she wants to in her own way. Cotton suggests that this is what was actually intended by the husband & in his judgement even sets out what he assumes the husband was thinking, *"I am the head of the family and it is laid upon me to provide properly for the members of my family – my children; my widow will succeed me when I die and I wish to put her in the position I occupied as the person who is to provide for my children."* He goes on in his judgement to suggest that it is merely the transfer of a moral obligation unto the wife which the husband has a feeling she will discharge accordingly.

In the case of *Comiskey v Bowring-Hanbury* [1905] however, there as a bit of a difference. The Husband left in his trust that *"on her death she will devise it to one or more of my nieces."* This is known as a gift-over clause. This is basically that kind of a gift that if the trustee does not use that property in a certain way, then that property will vest itself absolutely in the beneficiary. For example, if I leave you £200 to spend on my 5-year-old daughter & say that you must spend it on her before she turns 10, and you for some reason fail to spend it on her, then she will, as soon as she turns 10, get the absolute of that £200.

The difference between both cases is the gift over clause. With precatory words however, these alone cannot impose a trust. One will need to look at the entire circumstance surrounding the agreement & then determine if the agreement can be deemed a valid trust or not.

II. Sham Devices – much like in anything, property owners will try anything to keep a hold of their property and thus often refer to using sham devices to create fake trusts. In the case of *Midland Bank v Wyatt [1995]* he set up a trust on behalf of his wife & daughter at a time when his business was failing and was close to going bankrupt. The bank said that if he defaulted on his loan, they would take steps to repossess his home so in an attempt to stop this, he created the trust to try and say that the bank can't take the house because there are other beneficiaries to the house.

III. Informal declarations of trust – these are those cases where there is no obvious agreement between the parties that they want to enter a trust by official/formal agreement but rather there are merely informal declarations as such. In the case we looked at above between *Paul v Constance [1977]*, it can be determined that there was actually a serious plan to create a trust even though they didn't do so knowingly. They were required to create a trust by the bank manager when they signed up for what was effectively the joint tenancy of the bank account & thus this informal declaration between them wasn't a cause for concern & was deemed a valid trust.

In the case however of *Jones v Lock [1865]* where a wife was concerned that her husband wasn't doing enough by way of providing financial support for their baby, the husband reacted by pulling out a blank cheque, waving it in front of the baby & teasing,

"I give this to baby." In this case, the courts determined that there was actually no trust because he didn't actually do anything to create the trust as such. Waving a cheque plus going to your solicitor to talk about it isn't enough to create a trust; he knew he had to do more, but because he died, there was no trust. All it was, was a little bit of banter! (Ngl, man smashed it – he played his wife, made her happy, got her off his back & then decided to die before he had to act on his promise. I'm telling you; men are trash...)

### Certainty of Subject matter

Certainty of subject matter is the idea it must be known what property is being and is not being subject to the trust. This is particularly important because we need to know who owns a piece of property, what their interests in that property are, from whom did they get that interest, when & for how long etc. And for this, there are 3 key questions to be answered:

I. How will the property be divided? With any fixed trusts, you need to know to whom what property is give; the quantum of property has to be known. There is a bit more leeway for a discretionary trust because it is down to the trustee to determine what the beneficiary gets.

In the case of *Palmer v Simmonds [1854]*, the trust determined is the "bulk my residuary estate." This is often used when specific things are made known and whatever is left over, will be determined to be the residuary estate. This is then used by people who do not actually know what they own or what they have left over.

In the case of *Re Golay [1965]* a man got into a relationship with a mistress, Tussy, despite being married. In his will, he left a statement, "to let Tussy receive a reasonable income from my properties." The courts say that this trust was valid because we can look at what was reasonable by looking back at what she was given in is life span & whatever that was, would be taken as what we would define as being reasonable.

II. What particular property will be subject to the trust? This is basically the requirement of determining what is and what is not subject to the trust. In the case of *Goldcrop [1995]* there was a trust relating to 50 gold bars out of 200; 25% of the stock. The courts determined that the gold bars did not need to be segregated/separated because they were basically the same. However, in the case of *Hunter v Moss [1993]* there was a trust with regards to 50 shares out of 950. The High Court determined that there was no need to segregate the shares because they are completely the same; there is no difference between the two. The court of appeal said that there is a need to segregate if it is intangible property, because you need to be able to point it out but if they're the same, then you do not need to segregate. In the case of Hunter v Moss, the High Court suggested that the reason that there was no need to separate the shares was because they were effectively the exact same; the value, worth of each share was the same & there was no consideration of them being similar or different from each other.

The logic taken by the Court of Appeal was slightly different; they suggested that no, the reason why you don't need to separate between both is because shares are intangible & as they're intangible, it doesn't really matter which of the shares one receives, but if they were tangible, then it would be necessary to determine which of the subject matter was being referred to as being part of the valid trust. So, using the Court of Appeals logic, in the case of Goldcrop, even though all the gold bars were the same & there was no indifference amongst them, there would be a requirement to separate them, solely because they are tangible property.

In the case of *Re London Wine [1986]* was a case where the company went bankrupt and argued that they should be able to claim the bottles of wine they had paid for. The fine wine company had gone into receivership, and the remaining wine stock was a valuable asset. The bottles that the customers had bought had not yet been individually identified. The company had not even promised to provide wine from its current stocks. It was held by Oliver J that any alleged constructive or express trust of 50 bottles because the subject matter of the trust would be uncertain, at least until 50 specific bottles were set aside for the customers because all the bottles were different; there were different styles, sizes, types & to say any 50 is uncertain.

There is one situation where a problem can arise beyond the afore discussed problems. In the case of *Boyce v Boyce [1849]* the testator devised that all my houses on trust to convey one to the eldest daughter, Maria, whichever she may think proper to choose and the other to the other daughter, Charlotte. The problem that arose in this case, was that Maria passed away before she could stake a claim to either one of the properties, and thus the vice-chancellor held that the trust was an uncertain one because it could not be determined which of his 2 houses was actually to be held on trust for Charlotte; her one would have been decided once Maria had chosen her property & thus in Boyce v Boyce as the trust was invalid, the property was given in the end to his heir; his grandson. I don't agree that this judgement is fair because the settlor did indeed intend to leave at least one house for Charlotte & the fact

|  | Tangible | Intangible |
| --- | --- | --- |
| Similar | HC = NO SEGREGATION NEEDED<br>CoA = SEGREGATION NEEDED | HC = NO SEGREGATION NEEDED<br>COA = NO SEGREGATION NEEDED |
| Different | HC = SEGREGATION NEEDED<br>CoA = SEGREGATION NEEDED | HC = SEGREGATION NEEDED<br>CoA = NO SEGREGATION NEEDED |

that she was left with no house at all, wholly goes against what the settlor was attempting to do; he wanted Charlotte to get one of the houses!

III. Future property – this is the idea questioning whether or not future property can be validated against a trust or not. So, for example, if I firmly believe that when my Grandma dies (☹), she's going to leave me £1,000, if I create a trust on it, it will not be valid. This is because I do not have a right to that money until I have it!

On the other hand, however, if I have a piece of property out on rent & make a trust giving you the rent for the next 4 years, as I have a vested right in that rent, I can make a trust of it. This right already exists & you are creating a trust over the right, not over the money which I will make; the tenant may leave before 4 years are up & my trust is stating that any money received will be yours but if nothing is received, then that's part of the right of the vested right.

## Certainty of Object Matter

Just as an initial recap to help the understanding, the basics of express trusts, we considered the notion that for a trust, there must be the following certainties, which are:

I. Certainty of intention – must be a certainty that one intends to create an express trust
II. Certainty of subject matter - the idea that it must be known what property is being, and is not being subject to the trust
III. Certainty of object – the idea that it must be known who the beneficiary actually is; they must be known.

Certainty of intention & subject matter was something we have already considered the previous topic & now we look at certainty of object which is admittedly significantly more confusing and debated than the previous two, however, here goes.

Before diving into the notion of certainty of object matter, it is first important to have an understanding of a spectrum if you like, of trusts and power.

A fixed trust is what we discussed the previous topic & the idea that a settlor gives property to a trustee and directs them what to do with that property such that the trustee must adhere wholly in accordance with the demands of the settlor for the beneficiary.

On the other end of the spectrum is the idea of bare power; this is for example the situation where I give you x amount of money/property on a trust to give to anyone you want to. This is as though I am giving you an absolute gift; do whatever you want with this gift unto you. "I give you £2,000 to spend."

Discretionary Trust /Trust Power – This is the middle ground between a fixed trust and a bare power. This in today's context is the idea that I give you property for you to use for a purpose as you deem fit. For example, "I give you £2,000 to spend on the people of India as you see fit." There is a discretionary element attached to the trust because you are effectively given the freedom from me to spend that money in a manner that you see fit.

In the case of *Morice v Bishop of Durham [1804]* there was the establishment of how to determine if a trust was actually a trust, or if it was a power, which we look into below. With regards to this case specifically, Morice was a governor of Mallorca, an island in Spain, who left much of his will in the trust of his then 79-year-old Aunt. Under the influence of the Bishop of Durham, the Aunt amended her will such that it read, "such objects of benevolence and liberality as the trustee in his own discretion shall most approve of." What his meant was basically the will then began to look like a power, because he has no one person who can benefit from the trust as such anymore; and as there is deemed to be no subject of the trust, it's simple that it cannot be a trust, but would be seen to be a power instead. This is what was explained by the courts when they declared, "an uncontrollable power of disposition would be ownership, and not a trust...Every [...] trust must have a definite object. There must be somebody in whose favour the Court can decree a performance." The idea that they cannot decree performance is the idea that there is a requisite need for a beneficiary to actually stand & enforce the trust and the notion of list certainty was born.

<u>List certainty</u>

This is the concept that the beneficiary of a trust should be known, and made clear under 3 key categories:

I. Conceptual Certainty – this is the idea that conceptually one must be able to completely identify who is & is not a part of the class/list
II. Evidential Certainty – this is the idea that there must be relevant & sufficient evidence that the specific people who have been

conceptually identified, are proved to be who they are in reference to the trust

III. Ascertainability – this is the idea that those who have been conceptually and evidentially proven, must also be ascertained to be in continued existence; they must be alive

Once someone has passed all 3 of these tests, in old law, they would be seen to be legitimate to be added onto the list certainty and thus a beneficiary of the trust – an object of the trust, they could reverse the benefits of the trust.

The following are regular examples used to explain the difference which can often be left as proposed objects to a trust:

I. Friends – This cannot be declared when claiming to be a trust, because friends cannot be seen as being conceptually certain as such. There may be people that I'm acquainted & friendly with, but they may not be my friends. Likewise, there may be someone who I hardly see, ever talk to, but they're one of my closest & dearest friends – how can it conceptually be certified who is my friend. Because of this, as it is not conceptually certain, the object of the matter is not met & thus the trust would not be seen to be valid in that way.

II. Ex-Employees of Amazon – this meets the criteria of being both conceptually and evidentially certain; it can be ascertained if someone is an ex-employee of Amazon quite easily by checking Amazon's records of their past employees etc. However, with regards to ascertaining if they are alive or dead, it would be highly impractical to do so because the list of ex-Amazon employees would be huge & to track down the details of everyone to see if they're alive would be a huge task and quite impossible in practical term and thus it cannot be determined.

III. All SOAS LLB Graduates – Likewise, it would be difficult to ascertain if all SOAS LLB graduates are still alive or if they're dead; the task would be a mammoth one & not ascertainable in that way.

IV. My Daughters – this is indeed a valid trust; daughters can be conceptually, evidentially certain as well as it being simple to

> ascertain if they're alive or not because they're your daughters & there's probably not too many of them (unless...)!

The reason why a list certainty is needed because in a trust such as a fixed trust, it is a requirement to know how much the property/wealth needs to be divided/distributed by – how many people need to get a slice of the cake. For example, if I say I want to distribute £1,000 to the members of the SOAS LLB Class of 2019, I need to know how many students of SOAS LLB Class of 2019 there are, so the amount can be divided equally amongst them & they all receive the share they are entitled to from the trust.

<u>A Power as a Trust</u>

In the case above, of Morice v Bishop of Durham, there was a very strong distinction raised between a trust and a power. A power is basically the ability to do something with property but with a little less obligation than a trust. This is a grey area & has a great amount of controversy in determining the difference between a trust & a power & a large amount of the remainder of the topic goes into determining the differences between both as such.

Like a trust however, a power is dealt in a tri-partite system where:

I. Donor – the person who gives the power. In a trust, this would be the Settlor.
II. Donee – the person who gets the power. In the trust, this would be the Trustee.
III. Object of Power – this is the person who benefits from the power. In a trust, this would be the beneficiary.

In the example that I give you £1,000 to use for the benefit of my extended family as you seem fit, there's a real problem here – is this a trust or a power? It's actually a discretionary trust. These are those trusts which were introduced in the hope of immunising oneself from bankruptcy laws of repossession as well as then going out to be a tool/mechanism to be used for tax avoidance purposes. The majority, if not all cases that arise due to discretionary trusts, is due to tax avoidance schemes.

## The Foundations of Property Law

There's a problem with discretionary trusts, however. As it is a discretionary trust, the Trustee isn't actually compounded to fully do as per the wishes of the settlor. This caused a great deal of problems for the courts who as a remedy, for a long time under the old law, was that the beneficiary could go to court & then the courts would simply order the trustee to equally divide the property amongst all the beneficiaries. For instance, if I left behind £100 for my 2 daughters, one to have £60 & the other £40 to be spent on them as the trustee sees fit; if the trustee was not exercising his duties properly, the courts would simply give £50 to each of my daughters. Furthermore, under the old law, if there was no list certainty, then it would be declared by the courts that the discretionary trust would be deemed as invalid.

Likewise, could it not be deemed that the above example was actually a power. And this is the problem which has caused so much problem between the courts of defining if something is a power or a discretionary trust. The big difference between a trust & a power is the fact that a trust requires a list certainty, whilst a power doesn't actually require a list certain as such. Rather, what happens is that it must be looked into a power to determine whether there is a power or if there is a wider obligation to confer benefit and this is done by understanding in detail the words used in a trust document based on power appointment; this is where the trustee has the power to appoint beneficiaries.

With regards to this differentiation, there are 2 cases which highlight the difficulties which can arise. In the case of *Re Saxone Shoe Co Ltd Trust Deed [1962]* which gave rise to a trust for the employees of the company & their dependents with the clause in the trust being, "the fund shall be in the discretion of the directors be applicable…"

The second case of this type, was that of *Re Saver Trust [1956]* where similarly there was a trust for the employees of the company along with their dependents, but here, the clause was, "the management committee is empowered to make payments." In the Saxone case, there is an initial belief that due to the imperative 'shall' being included in the clause, it would be deemed as a trust. However, there is a problem with the consideration of the evidentiary certainty associated with regards to who the dependents are – there was no list certain as such; dependents could be anyone and thus it was not certain when the trust was created who would be the object of the trust as such & thus it could not be a trust & would be a power instead. In the case of Sayer, it's simply a power because there is an empowerment to make payments; the obligation is fairly small comparatively to the obligation associated to a trust. Additionally, for a power, there is no need for a list certainty, and thus the dependents do not need to be specified/defined as they would need to be in the case of a trust.

## The Evolution of the Law

Up until this point, we've looked at, in a considerable amount of detail, the notions associated with the old law & now we begin to look at how that law has changed overtime.

And we begin with the *Re Gestetner [1953]* case, where the clause of the will read, "4 named individuals, descendants of testator's father or uncle; any spouse widow or widower of such a person; any former employee of the settlor, or his wife, widow or widower; any director of Gestetner ltd; any director of a company of which the directors of Gestetner ltd were also directors." There is much that could be taken to be problematic with this, however, the courts took their key issue with the final clause, which basically suggests that an individual who was a director of Gestetner Ltd as well as another company, the other companies directors would also benefit from the trust of Gestetner. Under the old test, this would not have been a valid trust, however, this case departed from the old law & began the evolution of the requirements for a list certainty in trusts.

Mr Justice Harman was adamant to explain that there was an obligation on the trustees unlike that in a bare power. The trustees did indeed have an obligation which needed to be fulfilled as it had been imposed upon them. Their obligation/duty wasn't one to actually go out & distribute the property, but rather the duty on the trustees was to consider and investigate who is actually culpable of being a beneficiary of the trust. So effectively what is being said, is that the trustee's obligation wasn't to distribute the money, but rather they were just considering who can be a beneficiary of the property. It does indeed raise the question that what the hell is the actual difference – if they are investigating, then surely once a potential beneficiary knows that they can get some money, they will indeed pursue all avenues to ensure that money gets to them & thus the trustees will eventually have to distribute anyways. Thus, the point can be said to be that the primary consideration was not to distribute, albeit they would eventually have to distribute anyways.

In the case of *Broadway Cottages [1955]* a settlor left £80,000 on trust for a number of beneficiaries including a charity, Broadway Cottages. HMRC basically turned up & asked where you got the money from to which they said it was from a trust & thus you cannot tax it at the higher rate & must give it tax exemption because it is income to a charity. HMRC (being the wastemen that they are!) decided to question the validity of the trust & it was here that the court of appeal went back to the Morice v Bishop of Durham judgement that a list certainty was required in order for a trust to be deemed as being valid. They said that the settlor had left money of which it was not actually possible to obtain a complete list of who the beneficiaries were & thus there was no list certainty making the trust a void one suggesting that there was indeed a test, the list certainty test, that had to be passed in order for a trust to be deemed as valid with relation to certainty of object matter.

Yet the courts again a few years later decided they didn't like Morice again, and this was proven in the *Re Gulbekian Settlement Trust [1968]* where Gulbekian who was an extremely rich aristocrat in the Ottoman empire, gave a trust which gave power to whoever his son may from time to time be employed with or with anyone with whom he resided. The trustees of this trust were not sure what this actually meant and thus went to the courts seeking some help in order for them to properly understand what this request meant. The Court of Appeal said that the trust is valid so long as any one person falls into the class of people and if anyone falls into the class, then the class will be deemed as a valid one. This was known as the one-person test. This is the idea that a trust would be deemed certain so long as at least one person falls within the class of objects, even if you did not know who else fell into it. For example, you'd know that person A was in the trust, but B, C, D, E, F & so on, even if you had no idea if they were or were not a part of the trust, the trust would still be wholly valid. Denning here was basically suggesting that the distinction between the test for powers and the test for trusts should just get rid of but the House of Lords, who clearly weren't the biggest fans of Denning (welcome to my world!) greatly criticised the one-person test & said that the test for the validity of a trust & the validity of a power should still be different & the test for trusts should remain to be list certainty.

The Law of Today

And then we eventually come to a big case which is actually what our current law is based on & the authority for today's law; *McPhail v Doluton [1970] Aka Re Baden's Trust Deed (No. 1) & (No.2)* which was a case where both McPhail & Doulton were trustees to a trust & in essence they sued themselves in order to get some direction from the courts in aiding them to lawfully & correctly fulfil their duties as trustees onto the beneficiaries of this rather vague trust.

*(No.1)* In this case, Baden established a trust which had a clause that read, "trustees shall apply the net income... building of a sports ground for the benefit of any officers or employees, or ex-officers or ex-employees of the company or to any relatives or dependents of such person..." The question in this particular trust arose with regards to if this was a duty of discretionary distribution (a trust) or a power of discretionary distribution? The Chancery courts said that this was an instance of mere power & actually ignored the consideration of the term 'shall' in their judgement. The Court of Appeal agreed with the chancery court & too said that this was indeed a power. The House of Lords however, actually agreed with Denning's suggestion from the previous case, that the test for powers & the test for trusts should actually be different because Wilberforce felt that there was an artificial and narrow distinction between trusts and powers with his suggestion that, "The distinction [between trust and powers] may be one of degree rather than principle." And that "the wide distinction between the validity test for powers and that for trust powers is unfortunate and wrong." In essence what is being said, is that ownership of the contents of the trust is not exactly vital as such but rather the fundamental requirement is in the ascertaining of who the actual beneficiaries of the trust are; if this

can be determined, then even if you can't pinpoint a legal owner as such, so long as there is evident a person/group of people who will benefit from it, the trust will indeed be termed as being valid. He concluded this by bringing to life a new test for trusts; the is or is not test ascertaining the certainty of objects. He states, *"the validity of trust powers ought to be similar to that accepted by this house in Re Gulbekian's settlement trusts for powers namely that the trust is valid if it can be said with certainty that any <u>individual is or is not a member of the class.</u>"* This is known, as the is or is not test.

Basically, what this test looks at is determining whether or not someone can be classified to be a member of the class or are they not a member of that class. By finding this out, you can determine the certainty of the object & wholly understand who the beneficiary of the trust is!

Additionally, Lord Wilberforce was clearly on a role in this case (man was on fireeee in this case) & he decided to also look into changing the old law with regards to what happens if a trustee does not exercise their discretion. In the old law, the courts would just order the equal distribution of the property amongst all the beneficiaries. Wilberforce was wholly against this because he argued, correctly in my opinion, that this is completely against the intention/purpose of what the settlor asked for & thus he suggested 4 potential remedies:

I. Order the Trustees to exercise their discretion as per the wishes of the settlor
II. Replace the trustees with more compliant trustees
III. Ask the representatives of class (the beneficiaries) to devise a scheme which the trustee will then act in accordance to
IV. The courts themselves can step in & exercise the discretion

It is worth remembering & noting that this was a majority decision of 3 to 2 in the House of Lords wherein 2 members of the HoL actually determined that this was a power & their argument was simple; there is no list certainty & thus it cannot be deemed as a trust & has to be a power. But of course, with the development of the is or is not test, there was a constitution of a bit of leeway with regards to this.

*Baden (No. 2)* considers the problem with the clause & in particular the clause of "relatives or dependents." Is relatives & dependents surely not too broad and not comply with the requirement of conceptual certainty in a trust object matter in order. Dependents was certain on all counts, but relatives were way too broad to be conceptually certain. My Dad's brother's wife's uncle's sister in law is still my relative, so should she be included in the trust too? God knows – there is no conceptual certainty in the clause of the trust & thus it could not be deemed a valid one! This was the first case to apply the is or is not test to a trust; it has been applied to powers but never before to a trust.

But with regards to the 3 points of conceptual, evidential & ascertainable certainty, there was a difference of opinion between what is required:

I. Lord Justice Sachs – All you need is conceptual certainty; it doesn't matter about the don't knows of the trust – all you need to know, is who is a part of the trust. He says this in his statement, *"The court is never defeated by evidential uncertainty... Once the class of persons to be benefited is conceptually certain it then becomes a question of fact to be determined on evidence whether any postulant has on inquiry been proved to be within it: if it is not so proved, then he is not in it."*

II. Lord Justice Megaw – The is or is not test is satisfied as long as a substantial number of people are defined in the class. My personal problem with this is the idea of defining substantial – it's not very clear & quite vague in my opinion. But according to him, as long as a substantial number of people are in the class, then the trust would be valid.

What both Megaw & Sachs said, that the term relative eluded to the notion of a common ancestor which must be proven by the person who is suggesting to be an ancestor to the settlor. What this basically means, is that if I leave behind wealth for my relatives & you turn around & say you're related to me, it'll be down to you to prove that you're actually related to me through a common ancestor & it will not be the duty of my trustees do investigate & decide if you are or are not my common ancestor.

## The Foundations of Property Law

III. Lord Justice Stamp – As long as you can tell if someone is within or outside the class, the trust is valid. Stamp argued that there must be a statutory next of kin which was basically his way of saying that there must be conceptual certainty in order to deem them as a relative & this can be one through list certainty; he is hinting that in an ideal world there would be a list because statutory next of kin can be proven through a list because that is how next of kin is legally determined.

In essence, what Megaw & Sachs are saying is that as long as it is conceptually certain, the trust would be valid So no matter how far back you go in terms of relatives, as long as it can conceptually be proven, the trust would be valid. If it cannot be conceptually certain, then that's the end of that! The problem with this arises when you have only a small amount of property/wealth to be distributed amongst a potentially massive number of beneficiaries.

As a result of this, the courts have developed the principle of a duty to survey. This is where the trustee will try to ascertain who the beneficiary of a trust actually is & this will be done through 3 key steps:

I. Consider the person or classes that are object – have a sense/idea of who the class may be
II. There is no requirement of a complete list, but there must be an appreciation of how wide & big the list is going to be
III. After getting an idea of the scale of the class, look at the individual by individual case for whether or not they should be conjoined in the trust as a beneficiary or not.

Upon completing the duty to survey, or even whilst conducting the survey, the trustee may realise that the point of the trust is beyond reasonable administrative workability & is in fact highly incompatible with even pursuing – it makes absolutely no point to deem the trust valid, because there was no worth/benefit which can be derived from the trust reasonably. This is another way a trust can be deemed invalid. For example, used by Wilberforce in the McPhail judgement, "I leave £1,000 for all citizens of greater London." Now the fact is, to investigate who is conceptually, evidentially & ascertainably certain would be a mammoth task alone as there are at least a million residents in London & then to split £1,000 between them is just a joke – the fund is too small in relation to the class. Thus, if a trust, according to the judgement from *Re Manistry's Settlement [1974]* is capricious (fanciful) meaning it comes across as being crazy, then this seeing as crazy will negate any intention on the part of the settlor and thus the power would also be deemed as invalid. In *Re Hay's Settlement* the case we looked at before, it was developed that administrative unworkability is also conjoined with trusts and Manistry extended this to powers too.

In attempting to understand who the beneficiaries are from the point of being conceptually, evidentially and ascertainably certain, the courts have taken the idea on that the opinion of a 3rd party can actually cure a type of uncertainty. For example, as we discussed right at the beginning, if I leave money behind for my friends, I have failed the conceptually certain test. However, if I leave behind £1,000 for anyone whom my wife deems to be my friends, then this can then be a valid trust. This was brought to life in the *Dundee General Hospital v Walker [1952]* case where a will was left behind a gift subject for the sole discretion of the directors of the hospital. The courts deemed this to be a valid trust and this concept was developed in *Re Coates [1955]* where a man left behind in his will the following clause: *"If my wife feels that I have forgotten any friend I direct my executors to pay to such friend or friends as are nominated by my wife."* This was deemed to be a valid clause because the opinion of the wife was determined to cure the conceptual uncertainty which arose, because she could determine who was & who was not a fried of her husband. Obviously, this raises the question that what if there was a friend the wife didn't know about & the simple answer is, tough luck to that person!

## The Beneficiary Principle

In the Morice v Bishop of Durham case, the courts ruled, *"Every [non-charitable] trust must have a definite object. There must be somebody in whose favour the court can decree performance."* What this means is that there must always be someone who can enforce the trust as a legitimate beneficiary, be that a normal person or a corporate person like a bank.

## The Foundations of Property Law

Beneficiary Principle ensures those objects are able to enforce those duties and focuses on Beneficiary's rights. The principle is all about ownership of enforceability; in the McPhail case, the idea of ownership is loosened due to the categories of ownership because there are some people who we have no idea with regards to in relation to if or if not, they are deemed to be beneficiaries of the trust. Ultimately, the basis of a claim against a trustee for not exercising their discretion is based on the notion of there being a beneficial owner who is claiming for their beneficial title to be established as per the wishes of the settlor. It is important however to note that the difference between the beneficiary principle and the certainty of object is the idea with regards to in a certainty of object, the object does not necessarily need to be a person as such. Rather, if an object like a monument, animal and most significantly, a charity is deemed to be the beneficiary of a potential trust or power, then this can be upheld under the 3rd certainty of object matter.

In <u>non-charitable purpose trusts</u> again, usually there is a beneficiary who can stake claim to the beneficial title. For example, if I create a trust to "leave my money to be used for the purpose of education A's children" then A's children have a beneficial title to that money & can claim for the discretion to be exercised to entail them to have money spent on their education. However, in the case of *Re Astor [1952]* he left behind in his will, *"income from fund to be used to maintain good understanding between nations and for the preservation for the independence of newspapers"* This was deemed to not be a valid trust because quite simply, no one person can enforce the trust because there is no beneficiary of the trust who has the right to enforce it in that way.

In the example of *Re Denley's Trust Deed [1969]* the clause in the will was, *"Land to be conveyed to trustees 'to be maintained and used... for the purpose of a recreation or sports ground for the benefit of employees. And for the benefit of such other persons (if any) as the trustees may allow to use the same."* This is a ground breaking case because on the surface, it looks as though there is no one beneficial owner of the property; many will benefit however, you cannot pinpoint to one person to be the beneficial owner. However, this case ruled that the employees were deemed to be

## The Foundations of Property Law

sufficiently certain whilst at the same time, there was a beneficiary – the employees collectively had a standing – locus standii & as a result, they were able to enforce the trust.

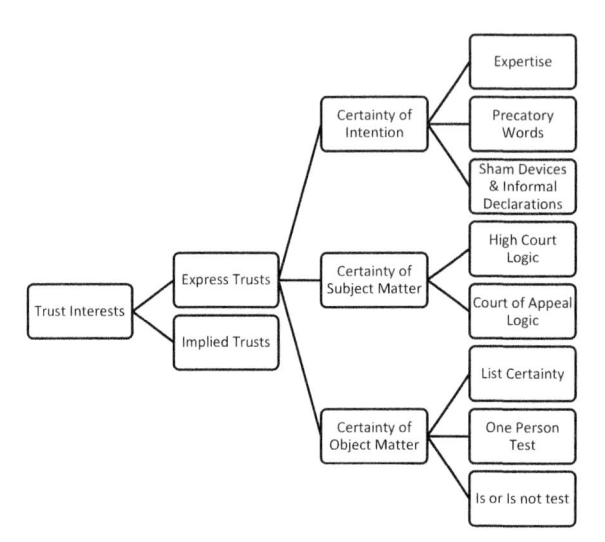

```
Trust Interests
├── Express Trusts
│   ├── Certainty of Intention
│   │   ├── Expertise
│   │   ├── Precatory Words
│   │   └── Sham Devices & Informal Declarations
│   ├── Certainty of Subject Matter
│   │   ├── High Court Logic
│   │   └── Court of Appeal Logic
│   └── Certainty of Object Matter
│       ├── List Certainty
│       ├── One Person Test
│       └── Is or Is not test
└── Implied Trusts
```

# Implied Trusts

I. What is an implied trust?
II. Resulting Trusts
III. Presumption of Advancement
IV. Basis of Presumption
V. Constructive Trusts
VI. Trusts in the family home
VII. Quantification

## What is an implied trust?

An Implied Trust is a trust which arise without an element of an express intention; there was no clear, obvious intention through which a trust could have come to life, which is what an express trust would be. We looked at in the previous topic which extensively covered one element of trusts, express trusts, and the requirement they have to ensure their validity, of the three certainties:

I. The certainty of intention
II. The certainty of subject matter
III. The certainty of subject matter.

It is important to remember, like we looked at in the preceding topic, that there is a clear division between legal and beneficial ownership in a trust; the trustee is a legal owner whereas the beneficiary is the beneficial owner.

There are two types of implied trust that we look at in considerable details in this and the next topic:

I. Resulting Trusts
II. Constructive Trusts

Both of these trusts have differing histories and thus, there is now a renewed appreciation of the different range of principles that underpin each of them respectively including estoppel.

The Foundations of Property Law

Resulting Trusts

These are actually not used much more in relation to land law, but there are two key categories through which they have been explained:

I. Automatic – this is where there is a gap in the beneficial interest which in essence will then lead to it being resulted back to the settlor. In other words, this is where it is not made clear who the beneficial owner is and as a result, it will go back to the settlor's possession. Or for instance, let's say that a settlor gives money for a specific purpose & once that purpose has been completed, there is still money left over, then it will be held that the settlor had left that property as an Automatic Resulting Trust & the leftover money will be returned to him.

II. Presumed Intention – this is where there are a set of facts through which it can be proven that 'x' happened and subsequently, the law can assume that 'y' happened/or was intended for it to happen. There are 3 such situations:
   a. When there was a money contribution to the purchase meaning that both parties had financially contributed to the purchase of the property.
   b. Where the property has been purchased in the name of the other such that one person may spend their money to buy a piece of property for another person. Here the assumption would be that the purchaser would have a resulting trust.
   c. Where there has been a voluntary conveyance of the property in that ownership of the property has been forfeited, again there will be the presumption that a resulting trust was intended.

In all 3 situations, the presumption is that only the legal title has been transferred, whilst the beneficial ownership is still owned by the donor; the equitable interest has been retained by the donor. This was proven in the case of *Re Vinogradoff* [1935] wherein it was determined that the grandma had put the name of her grandchild on the property; she purchased a piece of property in the name of another, her grandchild. When she died,

# The Foundations of Property Law

although the child was an infant, it was held by the courts that the property was to be held as a Resulting Trust for the adult's estate.

With the first two situations, as in based on a money contribution or when purchasing property in the name of another, the presumption will be as above. However, for the final one, with a voluntary conveyance of a property, it will be subjected to S60(3) of the LPA 1925 which is, much like S78 & S79 that we've looked at in previous topics, a word saving section which states, *"In a voluntary conveyance a resulting trust for the grantor shall not be implied merely by reason that the property is not expressed to be conveyed for the use or benefit of the grantee."*

Presumption of Advancement

The presumption of advancement is the presumption of a gift. The presumption of a resulting trust, however, is not applied in those cases where it is determined that the resulting trust that is applied is weak and as per the case of *McGrath v Wallis* [1995] comparatively slight evidence can also determine something as being a weak presumption. Other ways in which the advancement can be rebutted are through the following:

I. Where a father transfers to his child. The presumption in this instance would be that, as per the case of *Re Roberts* that the transfer was a gift. The burden of proof in this instance would be on the father to say that the transfer was not intended to be a gift, but rather was indeed a transfer with which the father intended to keep the beneficial interest for himself & subsequently stake a claim to a resulting trust.

II. A husband to a wife as per the case of *Pettitt v Pettitt* would follow the same principle as above in that it would be deemed a gift and the burden of proof will be on the husband to say that the transfer was not intended to be a gift.

It's interesting to note actually, that if there was a transfer from mother to child, or from wife to husband, the presumption would be that it was not intended to be a gift and that there would be a formation of a resulting trust. This means, that the burden of proof in these instances would be again on the child/husband to prove that the transfer was meant to be a

## The Foundations of Property Law

gift and should not uphold a resulting trust. This goes back to the idea of classical times that a woman typically cannot own property and thus the question would be that why they would be giving up property just like that. A father gives away property, but a mother needs her property!

However, it can be argued, based on a case by case basis, that in certain situations, a mother can be *Loco Parentis* meaning that in certain families a mother can play the role of the traditional father/bread winner of the family (patriarchal society thoughts, nonsense!) & therefore, in these instances, the presumption can be rebutted but this will obviously be determined on a case by case basis. This should no longer exist under S199 of the Equality Act 2010 but still has not been enacted – why? If this point of consideration was to come up in an exam, or in a situation in real life, then be sure to bring this up as a point of evaluation; the law will need to listen to your argument, because the Equality Act clearly states that this kind of situation should not exist, so show off with your knowledge & go slay!

The presumptions can further be rebutted by way of evidence and there are 3 ways in particular:

I.  Timing – evidence must be available before or at the time of the transfer of money. This can be seen in the case of *Shepherd v Cartwright* [1954] wherein the judge stated, *"The acts and declarations of the parties before or at the time of the purchase, or so immediately after it as to constitute a part of the transaction, are admissible in evidence either for or against the party who did the act or made the declaration. But subsequent declarations are admissible as evidence only against the party who made them, and not in his favour."* To say a transfer was a gift a while after the money has been transferred by the mother or wife, cannot used to prove that it was not a Resulting Trust – it is too late to make use of this evidence & thus there will still be the assumption that it was deemed as being a gift.

II. Illegality – The old law rooted from the case of *Tinsley v Milligan* [1993] wherein it was determined that the maxim/principle that a court of equity will not assist a claimant who does not come to equity with 'clean hands. In this case, Milligan had engaged in the transfer for an illegal purpose which would mean that the court would typically refuse to assist her even though the claimant can face prima facie establish that her claim. Because there was a participation in illegal activity, and they came to the courts without clean hands, the burden was on Tinsley to prove that the activity that they engaged in was not illegal. This has been overturned however in the case of *Patel v Mirza* [2014] where Mr Patel paid £620,000 to Mr Mirza pursuant to an agreement under which Mr Mirza would bet on the price of some shares, on the basis of insider information. Using advance insider information to profit from trading in securities is an offence under section 52 of the Criminal Justice Act 1993. The scheme did not come to fruition as the expected insider information was mistaken. Thereafter, Mr Patel brought a claim based on contract and unjust enrichment for the return of £620,000. Mr Mirza argued that no such obligation could be enforced because the whole contract was illegal. and any claim would be precluded by the principle of ex turpi causa non oritur action and the courts held that Mr Patel could recover his money as the Tinsley case is now referred to as old law because a person who satisfies the ordinary requirements for a claim in unjust enrichment should be entitled to the return of his property; he should not prima facie be debarred from recovering his property just because the consideration which had failed was an unlawful consideration. Mr Patel's claim should be allowed since it would have the effect of returning the parties to their positions prior to the conclusion of the illegal contract, as well as prevent Mr Mirza from being unjustly enriched.

III. Multi-factorial approach on admissibility – this is the fact that a variety of factors need to be looked at. Why was the transaction made illegal? Why was it made illegal? What would the public policy that would be damaged by admitting this illegal evidence? And is the remedy disproportionate? This is a much more discretionary approach.

## Basis of the Presumption of advancement

There are 4 ways in which the presumption can be rooted which are the following:

I. Orthodox view – this is the belief that the beneficial interest will naturally always be retained in a Resulting Trust. The general conception is that equity presumes a bargain, not a gift – why would I on my own will give up my property and put myself at detriment by giving up my property, therefore it will always be presumed that I intend to keep a Resulting Trust whenever a situation arises

II. Birks & Chambers Theory – this is the theory which states that there is an intention to not benefit a person in all types of resulting trusts, even automatic trusts. His argument was based on restitution and unjust enrichment. On this theory, resulting trusts arise on trust failure to prevent someone enjoying the benefit of property that he was never intended to benefit from. So, the focus is not on who A intended should have a beneficial interest (a proprietary concept) in the money, but on who A intended should benefit (a straightforward, non-legal concept) from the money. If for example, I did not intend that Katie should benefit from the money that I transferred to her, then Katie would be unjustly enriched if she decided to run away to an island and subsequently walked off with the money and enjoyed the benefit of it. In order to prevent this happening – as it might if we simply say that Katie is the legal owner of the money and doesn't hold on trust for anyone – we find that she holds the money on trust for me & I would be the one to take the L if Katie decided to walk away & it is she who would be unjustly enriched if she were allowed to walk off with my money. The assumption herein is really simple – one never intended for you to have the property.

III. Swaddling – This is where there is actually an intention to not keep when property is transferred. There was no intention for me to keep or retain it, I did not want it.

But put all of these together & a question is raised; are they just simply rhetoric? In the case of *Westdeutsche* [1996] where there was a contract to transfer property as a result of which, the bank lent money to Islington Local Council with a contractual intention to repay. However, this agreement was deemed as being void and the contract was a void one. The question to the courts now, was that, the council was given money under a void contract which means that there is now no contractual obligation as such on the local council/authority to pay the money back. The bank however, said that as it was a resulting trust, they should also be entitled to a share of the profits and also claim the higher rate of interest on the loan too. The Birks theory would say that this was an unjust enrichment to the local authority and the remedy would be restitution of the money to the banks whilst Swaddling would say that there was actually no intention to retain the money. However, the courts in this instance held that Westdeutsche bank could only recover its money with simple interest because it only had a personal claim for recovery in a common law action of money had and received. But the bank had no proprietary equitable claim under a resulting trust. There was no resulting trust because it was necessary that the council's conscience had been affected when it received the money, by knowledge that the transaction had been ultra vires and void. Consequently, it was necessary that there would be an "intention" that the money be held on trust, but this was not possible because nobody knew that the transaction would turn out to be void

The bank's argument makes sense when you look at it in light of this example. Let's say I give you £100 under a contract; however, it is determined later that the £100 contract was void. You then, go and spend some of that money to buy a lottery ticket & subsequently, by some miracle, end up winning the lottery. I would now go to the courts obviously & argue that no, I want my property back which is £98 & a lottery ticket – that lottery ticket was my possession & because it is my possession, I should be entitled to the lottery money that you won. The argument is very compulsive and makes a lot of sense.

Orthodox Constructive Trusts

Equity is a concept that acts in personam; this means that a person's conscience should be affected and if it can be proven that it should have been affected, then equity can be said to impose a constructive trust unto you regardless of what one intended and there are two types:

I. Remedial Constructive Trust – this is what is created by the court when a remedy appears to be just, the right thing to do
II. Institutional Constructive Trust – this is one which arises based on a set of facts, such as:
    a. A breach of a fiduciary duty
    b. Mistaken receipt of property
    c. A piece of property that is transferred with an obligation to do something else too

What we should have, is a remedial constructive trust where a court finds a set of facts in which there is a negative consequence as a result of which, the courts create a trust. There is no trust that exists as such, but the courts step in & create a trust which in turn gives the courts a significant amount of power & discretion.

# **Trusts in the Family Home**

- I. Trusts of the Family Home
- II. Quantification
- III. Estoppel
- IV. Tree Diagram

<u>Trusts of the Family Home</u>

In today's day & age, there is a huge increase in property ownership & this is becoming a significant aspect of law due to the expanding nature of property ownership. Both husband and wife are working people now & as a result, the whole traditional matrimonial setting has changed, leading to it being a lot more blurred by way of ownership in a matrimonial setting – where the husband would be the bread winner & the wife would up bring the family at home. The patriarchal society concept no longer exists or is no longer anywhere near as established in the Western world, as it used to be, or how it still is in other regions of the world.

What we look at now, is where legal title is held by one person (the rules are different if married) but if legal title is held by one person, then the other parties claim will need to go through two stages:

- I. A beneficial interest by way of a Resulting Trust or a Constructive Trust will need to be found
- II. The beneficial interest will need to be quantified – what is the size of the beneficial interest?

The first step requires for an interest to be established which requires the following steps to be taken:

If there is no express declaration of trust as per Section 53(1)b) of the LPA 1925 then…

- I. It will be dubbed an Implied Trust as per Section 53(2) of the LPA 1925
- II. Do you have a Resulting Trust?

## The Foundations of Property Law

       a. Was there a money contribution to the purchase? Remember, that the money contribution needs to be toward the purchase of the property itself and not to things leading to its purchase, such as solicitor's fees etc. Contributions to the purchase must be before or at the time of the purchase itself.
       b. Was there a purchase of a property in the name of another?
       c. Was there a voluntary conveyance of the property?

III. Or do you have a Constructive Trust? In the case of *Lloyds Bank v Rosset* [1991] it was determined by Lord Bridge that there are 2 ways to set an interest in a home which look at whether or not the conscience of the legal owner were affected & they are:

       a. Express Common Intention – this is where it is decided by looking at what was actually said, discussed and determined between the parties, rather than what it may be shown as being on the official title; intention and purpose will be looked at as proven in the case of *Springette v Defoe* [1992] which says that it must be proven that it was an arrangement that was agreed between both parties. Additionally, there must be an element of a detrimental reliance (links in with proprietary estoppel) which links in with the case of *Eves v Eves* [1975] where the claimant formed a relationship with the defendant who was married at the time but had separated from his wife. The claimant fell pregnant and changed her name by deed poll to take on the defendant's name. They intended to marry when their divorces came through. They purchased a house which was conveyed into his name alone. He told her this was because she was too young to have her name on the legal title and that if she had been old enough the house would have been in both their names. The purchase price was met with the proceeds of sale of his former house and a mortgage. The claimant did not provide any direct contribution to the purchase price but carried out substantial work on the property including redecoration, demolishing and building a shed, breaking up concrete and preparing the lawn for turfing. They had a further child and when the divorces came through, they agreed to marry but didn't. He then left the claimant for another woman. The courts held that the claimant was entitled to one quarter of the beneficial interest under a constructive trust

b. Inferred Common Intention – this is where conduct has taken place which leads to the understanding that there is a trust. There may be situations where direct financial contributions may not necessarily be directly related to the purchase of the property but paying things such as the bills may also be a factor which can be determined. Though the courts do hold that these contributions do not necessarily lead to a trust interest in the property, it can be argued against by the ideas of Hegel who would say that rulings of this nature is a failure to value non-financial contributions to the house. I would go beyond and say that it is sexist and links in with the traditional concepts of a patriarchal society. Also, this can be argued against by very persuasive authority which says that bills should count to financial contributions, such as *Abbott v Abbott,* [2007 *Stack v Dowden* [2007]. What these persuasive authorities along with Hegel are arguing, is that the interpretation in *Lloyds Bank v Rosset* is way too narrow. It is not appreciating the value of indirect financial contributions which quite simply is unfair & to require direct financial contributions & those only is not realistic sometimes in a family home.

So, in the following worked examples, let's see if the other can have a claim of having an Implied Trust:

I. Katie is the sole legal owner of Blackacre. Nabeel moves in & pays half towards the bills & does extensive landscaping. Does he have a beneficial interest? NO; there is no express agreement nor is there a possibility for an inferred common intention.

The Foundations of Property Law

II. Katie is the sole legal owner of Blackacre. Nabeel moves in & says "I'm so glad we have a place of our own." Katie is busy texting & doesn't reply. Nabeel then pays half towards the bills & also does extensive landscaping. Does he have a beneficial interest? NO; there was no **common** express agreement. Nabeel stated something, but Katie not replying can mean that there was no common intention for it. And as above, there is no possibility of an inferred common intention.

III. Katie is the sole legal owner of Blackacre. Nabeel moves in & says "I'm so glad we have a place of our own." Katie then says, "Yup, you now have a home." Nabeel then does extensive landscaping. Does he/she have a beneficial interest? Well… This is one here it is held that it will look at what is understood by the other party, rather than what was intended by the party that was making the statement. So, Nabeel understood that they now had an interest in the home = an express common agreement which followed by the landscaping = detrimental reliance = Express Common Intention Constructive Trust, which means he has a resulting trust interest!

IV. Katie is the sole legal owner of Blackacre. Nabeel moves in & pays half towards all the household utility bills & buys all the food for the house. Does he have a beneficial interest? Though there is no express agreement, it can be argued based on persuasive authority & the belief of Hegel, that there is sufficient conduct to infer a common intention.

V. Katie is the sole legal owner of Blackacre. Nabeel moves in & pays half of the mortgage. Does he have a beneficial interest? Though there is no express agreement as such, there is sufficient conduct to infer a common intention – by paying the mortgage, they are contributing to the purchase of the property.

However, in those instances now where legal title is not held in the name of a single owner, but rather in joint names, then it will be held that Equity follows the law & they will be joint tenants in equity too based on the case of *Stack v Dowden* [2007]. In this case, Ms Dowden and Mr Stack had been in a relationship since 1975. In 1983, they decided to purchase a house, which was exclusively paid for by Ms Dowden, In 1995, they decided to move to a new house, into a larger property, which would accommodate them and their 4 children. This house was brought on a mortgage, where both made mortgage payments, thus, the house was issued in joint names. In 2002, the marriage broke down & Mr Stack sought to claim a 50% interest in the house. However, Ms Dowden was insistent, that he was only entitled to 35% of the house.

In court, it was established, as can be seen in the judgement in Paragraph 92, that what happened in this extremely peculiar situation, was Ms Dowden had kept a record of who had paid what amount for the mortgage, through which she could mathematically prove that Mr Stack had only paid for 35% of the house. By keeping this figures, it was proof enough to the courts, that she didn't wanna share the house, but rather, wanted to split it through their shares – there was no express, nor any inferred common intention which could be cited.

The presumption which results from this case, therefore, would be that if you did not want to be a beneficial owner, then it would have been an expressly identified that you did not want to be a beneficial owner.

So, the steps taken are as follows:

I.   Is the home in the name of a sole legal owner:
   a. No, it is held in joint names:
      i. You need to move to quantification (comes up below)
   b. Yes, there is a sole legal owner:
      i. Need to establish beneficial interest under a RT or a CT
      ii. If doable, then the size of the beneficial interest needs to be quantified & if not, then there is no claim of a trust

Quantification

This is basically the size of your interest which determines what your remedy is/what you're going to get back once you've established a claim.

In a Resulting Trust, you basically get back the shared proportion of your contribution; you get your percentage back as per the case of *Laskar v Laskar* [2008].

In a Constructive Trust, it was determined by the case of *Stock v Dowden* that equity follows the law which means that as a Joint Tenancy, it will be divided equally Joint Tenancies & Tenancy in Common. This was proven in the case of *Clarke v Harlowe* [2005].

In the case of *Oxley v Hiscocks* [2005] it was said that there are a number of factors that need to be considered when looking at these situations & understanding the whole course of dealing between the couple & they are:

I. Discussions – how will the Beneficial interest be divided; this is a conversation that needs to be had between joint legal owners
II. Reasons why it is held as a JT
III. Children
IV. Length of relationship

But, the case of *Jones v Kernott* [2011] likes to make it known that intention can change over time as a result of which this must be considered too. The dynamic of a couple can & probably will change over time in terms of who's working, who is earning more, when are they being paid, are they still a happy couple etc.

Remedial Constructive Trusts

Lord Scott - For my part I would prefer to keep proprietary estoppel and constructive trust as distinct and separate remedies, to confine proprietary estoppel to cases where the representation, whether express or implied, on which the claimant has acted is unconditional and to address the cases where the representations are of future benefits, and subject to qualification on account of unforeseen future events, via the principles of remedial constructive trusts.

I am satisfied [the facts have] justified a remedial constructive trust under which David would have obtained the relief awarded him by the judge.

The Foundations of Property Law

Estoppel

This looks at whether that was reliance & detriment in the promise that was made. This is a form of protection for the party which has lost out. If there was a passive or active promise that was made which is followed by detrimental reliance, then regardless of what the above says, estoppel can be claimed to estop the party from not gaining anything. Though the remedy here will not be a property right as such, they will at the very least get some financial remedy which can help to compensate for what has been lost.

This is what we look at every time we do estoppel & the need for there to be:

I. Assurance
II. Reliance
III. Detriment

Top Tip: draw out a tree-diagram for this to help understand which method needs to be used in which circumstance

Tree Diagram

The Tree Diagram below is the perfect way to shape your answers and to follow logic. As a student myself, I found the best way to answering questions, was to establish and then follow a logic which made sense. What the tree diagram does, is give the foundation for that logic, which can then be built on easily and effectively, by adding in cases, judgements and scholarly thoughts on each of the different branches on the tree. The below covers the entire concept of trusts; both implied & express.

# The Foundations of Property Law

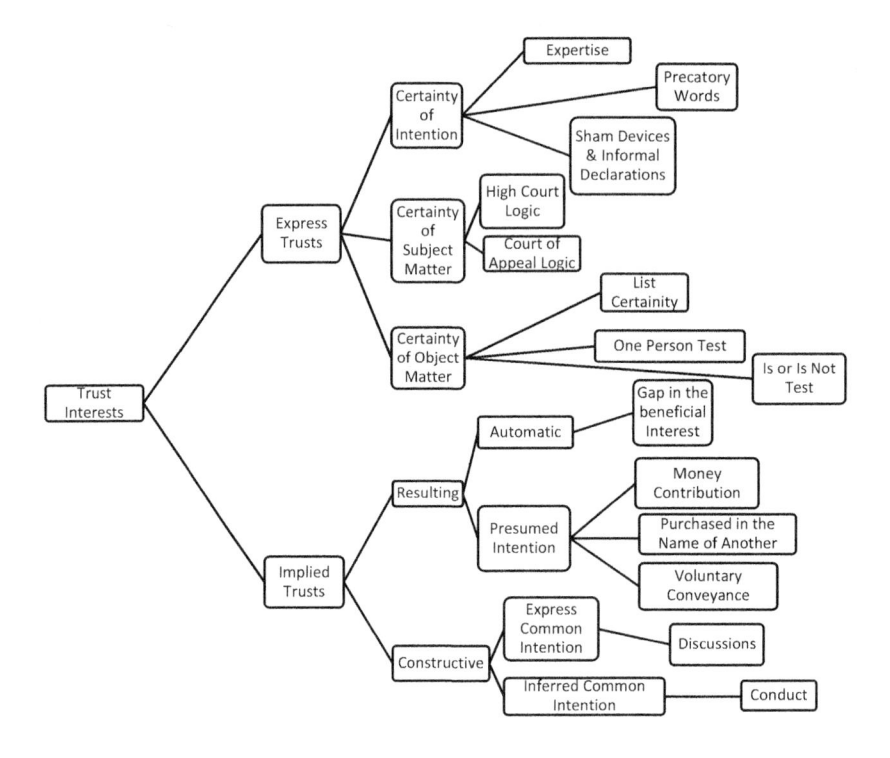

- Trust Interests
  - Express Trusts
    - Certainty of Intention
      - Expertise
      - Precatory Words
      - Sham Devices & Informal Declarations
    - Certainty of Subject Matter
      - High Court Logic
      - Court of Appeal Logic
    - Certainty of Object Matter
      - List Certainity
      - One Person Test
      - Is or Is Not Test
  - Implied Trusts
    - Resulting
      - Automatic
        - Gap in the beneficial Interest
      - Presumed Intention
        - Money Contribution
        - Purchased in the Name of Another
        - Voluntary Conveyance
    - Constructive
      - Express Common Intention
        - Discussions
      - Inferred Common Intention
        - Conduct

# Unincorporated associations & Rules Against Perpetuity

I. What is an unincorporated association?
II. How does an unincorporated association hold property?
III. What happens to the association's assets when its dissolved?
IV. Rules against perpetuity

What is an Unincorporated Association?

As we all know, it is possible for a person like you & me to own a piece of property/land with no questions asked. It is also widely known that that individuals can come together to actually own a piece of property. This is the idea of a corporate personality and the notion that companies are people who themselves have personalities, births, death, interests, identities, can be sued & be sued in their own rights and so on. And as a result of their position deeming them to be persons as such, they are recognised as a distinct legal entity that is different/apart from its members.

So, in the example of two different entities; a partnership & a company. A partnership is merely an agreement between two or more people who come together to form a business partnership amongst each other. The individual assets of the members of the partnership can be seized if there is a problem of let's say bankruptcy, which means that the partners are the identity of the partnership. On the other hand, if there was a company that went bankrupt, as the company is seen to be a distinct legal entity, the shareholder's assets would not be under any sort of danger because they are wholly different legal identities. The big difference is simple – the company is a different legal entity than those who make up the company.

As a corporation therefore, it has its own right to hold property. The problem however, for property lawyers, is in the situation where there are unincorporated associations involved. An incorporate association can be deemed to be a group of people who have joined together in order to form a club or society to pursue a common purpose such as playing sport or engaging in a common cultural activity but have not registered themselves as a company. As it is not a corporate association as such, it does not have a distinct legal entity apart from the members from that association. The problem is that you do not know if property is being held by the association or by the members of the association & so if property is left behind on a trust, has the property been left behind for the association or has it been left behind for the members of the association in their own right.

And this problem begs the question to be asked; what does an unincorporated association actually look like? We all know exactly what an incorporated association looks like; there are clear remarks/evidence with regards to who is the owner, the shareholders, the directors etc. But with an unincorporated association, it can be slightly more difficult to determine who or what is involved. And this is where the *Conservative and Unionist Central Office v Burrel [1982]* case gives us a guideline on how to determine what makes up an unincorporated association where Inland Revenue argued that the Conservative Party (formally the Conservative and Unionist Party) should pay a higher level of corporation tax because members' contributions took effect as an accretion to the funds, the subject matter of a contract, which safeguarded what happened with the members' funds. *Vinelott J [1980]* held that each contributor enters a contract with the treasurer, who undertakes to use the subscription for the association's purposes. Breach would mean liability in contract. In the Court of Appeal, it was held that an unincorporated association would have the following features which is effectively the root/foundation of determining if something can be defined as being an unincorporated association & they are:

I. Two or more persons bound together for one of more common purposes, not being a business purpose – you cannot have an association of one person by themselves
II. Having mutual rights and duties arising under contract between them – in amongst themselves, they enter into a contract such as paying a subscription fee, signing the terms & conditions or something like that which effectively forms a common contract that binds all members of the association

III. In an organisation with rules to determine who controls it and its funds and how; and
IV. In which members must be able to join and leave at will.

The question still remains for property lawyers that how does an unincorporated association hold property? Does it hold the property in its own name or in the name of its members? It cannot be said that a property is owned by an unincorporated association. Likewise, if a company owns a piece of property, it cannot be said that the company owns the property because they are 2 distinct legal entities; the company is its own legal entity whilst the shareholders are separate legal entities & thus the company owns the property for its own benefit. But in an unincorporated association, as there is no actual legal distinction between the members & the association, so who actually owns the property? Do all the members have ownership in that piece of property or do the office bearers hold the property on behalf of the members of the unincorporated associations. And surely, if they're holding it on behalf of the members of the association, does this not then sound like a trust agreement?

The case of *Re Bucks Constabulary Widows and Orphans' Fund [1979]* gave us the answer to this question – this case explains just how a piece of property is to be held by an unincorporated association. Associations have, for practical purposes, one or more persons to act in the capacity of treasurers or holders of the property such as office-bearers, secretaries etc. These people hold the assets of the association in trust for members of the association, subject to the contractual claims of the members inter se. So, the treasurer/office bearer of the association hold property on trust for the members of the association, subject to a contractual agreement between the members of the association. But this raises a question – as people can join & leave the association at will, which members are actually objects of the trust; past members, present members? And if it is only present members, how on earth do present members get their interest from the past members.

And this is something that is explored in the Privy Council case of *Leahy v AG of New South Wales [1959]* wherein a wealthy man in Australia died leaving behind his estate with the following two clauses in his will:

I. 3 - As to my property known as 'Elmslea' ... upon trust for such order of nuns of the Catholic Church or the Christian Brothers as my executors and trustees shall select – the problem with this clause is with the certainty of object; there is no guidance in the will with regards to who will or will not be a beneficiary or rather, there is no list certainty to the trust in relation to which nuns or Christian Brothers will be beneficiaries of the trust.

II. 5 - As to all the rest and residue of my estate both real and personal ... upon trust to use the income as well as the capital to arise from any sale thereof in the provision of amenities in such convents as my said executors and trustees shall select either by way of building a new convent... or the alteration of or addition to existing buildings... With this one, this is determined to be a purpose trust which is to be used for building stuff for the catholic church which as we know, purpose trusts are void & can never actually be valid except in the case of certain circumstances

In response to this, his widow & children challenged the validity of his will. And with regards to this, the Privy Council laid out 3 possible constructions trying to determine his trust:

I. Charitable Trust – this will fail the trust quota based on what we will discuss in the coming topics.
II. A gift for each individual member – this would have failed too because there was no list certainty and thus there was no object matter as such. If he had specified which Christian nuns & brothers, he wanted to give it to, then it would've been a different story, but because there was no list, then it cannot be deemed valid
III. An endowment for present & future members – this fails too with regards to the Law of Perpetuities which we look at later on in this topic.

# The Foundations of Property Law

This trust was actually saved by a statute which was specific to New South Wales which allowed the giving of bequests despite the lack of a certainty of object; there was a lack of standard for the certainty of object & let them get around the problem of no object in the trust.

In the case of *Neville Estates v Madden [1962]* there was a gift to a group of Synagogues in North London who tried to turn around & sell the land to a property developer in order to build some flats. The question in this case arose whether or not it was permissible for them to do this; to actually sell the land because there was a question of how a gift is held by an unincorporated association. The question was answered by the courts by declaring 3 ways to potentially approach it:

I. On its true construction, be a gift to the members of the association at the relevant date as joint tenants, so that any member can sever his share and claim it whether or not he continues to be a member of the association. This raises the question that how do you actually sever a relationship in this way/a joint tenancy without taking the property away from the synagogue – to understand this, we need to understand the concept of a joint tenancy. In a joint tenancy, if you sever your agreement, you receive an equal share of the property & can leave. This means that you take away from the value of the property; in this case, if that is done, you take some of the money away. In this case, if you did that, you'd be taking money away from the synagogue which would be of no benefit to them & makes it a loss. Additionally, as members join & leave freely, there would be no unity of time which makes it difficult for it to be declared as a joint tenancy as such. Of course, this is more of an analogy from the courts rather than a legal test. But to counter the former point, the court determined a second test.

II. It may be a gift to the existing members not as joint tenants, but subject to their respective contractual rights and liabilities towards one another as members of the association. (contract holding theory) – so if & when the members choose to leave the Joint Tenancy, you are able to take the share & leave but in doing so, you cannot sever your share which is a declaration that you are simply giving up your piece of property in the association; giving it back to the association.

III. The terms or circumstances of the gift or the rules of the association may show that the property in question is not to be at the disposal of the members for the time being, but is to be held in trust for or applied for the purposes of the association ... In this case the gift will fail unless the association is a charitable body.

So, in essence, there are 2 ways in which an unincorporated association can hold property; through a pure joint tenancy or a joint tenancy which is subject to a contract (contract holding theory.) So in the example of *Bertram wants to leave money to an unincorporated book club to give an annual prize for the best non-fiction to come out of Hackney* it is clear that he would prefer the 2nd option because if he gives it on a pure Joint Tenancy, one tenant could sever the agreement & simply walk away with some of the money!

So, the Contract Holding Theory basically incorporates the following ideas:

I. It is a gift to the members as joint tenants
II. They are subject to a contractual obligation which cannot be severed & for which the rights are surrendered on one's death or resignation.

Yet even this isn't a perfect option. In the case of *Re Reacher [1972]* was one where the testator's will on 23 May 1957 gave some of the residual estate to the Anti-Vivisection Society, at 76 Victoria St, SW1, which was construed as being 'the London and Provincial Anti-Vivisection Society'. But this had wound up on 1 January 1957 and amalgamated into The National Anti-Vivisection Society of 27 Palace Street, SW1. Neither were charities. She died in 1962. In her will, there was no expression of an express trust in the society's by-laws which suggested that there was no was no explanation in their internal laws to say how property was to be held except for the clause in the will. What Brightman J said about this, was, *"In the case of a donation which is not accompanied by any words which purport to impose a trust, it seems to me that the gift takes effect in favour of the existing members of the association as an accretion to the funds which are the subject-matter of the contract which such members have made inter se, and falls to be deal with in precisely the same way as the funds which the members themselves have subscribed."* There is no idea as to what should take preference – do the rules take preference or do the terms of the gift take a preference? This is a grey area which needs to be fixed in order to best make use of this theory.

In the case of *Re Lipinski's Will Trusts [1976]* a housing society was given in the will a mandatory condition which stated, "only for the construction of new buildings for the association." The terms of the association did not have anything with regards to the building of new buildings; they had terms for the maintenance but nothing for the buildings. The court however said that don't worry about the terms of the association, we can declare this to be an absolute gift to the members of the association, meaning that they can use the money as they wish.

However, in the case of *Re Grant's Will Trusts [1979]* there was a will which left behind the residuary estate of a member to the Labour Party for the benefit of the Chstersey HQ of the Constituency Labour Party for them to basically build a new HQ. The court determined that it did not look like a gift to the members of the labour party, nor was it a gift to the members who were beneficiaries of the contract but rather looked like a purpose trust for the trustees which as we know, makes the trust void; it was an absolute bequest!

The main reason why we are concerned with how property is held by unincorporated associations is because of what happens to property when it becomes dissolved. In the Bucks Constabulary Widows & Orphans Fund case when they eventually joined together with another constabulary, it was determined that the fund was sat there with no one doing anything with the fund for so long & it was eventually decided that something had to be done with regards to the fund to decide what to do with the money. There were no rules of the society said how the assets should be dealt with when it wound up. If it was a joint tenancy, then the funds should simply be divided between amongst all the members. But the courts said no, we have to apply it to all the types of funds which were received by the constabulary

& as a result, it was determined that they were receiving funds from 4 main sources:

I. Contributions from past & present members – this is a contractual contribution, but because there were actually no members left of the fund, this was also determined as being Bona Vacantia
II. Proceeds of raffles – this was bona vacantia; this is the idea that it is ownerless property which means that once it is declared, it is taken by the crown because no one actually owns that property as such
III. Anonymous collection contribution boxes – this is the same as B.
IV. Donations & legaices – Donors could be presumed to wanting their money back because it hadn't been used in the way they had stipulated when they were donating & thus it would be said that the fund is holding the money on trust for the donors until they want their money back

Rules against perpetuity

This is basically the idea that you cannot bind a piece of property forever & ever because it is a capital & should not be locked up in safe trusts because this is highly wrong & unfair. Additionally, it needs to be available be available for entrepreneurial activities & simply should not survive death!

The old common rule is that *"No interest is good unless it must vest, if at all, not later than twenty-one years after the death of some life in being at the creation of the interest."* Basically, what this means, is that within 21 years of the person to whom the property was initially left, the property must vest with someone else before that 21 years is up. This can best be understood using 3 examples (how Abdul was allowed to name his daughters Britney & Alice is beyond me!):

I. On January 30, 2017, Abdul leaves property to Britney and then to their daughter Alice. In this example, Britney is the life in being & within 21 years of her passing, Alice will definitely be the vested owner of the property; in fact, immediately after her death, Alice would be the owner.

## The Foundations of Property Law

II. On January 30, 2017, Abdul leaves property to Britney and then to their daughter Alice when she turns 30. In this example, though Britney is the life in being owner, there's a problem. When the bequest is made, it is possible that Alice is only 2, 3 years old which means that by the time 21 years come to pass, she still won't be 30 years old meaning that she cannot actually take possession of the property meaning that this bequest would not be valid.

III. On January 30, 2017, Abdul leaves property to Britney and then to their daughter Alice on the condition that she becomes a lawyer. Likewise, in this case, there is no guarantee that Alice will actually go on to become a lawyer & there is also no guarantee that if she does, she'll do so within 21 years of Britney dying.

Now what actually happens when a trust is uncertain in that way, is based on the two Perpetuity and Accumulation Acts which are in English Law. The 1964 Act was one which allowed the settlor to specify a perpetuity period of 80 years instead of life in being + 21 years & adopted something called a wait & see approach. This lives on till today thanks to the 2009 Act which only changes the length of time a perpetuity can be held for; they will now have will have a perpetuity period of 125 years or shorter if stipulated. But the wait and see approach is basically the idea that you wait & see what happens; is it possible, in the 3rd example, that Alice does indeed become a lawyer by the end of the 21 years. Well in order to determine it, you have to wait & see! In the common law however, if there is even an element of doubt in that regard, it would be held that the trust would be void from the very offset.

However, the common law approach/rule only applies to non-charitable purpose trusts which means that this provision for normal people trusts is still life in being + 21 years.

Where there is no life in being as such, it would be concluded that the trust will be valid for 21 years after which it cannot be upheld at all.

# Charities

I. Charitable Organisations
II. What are the legal tests for a valid charity?
III. Benefits of becoming a charity

Charitable Purpose

Historically, charities were registered as a form of trust & the basis of the charity law is one of a trust. Now days, we can have charities as an Unincorporated Association, a company or even as an Incorporated association as such. The first distinct recognition of a charity came preamble the Charitable Uses Act 1601, which recognised the purposes of a charity as being, *"some for Relief of aged, impotent and poor people...for the maintenance of sick and maimed soldiers and mariners, schools of learning, free schools and scholars at universities, some for repair of bridges, ports, havens causeways, churches, sea-banks and highways and some for education and preferment of Orphans... relief, stock or maintenance of houses of corrections, marriages of poor maids.. Support for young tradesman, and persons decayed..."* It can be determined from this that even at this early stage, it could be seen that a charity should have one of potentially 2 key underlying purposes:

I. A Public benefit
II. A mechanism for support

Despite this, there was actually no official definition of what a charity is until 2006 & the Charities Act 2006 which gave the first proper definition of what a charity & its purpose is but until then, it was left wide open for courts to basically try & figure out if something was a charity or not. This lack of definition came to light in the *IT Special Purpose Commissioners v Pemsel [1891]* case whereby deed in 1813 Mrs. Bates conveyed certain lands to trustees upon trust, the rents from which were to be used in the following way:

I. As to two-fourths, for the general purposes of maintaining, supporting and advancing the missionary **establishments among**

**heathen nations of the Protestant Episcopal Church, known by the name of Unitas Fratrum, or United Brethren...**

The clause in bold writing was the one that caused the courts a problem because up until 1886, there was a special exemption from Income Tax for charities/charitable purposes as a result of the Income Tax Act 1842. As a result, the trustees of the establishment filed to compel the Income Tax commissioners to grant an exemption to them as they were a charity/charitable purpose. This writ of mandamus failed at the first courts & got all the way to the House of Lords in an attempt for them to grant an exemption to them for the income tax. The court of first instance said that the definition of a charity is limited to be a means of relief to those from poverty, be that in the form of giving alms or assistance to the physically disabled. The Court of Appeal disagreed with this narrow definition of a charity, but still went so far to link the definition of a charity to supporting those in poverty. In the Court of Appeal, Lord Macnaghten went beyond the definition of charity for poverty & extended it to also include:

I. Advancement of Education
II. Advancement of Religion
III. Other purposes which are beneficial to the community by large

This very limited definition was the only definition of charities we had through 1 & a half centuries up until the 2006 Act which was then repealed by the Charities Act 2011 which is seen as good law today. Therefore, when the Charities Act 2011 came about, the very first thing it did was set out a very clear definition of what a charity was in Section 1(1) of the Act. It states, *"an institution which is established for charitable purposes only' and which is subject to the control of the High Court"* suggesting that you cannot have a charity for both charitable & non-charitable purposes. This act also makes clear under S(3(1)) that a charity must be for public benefit which means that what this act did as a whole, was break out the definition of a charity into 2 main aspects:

I. Must have a charitable purpose
II. Must be for public benefit

## The Foundations of Property Law

What is a public benefit? Well this is nicely defined for us in Section 3(1) of the act which states:

a. The prevention or relief of poverty;
b. The advancement of education;
c. The advancement of religion;
d. The advancement of health or the saving of lives;
e. The advancement of citizenship or community development;
f. The advancement of the arts, culture, heritage or science;
g. The advancement of amateur sport;
h. The advancement of human rights, conflict resolution or reconciliation or the promotion of religious or racial harmony or equality and diversity;
i. The advancement of environmental protection or improvement;
j. The relief of those in need because of youth, age, ill-health, disability, financial hardship or other disadvantage;
k. The advancement of animal welfare;
l. The promotion of the efficiency of the armed forces of the Crown or of the efficiency of the police, fire and rescue services or ambulance services

What happens in attempting to prove that your association is indeed a charity, is through developing analysis – if it cannot be located in one of the categories above, then there will be an attempt to fit it into one of them by likening it to one of the categories. Once it has been fitted into a category, then it moves on to proving that it has a public benefit. This is pretty simple; however, a question was raised to the courts with regards to the validity of political activity as being charitable. Political activity can indeed be argued as being for public benefit, but this distinction was made in a couple of cases before the courts.

In the *Bowman v Secular Society [1917]* case, *'a trust for the attainment of political objects has always been held invalid, not because it is illegal, for everyone is at liberty to advocate or promote by any lawful means a change in the law, but because the Court has no means of judging whether a proposed change in the law will or will not be for the public benefit.'* What the courts have basically said in this case, is a political object considered as being a public benefit or not? They decided here that of course it isn't!

So how do you actually determine if something does have public benefit? There are 3 rather vague & quite useless tests which attempt to help us unravel this question & they are:

I. Personal nexus test – this test is best understood by looking at the case of *Oppenheim v Tobacco Securities [1950]* where the Trustees were directed to apply certain income for 'the education of children of employees or former employees' of a limited company or any of its subsidiary or allied companies. The number of eligible employees was over 110,000. Charitable status was claimed but the courts judged that it was not a charity because the class of beneficiaries of the charity was based on a personal nexus to the donor; they had personal links to the donor & thus the class's ambit was quite simply not wide enough to be determined as being for a public benefit for the community by enlarge. There was no doubt that this was a charitable purpose, but the question marks occurred when determining the public benefit, which was decided to not actually exist.

II. Question of degree – This test came about as a criticism of the personal nexus test in the case of *Dinge v Turner [1972]* where the question was raised with regards to Whether a trust created for the poor employees (those who were aged or incapacitated) of a company would be charitable. What this test is basically deriving is that if you are benefitting so many people, to deny them a charitable status is wholly wrong. Look at the surrounding circumstances & then at the purpose of the trust insofar as to what its purpose was essentially & if at large there was a public benefit to a number of people, call it a charity! So, in the case of *Oppenheim v Tobacco Securities [1950]* as there was over 110,000 people who would've benefitted, this test would've passed it as being a charitable public benefit purpose too! The courts words exactly are, *"In truth the question whether or not the potential beneficiaries of a trust can fairly be said to constitute a section of the public is a question of degree and cannot be by itself decisive of the question whether the trust is a charity. Much must depend on the purpose of the trust"*

III. Class within a class – This is the vaguest of the 3 tests in that the class has to be wide enough to be determined as being a class for public benefit & to have conditions which make the class smaller & more focused, makes it considerably less likely to be determined as being for public benefit.

Exceptions for Charities

There are a number of benefits for charities, including:

I. Exemptions from numerous forms of taxes & on top of that, receiving gift aid which is basically money from the state to support them for every pound they receive from donations
II. They are exempt from the beneficiary principle and the certainty of objects so long as they are solely for charitable purposes
III. Exempt from the laws against perpetuity which means a gift can be made to a charity such that it can be vested well after the stipulated 125-year periods for non-charitable purpose trusts
IV. They benefit from the cy pres rule which is effectively the notion that a charitable trust will be upheld as far as possible so that it can be as close as, as near as/near enough to the original purpose; the state will work to morph the purpose of the charitable trust as close to the original purpose if the original purpose for some reason is made to be invalid.

The Foundations of Property Law

# **Formalities & Proprietary Estoppel**

I. Interests that exist under law & equity
II. Formalities for creating legal & equitable interests
III. Formalities for transferring legal & equitable interests
IV. Proprietary estoppel; how does it work & does it undermine formalities of transfer

This is where the course starts to get a lot more technical in the sense that we start looking more at the nitty gritty of the law itself in determining what the actual process is & how we tie in everything we've learnt so far into understanding how it plays out in real life. This can be seen as a rather complicated board game but nonetheless, we will go about playing it, one move at a time.

Title & Interest

There is a clear but often missed difference between title & interest in English Law because both are used interchangeably. Title describes the strength, the cumulative hold you have on a piece of property such as the legal & equitable hold/title that you have attached to a piece of land, the difference between registered & unregistered titles to land & the notion of the title which is attached to you when you are in ownership of a land as opposed to possession. For this final point, it may be worth thinking back to when we considered fixtures & the *Parker v British Airways* case which looked into the difference of possession & ownership & this is something too that'll be considered here. Possession will always be protected against the rest of the world except against a person who has a better title than you, typically the owner of the property which you may be in possession of.

Interest on the other hand is more like the essence of the property, the actual content of the property right & the extent to which you have a hold on the rights to the property. This could be freehold interests, leasehold interests or even interests such as an easement (right of way), a mortgage etc.

## Formalities for creating & legal equitable interests

But in a legal sense however, it is important to know this – legal interests in land can only exist in one of two ways:

I. Freehold
II. Leasehold

This is derived from Section 1(1) of the Law of Property Act 1925 which states:

*"1 Legal estates and equitable interests*

*(1) The only estates on land which are capable of subsisting beyond conveyed or created at law are-*
 *a) An estate in fee simple in absolute possession*
 *b) A term of years' absolute*

But a questions arises that what estates can be legal? This is answered in Section 1(2) of the LPA 1925 which states,

*(2) The only interests or charges in or over land which are capable of subsisting or of being conveyed or created at law –*
 *a) An easement, right, or privilege in or over land for an interest equivalent to an estate in fee simple absolute in possession or a term of years' absolute;*
 *b) A rent-charge in possession issuing out of or charged on land being either perpetual or for a term of years' absolute*
 *c) A charge by the way of legal mortgage;*
 *d) [...] and any other similar charge on land which is not created by an instrument;*
 *e) Rights of entry exercisable over or in respect of a legal term of years' absolute, or annexed, for any purpose, to a legal rent-charge*

Basically, what this is saying that the only estates capable of existing at law are easements, rent-charges, mortgages, or rights of entry annexed to a rent-charge. Any form of estate beyond this, can only be that with an equitable interest.

## The Foundations of Property Law

So, in that case, what is the actual procedure for creating legal interests? Well it's pretty simple (I lie sometimes but you know, life's hard!) & all you have to do is adhere to 2 conditions:

I. Must fall in Section 1(1) or (2) of the LPA mentioned above
II. It must be contained within Section 52 of the LPA – but this raises the question that what does Section 52 say? Well Section 52(1) states, *"All conveyances of land or of any interest therein are void for the purpose of conveying or creating a legal estate unless made by deed."*

What this basically means, is that these 2 conditions must be upheld; they must be one of Section 1 or 2 in the LPA & be conveyed by deed. Before looking at what a deed is however, there are a couple of exceptions to the requirement that a legal estate has to be created by a deed which is what is considered in Section 54(2) of the LPA which states, *"Nothing in the foregoing provisions of this part of this Act shall affect the creation by patrol of leases taking effect in possession for a term not exceeding three years (whether or not the lessee is given power to extend the term) and the best rent which can be reasonably obtained without taking a fine."* What this means, is that if a lease is one which at the time of creation is intended to last for nothing more than a period of 3 years, then it can be created by parol, which means orally & thus for this there is no requirement that there be a written deed for it as such.

Additionally, something to note for we will delve into this later on in the course, that if a lease is for 7 years or more on registered land, then it must be in writing & if it is not a registered piece of land, then before agreeing to the lease, it must become a registered piece of land first.

If you already have an interest in land, to transfer it also requires a deed. The same exceptions apply with regards to leases under 3 years & the requirement for land to be registered if a lease is beyond 7 years.

Completion requires two steps for the creation of a new legal interest or the transfer of an existing legal interest which will almost always be preceded by an agreement between the two parties. The two steps are:

I. Exchange of contracts as per Section 2 of the Law of Property (Miscellaneous Provisions) Act 1989 – LP(MP)A 1989
II. Completion as per Section 52 of the LPA as well as Section 1 of the LP(MP)A 1989

Section 2 of the LP(MP)A 1989 states the following:

*(1) A contract for the sale or other disposition of an interest in land can only be made in writing and only by incorporating all the terms which the parties have expressly agreed in one document or, where contracts are exchanged, in each.*

*(2) The terms may be incorporated in a document either by being set out in it or by reference to some other document.*

*(3) The document incorporating the terms or, where contracts are exchanged, one of the documents incorporating them (but not necessarily the same one) must be signed by or on behalf of each party to the contract.*

It can be derived from here that there are 3 main requirements for a sale/transfer of interest to be fulfilled & these requirements are:

I. Must be in writing
II. Must incorporate all the terms
III. Must be signed by both/all parties

However, these 3 key requirements are not required for 3 situations:

I. Leases which are for less than 3 years which can be agreed by parol
II. Creation of resulting, implied or constructive trusts – to be done later in the term
III. Proprietary Estoppel – looked at later in the topic

So that considers the first part of the 2 requirements; exchange of contracts & now we look at completion & the concept of what happens if the essence of completion doesn't actually occur despite the exchange of contracts. The best way to understand this is by way of example. Chloe sells her mansion to me; we sign the contracts & everything but there is no completion in the sense that despite purchasing it from her & giving her the money, she decides that she's not going to give me the keys to the house... I mean mansion! In this instance, what the status would be, is that Chloe will still have the legal title & I will have the equitable title. But because the exchange of contracts has occurred, I can go to court & ask the court to issue something called **specific performance** which will enforce Chloe to transfer the property to me; give me the keys to the mansion or something along those lines.

The courts would order that because of another equity maxim/saying, **"Equity looks as done what ought to be done."** If completion does not occur, the buyer has a right to compel completion from the seller (so Chloe, I'll have my mansion please, thanks ☺)

This equitable title/interest that I hold in the period that Chloe refuses to complete the transaction is known as me having an estate contract & despite having an estate contract, until Chloe doesn't complete the transaction, because I do not have legal title until she does complete it, I cannot grant subordinate rights/titles to anyone ese meaning I cannot grant lease, licences, easements or even get a mortgage on the property until I become the legal title holder too.

So, breaking this down, if we have a valid contract as per Section 2 of the LP(MP)A 1989 which requires for our contract to be in writing, with all terms incorporated & for both of us to have signed the document. If that is deemed as a valid contract, then it will be declared that:

- I have acquired an estate contract which is effectively an equitable title to the property
- Chloe now holds the property for me on constructive trust
- So, I can sue Chloe (sorry ☹) for specific performance enforcing her to get the legal title transferred to me!

This was something looked into in the *Walsh v Lonsdale [1882]* case where there was an agreement to lease Providence Mill for a period of 7 years, but the lease was not actually granted, meaning that there wasn't actually an official deed as such for the agreement. However, based on the maxim stated above, despite the fact that there was no deed, the courts ruled that this should not be a means to prevent the lease from being enforced & this specific performance can be relied upon in court. The courts specifically said this, *"The tenant holds under an agreement for a lease. He holds, therefore, under the same terms in equity as if a lease had been granted, it being...that relief is capable of being given by specific performance. That being so, he cannot complain of the exercise by the landlord of the same rights as the landlord would have had if a lease had been granted. On the other hand, he is protected in the same way as if a lease had been granted."*

### Deeds

What are the requirements for a deed?

> I. Must be in writing
> II. Must be clear that it is intended to be a deed as per Section 1(2)(a) of LP(MP)A 1989
> III. Signed as per Section 1(2)(a) of LP(MP)A 1989
> IV. Need witnesses to prove signature as per Section 1(3) of LP(MP)A
> V. Delivery to show that parties are actually bound by the contract as per Section 1(3) LP(MP)A

*Top Tip: Get all these statutes highlighted in your statute book well before your exam! Use different colour highlighters/sticky notes for different formalities*

Now the question is, that sometimes deeds may for some weird & wonderful reason, not comply with Section 1 of the LP(MP)A in the sense that it may not have been clear, signed, seen and/or delivered. The simple answer for this, is that no problem, because equity will see as done what ought to be done based on the Walsh v Lonsdale case discussed above. This will only be done however, if there is an actual contract preceding the half-done deed.

### Creating & transferring equitable interests

This is something considered by Section 53 of the LPA 1925 which states:

**Instruments required to be in writing.**

*(1) Subject to the provision hereinafter contained with respect to the creation of interests in land by parol—*

*(a) no interest in land can be created or disposed of except by writing signed by the person creating or conveying the same, or by his agent thereunto lawfully authorised in writing, or by will, or by operation of law;*

*(b) a declaration of trust respecting any land, or any interest therein must be manifested and proved by some writing signed by some person who is able to declare such trust or by his will;*

*(c) a disposition of an equitable interest or trust subsisting at the time of the disposition, must be in writing signed by the person disposing of the same, or by his agent thereunto lawfully authorised in writing or by will.*

*(2) This section does not affect the creation or operation of resulting, implied or constructive trusts*

The difference between section 1(a) & 1(b) is that (b) can be made orally & then proven by writing whereas in (a) it must be in writing & then signed; oral agreement alone quite simply is not enough in (a)

And once this interest has been created, then there are 2 conditions which must be adhered to in order to then transfer these equitable interests if one desires to do so & they are

I. Comply with Section 2 LP(MP)A 1989 – the formalities must be adhered to
II. Comply with Section 53(1)(a/c) of the LPA 1989 – it must be signed by writing

<u>Proprietary Estoppel</u>

This is a doctrine which comes into play to act as a protection to ensure fairness in the matter of deeds & all the formalities attached to property law in the sense that what happens if the strict formalities are not complied with, maybe because of a lack of knowledge or a genuine mistake. Would it be fair to deprive someone of their property interest if they have not completed a formality properly? Of course not!

## The Foundations of Property Law

Estoppel is something which we've already looked at in contact law with the notion of promissory estoppel & truth be told, this isn't too dissimilar. This is a doctrine that prevents a person from asserting something contrary to a previous action or statement. The key & underlying difference between proprietary estoppel & promissory estoppel is that the formed can be used as a defence & as a claim; or in more familiar words, as a shield & as a sword too!

There are effectively 3 key elements of PE & they are:

I. Assurance – the landowner must have some kind of assurance to the claimant that he would refrain from exercising his legal rights over his own land

II. Reliance – The claimant has to rely on the assurance in the sense that he behaved differently than he would otherwise have behaved because of the assurance made unto him

III. Detriment – The claimant must prove that they have suffered some form of loss/detriment in reliance of the assurance made unto him

The whole doctrine was recently put to the test in the *Cobbe v Yeoman's Row Management Ltd & Anr [2008]* where A orally agreed to sell B a piece of property in Knightsbridge to build some posh apartments for a price so long as applies for and obtains planning permission for the redevelopment. No other terms were discussed as they were to be negotiated. Now obviously B spent a lot of time & money in attempting to obtain planning permission for redevelopment, but once the planning permission was obtained, A asked for a higher price than that which was agreed upon. B however, according to the HoL was not able to use PE against A.

The HoL said that yes fair enough A's behaviour may have been unconscionable, but this does not automatically raise the case for estoppel. They said, *"It was not an expectation that he would, if the planning application succeeded, become "entitled to a certain interest in land." His expectation was that [they] would sit down and agree the outstanding contractual terms to be incorporated into the formal written agreement, which he justifiably believed would include the already agreed core financial terms, and that his purchase, and subsequently his development of the property, in accordance with that written" agreement would follow. This is not, in my opinion, the sort of expectation of a "certain interest in land."*

What they are effectively saying, is that PE cannot be used in a case where there is no contract which has been entered into & there was actually no interest in the property because all of that was still subject to negotiation. So, PE doesn't always have your back!

But in the case of *Thorner v Major [2009]* Thorner was a nephew who worked on his uncle's farm for 30 years without pay. He gave up his own land because his future lay in his uncle's land. Uncle did not tend to speak directly in the sense he would often communicate obscurely & in 1990, he said to Thorner upon giving him his life insurance policies, "That's for my death duties." Thorner understood from this that he would inherit the farm (mission accomplished! ☺) In 1997, uncle made a will which left most of the estate to Thorner but also some to other legatees but before his death in 2005, he cancelled the whole will because he had a fight with the other legatees.

In this instance, the HoL said that there was no reliance on the will in the sense that Thorner had already left his own land well before his uncle had made the will & thus if there was no reliance, there could be no detriment. But the courts did decide with David because the assurance was made to him.

They also stated which could be quite important, that PE in this regard can also be raised with regards to agreement by silence.

# Doctrine of Notice & Overreaching

   I.   Equity's Darling & the Doctrine of Notice
   II.  Overriding Interests
   III. Overreaching

For each of these topics, the main question that we are asked to consider is this; if there is an equitable interest that is held in a piece of land and that land is subsequently conveyed to another person, what role does that equitable interest actually play? So, let's say I sell my land, what will happen to the equitable interest which may be held by someone else before I sell it?

Equity's Darling & the Doctrine of Notice

Equity's Darling is the notion that someone who acquires the legal estate in the state that they are:

   I.   Acting in good faith; AND
   II.  Giving Value to the estate; AND
   III. Having no notice

This is also known as *"Bona fide purchaser of a legal estate for value without notice,"* which is another exception to Nemo Dat. But briefly, it's the idea, Nemo Dat says that you cannot give a better title than the one which you have. For example, if I steal a car & I sell it to you, the basic rule states that you cannot get a 'good' title from me because I don't have/possess a good title to transfer to you.

Equity's Darling's first case where it was raised was in that of *Pilcher v Rawlins [1871]* where a person was made a trustee for a piece of land on behalf of his nephews & nieces who were the beneficial owners of that land. The trustee mortgaged the property to a third party, who as a result of the security achieved through the mortgage, lent the trustee some money. Now however, it gets a little bit complicated & feisty.

The trustee & the third party to whom he mortgaged the property & subsequently was lent money from, entered into a conspiracy together. The

## The Foundations of Property Law

money lender was a solicitor so what he did was he returned the trust deeds and made it look like, to the world, that the mortgage had come to an end which would mean that it was now no longer subject to the trust. Basically, what they did, was to make it look like the trustee had the absolute fee simple of the property when the reality was that the solicitor still held a mortgage to the property too, hence making it subject to the trust. What happened next was that the trustee went further and used the property as a security in order to get a loan of money from the Savings & Loan Bank who remember, now that they had the property as security, were equity's darling. Why? Because they were bona fide purchasers, of value with no notice; they were the subject of a fraud by the trustee & the solicitor through absolutely no fault of their own.

The nephew & niece who are the original beneficial owners of the property obviously had a problem with the idea that the bank could be equity's darling & therefore be protected. The question before the courts was simple; who had the ownership of the property? The court decided that in this case, S&L were indeed equity's darling & as a result, this is what the courts said: *"Such a purchaser...once he ...has satisfied the terms of the plea of purchase for valuable consideration without notice, then, according to my judgment, this Court has no jurisdiction whatever to do anything more than to let him depart in possession of that legal estate, that legal right, that legal advantage which he has obtained, whatever it may be."*

This is something that was built on in the case of *Kingsnorth v Tizard [1986]* which is a case where the husband & wife co-owned a piece of unregistered property; the husband had legal title whilst the wife too had contributed to the purchase price, improvements & general maintenance of the house. It could be said, that they had engaged in a joint tenancy or even in the sense that the husband was the trustee & beneficiary whilst the wife was a simple beneficiary of the trust, because legal title was held by the husband. Two decades later however, the marriage broke down (awwwww ☹) The wife agreed that she'll move out to live with her boyfriend but would come back to the family home every day to take care of their two children, which meant that most of her clothes & belongings remained in the guest bedroom of the house; this continued for a year or so until one day she

The Foundations of Property Law

came home to look after the kids when all she found was a note. "Darling, me & my son have gone on a short holiday & we will be back soon!" (NB: This isn't what the note said, it's me just simply paraphrasing it) It just so happened, that this short holiday was actually intended to be him going away forever and ever and ever and ever and ever! And it only got worse for the wife...

Little did she know that before departing, the husband had taken out a mortgage on the property from Kingsnorth Finance and as a result was given £66,000 (which I'm assuming he used to finance his lifelong holiday!) Before issuing the mortgage however, the bank hired a consultant to do inspections of the property & look into the potential owners & the state of the property in all senses. There were signs for both the bank & consultant to see that there may have been a wife/partner who else was living at the, house & yet they did nothing to address it. At different times in the process, the husband said that he was married but separated whilst at other times he explicitly said that he was single; surely if the documents were checked properly, they would've seen this irregularity from the husband & would've flagged it up. They then came to check the house which of course the husband planned such that it was done whilst the wife was away with her new boyfriend & the inspectors saw that the wife's belongings were all still at the house but the husband said that she was using it as storage & guess what, they just accepted it & believed him. After this, they saw the children's room (daughter & son) & the inspectors didn't take a moment to try & add one & one together but just ignored it.

What happened after this inspection was that he obviously got his £66,000 but he, as happens in all cases, defaulted on his repayments because he'd basically ran away & so the bank sued for possession of the house. The problem that arises is simple; is Kingsnorth Finance Equity's darling? If they are, then they can claim possession, but if they're not, then they cannot claim possession.

And in this instance the courts ruled that the bank may have been bona fide & given value, but they did have notice, which means that they would not have been equity's darling. This is for 2 reasons; there was the contradictory statements by the husband should have raised questions & the presence of the kids should've raised questions too; who's their Mum? Does she have a property interest? The question had to be asked by the inspector & it's shocking that he didn't relay this information back to the bank or if he did, that the bank didn't raise any questions about it. Therefore, the bank's claim for possession failed. Here though the inspector didn't tell the bank, the notice was imputed & so the inspector was effectively seen as being the bank & his having these hints of notice means that they could not have been equity's darling.

But what would have happened if they didn't have notice. What would've happened to the wife's interests? This is where our next concept steps in.

Overreaching

There are 2 views which consider what overreaching actually means & we will look at them both but for the beginning, they are this:

I. Equitable interests of a beneficiary are transferred from the property to the proceeds of the sale (capital money) by two trustees. What this means, is that the beneficial interest holder will no longer have an interest in the property but rather in the proceeds of the sale.
II. "A process whereby existing interests are subordinated to a later interest or estate created pursuant to a trust power."

The first view arises from two key sections of the LPA – Section 2 & Section 27 respectively.

The relevant sub-sections in Section 2 & 27 states:

I. *A conveyance to a purchaser of a legal estate in land shall overreach any equitable interest... affecting that estate, whether or not he has notice thereof if ...*
    a. *the conveyance is made by at least two trustees or a trust corporation. (Section 27)*
    b. *For value. (Section 27)*
    c. *The interests are capable of being overreached (Section 2(3))*

## The Foundations of Property Law

The main thing to notice with regards to the difference between equity's darling & the doctrine of overreaching is:

I.   There must be 2 or more trustees at the very least
II.  There is no requirement of having no notice – can overreach even with notice

<u>Overriding interests</u>

There are instances however, where you can have an overriding interest the would move to bind the purchaser of the property regardless of whether or not they had notice. These are a number of things under Section 70 of the LRA 1925 which has now been repealed by Schedule 3 of the Land Registration Act 2002.

To have an overriding interest, you need two things according to Section 70 of the LRA 1925:

I.   A Property Interest
II.  Actual Occupation of the Property

This came to light in the case of *William & Glyns Bank v Boland [1979]* wherein both the husband and wife contributed to the purchase of a property, but during registration (as per the LRA 1925) the register was made to reflect only the husband's name; he was the registered owner of the property because he held the legal title whereas the wife only held a beneficial title. The husband then proceeded to take out a loan using the house as security, but as always, defaulted on the loan and the bank sought to possess the else. The husband's title can be liable because it's his own fault, but what about the wife's interests? The question for the court was whether or not the wife's interest could be overreached.

And the court in this case decided that no, of course the wife's interest could not be overreached. This is because, she had an actual occupation of the property; she had an overriding interest. And though her property can be overreached, her overriding interest protected her. Additionally, in this case, there was only one trustee which means that according to Section 2(2) of the LPA, her interests couldn't even be overreached. Ormond J said with regards to the two-trustees rule, *"I think...that the answer to both points is* that the wives' interests have not been overreached and are not capable of being overreached because in each case the land was held by a sole trustee who has no overreaching powers. The fact that the sole trustee might have appointed a second trustee and so acquired overreaching powers is nothing to the point unless and until a second trustee is appointed, which may afford some protection to the person whose interest is overreached."

The Two-Trustees rule originates from the LPA under Section 2(2) which states:

I. "Where the legal estate affected is subject to a trust of land, then if ... a conveyance... made by the trustees, the trustees are either
    a. Two or more individuals...
    b. A trust corporation
    c. And capital money is paid to them

Any equitable interest... shall... be overreached by the conveyance..."

It is also found in Section 27 of the LPA which states, "Purchaser not to be concerned with the trusts of proceeds of sale (capital money) of which are to be paid to two or more trustees or to a trust corporation."

Trustees get their powers from Section 14(1) & (2) of the Trustees Act 1925 which state:

(1) The receipt in writing of a trustee for any money, securities, investments or other personal property or effects payable, transferable, or deliverable to him under any trust or power shall be a sufficient discharge to the person paying, transferring, or delivering the same and shall effectually exonerate him from seeing to the application or being answerable for any loss or misapplication thereof.

(2) This section does not, except where the trustee is a trust corporation, enable a sole trustee to give a valid receipt for—

    (a) proceeds of sale or other capital money arising under a trust of land;

    (b) capital money arising under the Settled Land Act, 1925.

The Foundations of Property Law

So, what interests can actually be overreached?

This roots from Section 2(3) of the LPA which effectively ultimately states that the only equitable interests that can be overreached are beneficial interests under trusts:

I.  2(3): The following equitable interests and powers are excepted from the operation of subsection 2...
    a. Any equitable interest protected by a deposit of document relating to the legal estate
    b. The benefit of any covenant or agreement restrictive of the user of land
    c. Any easement, liberty or privilege... Affecting land and being merely an equitable interest
    d. ...contract to convey or create a legal estate...
    e. Any equitable interest protected by registration under the Land Charges Act, 1925

This came to life in the *City of London Building Society v Flegg [1988]* case wherein a married couple purchased a house for themselves and for the wife's parents. The wife's parents, being the lovely people that they were, contributed to the purchase price of the house. The couple, however, were the registered owners, whilst the parents only had a beneficial title to the property, but they were all occupants in the house.

The couple, in need of money, took out several mortgages on the property which were all repaid after the taking out of a loan from the building society; this loan was something the parents didn't know about!

The trial judge held that the parents did have an overriding interest in the property because they were in actual occupation of the property as per Section 70 of the LRA 1925, but these interests had been overreached because there were to trustees (the couple) which meant that possession was granted to the building society. The Court of Appeal relied on the Boland case & said nahhhh fam are you maddd, if you're in actual possession, your possession cannot be overreached because you have an overriding interest.

## The Foundations of Property Law

The House of Lords however, it was argued exactly that by the parents; we have an overriding interest, so we cannot be overreached. Lord Templeman however said that in order to claim an overriding interest, you need to have an interest in the land & actual occupation & for some reason I'm not too sure about but I'll get confirmed, the parents interest was overreached & thus their interest no longer remained in the property, but rather in the proceeds of sale. I think it occurred because there was two or more trustees & thus as per the two-trustee rule, their interests could successfully be overreached.

### Rationale for Overreaching

In the judgement of the above case, Lord Templeman stated, *"One of the main objects of the legislation of 1925 was to effect a compromise between on the one hand the interests of the public in securing that land held in trust is freely marketable and, on the other hand, the interests of the beneficiaries in preserving their rights under the trusts. By the Settled Land Act 1925 a tenant for life may convey the settled land discharged from all the trusts powers and provisions of the settlement. By the Law of Property Act 1925 trustees for sale may convey land held on trust for sale discharged from the trusts affecting the proceeds of sale and rents and profits until sale. Under both forms of trust the protection and the only protection of the beneficiaries is that capital money must be paid to at least two trustees or a trust corporation."* What this means is that overreaching allows the land to be taken free of charge and allows the beneficiaries to make a claim on the money. There are 2 problems with this however;

I. The beneficiaries lose their home
II. Usually it happens because the trustees have defaulted on the loan & have no money, so how on earth are the beneficiaries going to sue when the trustees don't have any money to pay out!

In the case of *State Bank of India v Sood [1996]* there was a situation where two people had legal title to the house, with 4 individuals being the beneficial title holders with a beneficial interest in the property. The two trustees had existing liabilities and what they did was they executed a mortgage using this property as security in order to pay off their existing liabilities & used the house as collateral in order for them to delay their existing debts. What happened, as has happened again & again in today's cases, is that the trustees defaulted on their loan & the bank sought possession of the property. What the beneficial owners claimed was obvious; we're living in the property & thus have actual occupation, so you definitely cannot overreach our interest because we have an overriding interest to protect us!

They also raised another couple of questions including What is capital money? It obviously includes money, but anything else? Because what their argument was that there was no payment of capital money by the trustees so there could be no overreaching interest for the bank. The Settled Land Act, 1925 defines Capital money as including "securities representing capital money". The overreaching powers include power to convey by an exchange or lease as well as by a mortgage or charge where capital money may not arise." So effectively the courts took this opportunity to define capital money as not only hard cash/money but also anything in security which represents money/monetary value.

The second question that raised was that did the capital money have to arise under the conveyance? Let's say only a part of the money was paid, at the time of the execution. Would that suffice? No because related to the answer to the last question; capital money can also be the security which was the property

Overreaching occurs upon execution of the charge, meaning that as soon as the mortgage/security on the house was taken out, overreaching had occurred for the ban. What Pill J said with regards to Section 2(1) was that, *"The paragraph does not expressly require the payment of capital money as a prerequisite of overreaching but does provide that the statutory requirements respecting the payment of capital money arising are complied with."* What this means is that the capital money does not need to arise contemporaneously for the execution of the charge for overreaching to occur.

So, there are two main concluding points:

I. Overreaching allows a process by which beneficial interests under a trust can be transferred for an owner of an equitable/beneficial interest from the property into the proceeds of the sale
II. But if there are two trustees or a trust corporation and capital money is paid, then the purchaser will take the property regardless of any overriding interests which are:
    a. Property Right
    b. Actual occupation

# Trustee Powers & Duties

I. How are trustees appointed & removed?
II. Duties on Appointment
III. Duty of Care
IV. Section 11 of Trustee Act 2000
V. Powers of Investment
VI. Standard Investment Criteria
VII. Identify Interests under the Land
VIII. Trustee Act 1925 Section 31
IX. Trustee Act 1925 Section 32

How are trustees appointed & removed?

There are a number of ways in which a trustee can be appointed &/or removed, however, before looking into them, the first thing to remember is to check the trust document first. Ideally, there will always be a trust document, but obviously there will be some oral trusts which do not have a trust document. But if there is a trust document, that is the first document to check, because that more often than not, will have details on how to appoint & remove trustees from the trust. What we look at below, will only occur if there is no trust document.

**Appointing Trustees**

There are 4 ways to appoint a trustee & they are as follows:

I. By a Settlor (a trust)/Testator (from a will) can ask someone to become a trustee. Once this position has been accepted, and you have been appointed as being a trustee, it is very important to know that you cannot simply just turn around & say you no longer want to be a trustee anymore.
II. Following Section 36 of the Trustee Act 1925, one trustee can appoint another trustee. This is because, there usually cannot be only one trustee to land; there is the two-trustee rule which requires there to be two trustees per piece of land & thus Section 36 allows for another trustee to be appointed.

III. Beneficiaries of a trust can appoint a trustee as per Section 19 of ToLATA (Trust of Land and Appointment of Trustees Act) 1996 where the requirement is that all beneficiaries must act unanimously in that they must all agree for the appointment of a trustee to the trust. The requirement for them to all act unanimously is simply to ensure that there is no disagreement or problem which may occur later on which causes a problem between the beneficiaries. The trustee, which is being appointed must be Sui Juris, as we looked at last year, which is the requirement that they must be 18 years of age and not be mentally incapacitated.

IV. The courts themselves can appoint a trustee as per Section 41 of the Trustee Act 1925.

**Removal of Trustees**

There are 3 ways of removing trustees & they are the same as above:

I. By other trustees as per Section 36 of the Trustees Act 1925 where it can be proven that there is a severe incompetence on the part of the trustees in not doing their jobs properly

II. By a unanimous decision of the beneficiaries as per S19 of ToLATA 1996

III. By the courts as per s41 of the Trustees Act 1925 wherein the court would have to be satisfied that it is essential for the good running of the trust in that they must have a high degree of certainty that the trustee be removed from the trust. S41 actually states, *"In particular and without prejudice to the generality of the foregoing provision, the court may make an order appointing a new trustee in substitution for a trustee who . . . lacks capacity to exercise his functions as trustee, or is a bankrupt, or is a corporation which is in liquidation or has been dissolved.*

<u>Duties on Appointment</u>

The very first & most essential thing for a trustee to do, is to examine the actual trust documents & come to grips with what the trust actually is, what the trustees' duties & responsibilities are etc. If this is not done, then the trustee will be seen to be in breach of their duty right from the offset! In fact, when examining the trust & other related trust documents, the things that must be considered link in with what we looked at last year:

I. Certainty of Intention – what was the purpose of the trust
II. Certainty of Subject Matter – what is the trust property & what property has been vested in the trustees
III. Certainty of Object Matter – who are the beneficiaries, what are they entitled to; looks back at the moot topic from last year & all the research into *McPhail v Doulton* [1970].

There is a requirement for trustees to make sure that there are no existing breaches on the trust & must take the required steps to correct any breaches before doing anything else with the trust. This is because, continuing to act on the trust before correcting any breaches, can be seen as a continuation of a breach & will be determined as a way of ensuring that a trust is run properly. If there is any breach, then claims must be brought against any trustees who have breached their duties/responsibilities.

Additionally, there are often specific duties for the trustee which can be specified in the trust document itself or other trust related documents. The important thing to note here however, is that with these documents specifically, a beneficiary has very limited rights to access these trust documents. They can see the trust documents, but beyond that, all the stuff that relates to the trustees, the way they're choosing to manage the trust etc. can be limited for the beneficiaries in that they can be limited in not being able to see this. In essence, if a trustee is exercising their discretion on a trust, then the beneficiary does not have access to this/a right to see documents relating to that. This roots from the case of *Schmidt v Rosewood* where it was decided that if the beneficiary thinks that there is fraud happening, then the courts can be asked to review the trust documents which may give rise to evidence of fraud but the beneficiary themselves cannot do anything. Yes, if the courts find evidence of fraud, then they can rule for the documents to be handed over to the beneficiary.

This is mainly done to ensure that, the trust is protected as this is the overwhelmingly main purpose of the trustees; they have a fiduciary duty to protect the trust assets for the beneficiary & in order to regulate this, there are certain statutory powers to ensure the trust assets are protected under the Trustees Act 1925 & 2000 respectively. It is important to note here, that both acts are still in action & therefore when talking about the Trustee Acts, one must specify which Act is being referred to.

Duty of Care

There are two standards when it comes to the duty of care & they are:

I. Statutory Duty of Care as per Section 1 of the Trustee Act 2000
II. Common Law Duty of Care as defined by the case of *Speight v Gaunt* [1883] which defined the duty of care as acting as per 'ordinary prudent man of business' in that you do not take any unnecessary risks. It is important to note that the Common Law duty only applies where the Trustee Act 2000 is not applicable.

The Common Law standard had been initially defined by a couple of cases, from which the rulings helped to form the Trustee Act 2000. The first case was *Bartlett v Barclays Bank Trust Co Ltd* [1980] wherein Barclays Bank was the sole trustee of the Bartlett trust, set up by Sir Herbert Bartlett. The sole asset of the trust was 99.8% of the issued shares in the family company. On the company board were two surveyors, an accountant and a solicitor. The trustee appointed none. In an attempt to raise cash, the trust appointed merchant bankers to consider taking the company public. The bankers advised that a public offering would be much more successful if the company expanded its business from managing property to developing property as well. Barclays Bank as trustee agreed to this policy (so long as the income available to the beneficiaries was not affected). The board then embarked on speculative developments, one of which ended in disaster when planning permission could not be obtained for a large development (the Old Bailey project), and the trust suffered a significant loss. It was here held by the courts that there was a duty for the bank to go above & beyond the information that is available to the public, or available in the public domain. This is imperative because they are setting a standard which means that there is a duty to take an active role and this role will be defined by the level of expertise one has. The higher the expertise, the higher the duty attached to it. Basically, the facts of the case are long & boring, so what you need to know from this case is quite simple – an ordinary prudent man of business will still supervise his business in that he will not delegate all the duties, especially not the duty to supervise. One must go beyond the publicly available information when dealing with a trust. The higher the level of expertise, the higher the obligation upon them.

The second case, of *Nestle v National Westminster Bank Plc* [1992] was a case where a testator died in 1922 and named his widow, two sons and wives and one grandchild as the beneficiaries. The wife got the family home as a life interest and a tax-free annuity. The two sons got annuities between age 21 and 25 and life interests in half the trust with a power to appoint income to their wives and Georgina, the grandchild, got the remainder. In 1922 there was £53,963 and in 1986 when Georgina became entitled, there was £269,203. She claimed that had the fund been invested properly there would have been €1.8m. The trust company had failed to conduct periodic reviews of investments. They invested in tax-exempt gilts because the sons were domiciled abroad, meaning exemption from inheritance tax. The argument here was that the trustees should've acted in a more prudent manner which would have allowed there to be a higher return on the money. The court however, said that this, although fell woefully short of the value they could have had, was not a breach of the duty on the part of the trustees. The courts said that in hindsight it can be seen as unwise, but at the time, the trustees were acting as per the 'ordinary prudent business man' & having hindsight only makes a fool wise. To impose a liability here on the trustees, would have been a step too far & unfair too.

The Statutory Duty of Care roots from Section 1 of the Trustee Act 2000 which states:

**1The duty of care.**

(1)Whenever the duty under this subsection applies to a trustee, he must exercise such care and skill as is reasonable in the circumstances, having regard in particular—

(a)to any special knowledge or experience that he has or holds himself out as having, and

(b) if he acts as trustee in the course of a business or profession, to any special knowledge or experience that it is reasonable to expect of a person acting in the course of that kind of business or profession.

(2) In this Act the duty under subsection (1) is called "the duty of care".

What this means, is that if declare yourself as someone who has special knowledge, or an expert in a field, even though you may be gassing yourself & chatting absolute nonsense, the courts will judge you based on what you refer to yourself, suggesting that there will be a higher degree of a duty of care over you; you will be judged as per a higher standard which will be the standard of that profession.

However, the duty of care can be excluded in a trust document, as per the case of *Armitage v Nurse*. This is because the responsibilities & obligations which a trustee is burdened by are so intense, no one wants to be a trustee anymore. It is an unpaid, stressful role which requires a lot of work, so to allow the duty of care to be excluded is seen to be a method of trying to ensure that people still do want to become trustees. Literally, anything but fraud can be excluded for liability.

## Section 11 Trustee Act 2000

One of the ways in which the roles of trustees are made easier, is through the implementation of Section 11 of the 2000 Act.

*11 Power to employ agents.*

(1) Subject to the provisions of this Part, the trustees of a trust may authorise any person to exercise any or all of their delegable functions as their agent.

(2) In the case of a trust other than a charitable trust, the trustees' delegable functions consist of any function other than—

(a) any function relating to whether or in what way any assets of the trust should be distributed,

(b) any power to decide whether any fees or other payment due to be made out of the trust funds should be made out of income or capital,

(c) any power to appoint a person to be a trustee of the trust, or

(d) any power conferred by any other enactment or the trust instrument which permits the trustees to delegate any of their functions or to appoint a person to act as a nominee or custodian.

This allows for certain responsibilities held by the trustees to be delegated such as who manages the trust on a day to day basis etc. However, it is imperative to note, that as per Sections 21 & 22 respectively, even after delegation, there is a fierce requirement for trustees to ensure that these functions are kept under review. This would include doing things like considering any needs to revoke the appointments or exercising any powers they may have in order to give directions to the delegates. This requirement to review & supervise the delegates is a duty of the trustee & if they do not, then it can be determined as being a breach of a duty of care & they can be held liable for it.

There are a few things which cannot be delegated such as:

I. Decisions relating to the distribution of assets
II. Payment of fees from capital or income
III. Powers of appointment
IV. The power of delegation

Powers of Investment

The powers of Investment have changed as per Section 3 of the Trustee Act 2000, which changed the previous Common Law Rule which had been determined through the case of *Re Wragg* [1918] which had a requirement that if there are to be any investments, they must be followed up with an income; an income must be generated from any investments. So, let's say for instance, with trust money, you invest in a property on the knowledge that you buy the house for £100,000 but in 10 years' time, the value of the house will be £300,000. With shares on the other hand, dividends will be the income & the price of the share will be the capital income. Under the Common Law Rule, if this house was not receiving an income, meaning there was no rent coming in from the property, this investment would not be valid as per the Common Law duty of care. The house price rising would be deemed as a capital rise, not income as such. This was extended by Section 6 of the ToLATA 1996.

However, this was changed by the Trustee Act 2000 and Section 8 within it, which stated capital growth investments can be allowed including for land. The land must however be in the UK & not be overseas, unless of course the trust document allows for it to be overseas.

In the case of *Harries v Church Commissioners* [1992], this is a case where the trustees engaged in legal tax evasion, much like the recent Panama & Paradise Papers news blasts. Nicholls VC held in this case, *"prima facie the purposes of the trust will be best served by the trustees seeking to obtain there from* **the maximum return, whether by way of income or capital growth, which is consistent with commercial prudence."** This is interesting because the trustee has the responsibility to make sure that they are doing absolutely everything to ensure that the trustee gets the best return on their investment & must explore all legal avenues in order to ensure that this happens, including legal tax evasion. They have that duty otherwise they will be breaching their duty of care!

In the case of *Cowan v Scargill* [1985], the trustees of the National Coal Board pension fund had £3,000 million in assets. Five of the ten trustees were appointed by the NCB and the other five were appointed by the National Union of Mineworkers. The board of trustees set the general strategy, while day to day investment was managed by a specialist investment committee. Under a new "Investment Strategy and Business Plan 1982" the NUM wanted the pension fund to cease new overseas investment, gradually withdraw existing overseas investments and withdraw investments in industries competing with coal. This was all intended to enhance the mines' business prospects. The five NCB nominated trustees made a claim in court over the appropriate exercise of the pension fund's powers. The court said that whatever the trustees need to do for the best financial interest for the trust, that is what they're entitled to do & they can do that with their absolute discretion.

The case we looked at above, *Nestle v National Westminster Bank Plc* [1988] considers a whole portfolio approach, with regards to which Hoffman J states, *"modern trustees acting within their investment powers are entitled to be judged by the standards of current portfolio theory which emphasizes the risk level of the entire portfolio rather than the risk of attaching to each investment in isolation."* If one has a large trust, then the trust should be diversified with some high-risk investments balanced with some low risk investments.

Standard Investment Criteria

These are covered in Sections 4(1) & 4(2) of the Trustee Act 2000 which state:

(1)In exercising any power of investment, whether arising under this Part or otherwise, a trustee must have regard to the standard investment criteria.

(2)A trustee must from time to time review the investments of the trust and consider whether, having regard to the standard investment criteria, they should be varied.

There are two stages to defining whether or not something is a suitable investment and that is:

I. Suitability – in general, would this investment be a good one? If yes, Suitability – would this specific investment into this category be a good investment?
II. Diversity – do not put all your investments into one trust/investment, but rather spread payments out to manage the risk; balance a high-risk investment with a low risk one

Section 5 of the Act requires that you have to take advice. To say that you did not have the knowledge isn't enough because the court will say well you didn't ask for help or advice, therefore we're going to say that you felt that you had enough expertise. The Act itself says:

**5Advice.**

(1) Before exercising any power of investment, whether arising under this Part or otherwise, a trustee must (unless the exception applies) obtain and consider proper advice about the way in which, having regard to the standard investment criteria, the power should be exercised.

(2) When reviewing the investments of the trust, a trustee must (unless the exception applies) obtain and consider proper advice about whether, having regard to the standard investment criteria, the investments should be varied.

(3) The exception is that a trustee need not obtain such advice if he reasonably concludes that in all the circumstances it is unnecessary or inappropriate to do so.

(4) Proper advice is the advice of a person who is reasonably believed by the trustee to be qualified to give it by his ability in and practical experience of financial and other matters relating to the proposed investment.

If advice is not sought by a trustee in relation to an investment & they do not have a good reason for not seeking advice, then this will constitute as a breach of duty.

**Just a general piece of legal advice, do NOT ever become a trustee. Just don't. Okay? DO NOT DO IT! NO! Thanks x**

## Identify Interests Under the Trust

Let's say for example a trust is as follows for which you are the trustee:

Matthew for life and then to Katie.

Life interest holder will get income. The remainder interest holder will get the capital income.

In this example, I have a life interest & my interest will be an income generated interest which means that any income that comes from this, will go to me because I have the life interest. Katie will have the capital interest in it. As a trustee however, you will be responsible for protecting both our interests. So, you will need to make sure both the income & the capital of the trust is protected; the income/rent of the trust is high & the capital value of the trust property is also maintained. Both of these are vested interests.

### Trustee Act 1925 - **Section 31 of the Act**

This looks at the powers of maintenance & advancement. This was amended by Section 8 of The Inheritance and Trustees Powers Act 2014. And it effectively now allows for a beneficiary, who is entitled to an income, to ask the trustees to give them that income. This will apply to both vested and contingent trusts. For the purpose of the exam, please note that it is now, as per the 1st October 2014, not limited to a reasonable amount any more.

I. If the beneficiary is over 18, then the trustee has a duty/obligation to give the income generated to the beneficiary, unless of course the trust document states otherwise.

II. If the beneficiary is under 18, then the beneficiary has the right to apply for some of the trust property, but it will up to the trustee to decide if they are entitled to that property. They will then get the money for sure once they reach 18.

What now happens, is that income, which was not applied, as in could not be collected because of age or mental capacity, will be accumulated. Trustees are required to keep the accumulations in a separate pot of money, away from further income/capital accumulations which may occur after the age of 18. With this, there are then two options:

I. For vested interests, accumulations can be obtained when the beneficiary turns 18. The beneficiary cannot take ownership of this property until the beneficiary turns 18, because then & only then, are they capable of being owners of property. They will receive all of the unspent income/accumulated incomes when they reach 18.

II. For contingent interests, accumulations will remain with the capital & will be collectable upon reaching the contingency age but will be entitled to the income itself as soon as they turn 18. The accumulations will be frozen until they reach that contingency age.

So, for example, let's look at the Trust example below.

Amina is to have trust property if she reaches the age of 25 (so this is a contingent trust.) The trust generates £10,000 a year. Aged 15, she wants to go on a school exchange programme which costs £2,000. She asks the trustees of the trust for which she is the beneficiary, to pay for the trip. As this is spending the property on something which is beneficial to her (education, maintenance or building) they have the discretion to pay for the trip. So, for that specific year, only £8,000 will remain in the trust income generated.

When she turns 18, she will be entitled to get the £10,000 each year automatically; she will not need to wait till she turns 25. However, the money which was accumulated from when she was 15 till 18, will be accumulated & will only be received by her when she turns 25. So, the £28,000 will be held for her & she'll only receive this when she turns 25. (I want a trust like this!!!) This is because this was a contingent interest as per Section 32 of the Trustee Act 1925.

If it was a vested interest, then she would've got both the income & the £28,000 of accumulations automatically as soon as she turned 18.

The difference is big & very important so:

I. Vested Interests: Accumulations & Income both received as soon as one turns 18
II. Contingent Interests: Income received at 18, but accumulations held till beneficiary reaches age of contingency.

In summary of Section 31 of the Trustee Act 1925, the following stages have to be taken to properly understand it & how to use it:

Does the beneficiary have a beneficial interest in the income?

## Section 32 of the Trustee Act

This applies to the beneficiary who is entitled to the capital of the trust. This has been amended by S9 of the Inheritance & Trustees Power Act 2014.

For new trusts, all trust capital can be advanced to/handed over to the beneficiary. However, for old trusts, it was limited up to half of their potential interest only. When deciding to give them their capital, the common law duty of care must be used & used in such a way that the capital must be used for their advancement, meaning the advancement for the beneficiary. This advancement could be something like starting a business, education or something which can broadly mean their benefit.

So, this is much more straight forward than Section 31 in essence. Remember, old trusts will only be half of the presumptive share. New trusts are any trusts created after the 1st October 2014.

However, it must be noted that if capital is taken out, then this must still ensure that the standard investment criteria is not violated & also the prior interest holder (of the income holder) must be consulted & his consent must be valid. There is a requirement that the income holder consents of the using of the trust in this way. This is simply because, any advancement of the capital, will change the income levels & therefore the income holders/prior interest holders income levels will be affected, therefore, their consent must be sought. What this looks to protect is the alternative remedy trustees can give to the remainder tenant – if they ask for something, then potentially the trust could purchase it for them as trust property & then as a beneficiary, they can be entitled to benefit from it & use trust property. All it must do is comply with the requirements we look at above in relation to the Standard Investment Criteria laid out in Section 4 of the TA 2000.

However, sometimes, it can be so that under S3 of the Trustee Act 2000, allows for a potential solution that the land (capital sought land) can be invested into, so long as it adheres to the standard investment criteria.

# Breach of Duty & Fiduciary Duties

I. Trust Duties
II. Fiduciary Duties
III. Remuneration, Payment – Fiduciary Duty
IV. Secret Profits
V. Information – Fiduciary Duty
VI. Breaches
VII. Personal Remedies
VIII. Defences
IX. Primary & Secondary Liability
X. Disgorgement Remedy

Trust Duties

There is a very heavy burden on trustees to ensure that they do not breach their trust duties & obligations, as there are very significant repercussions for any breaches. It was stated in the case of *Armitage v Nurse* that, *"A breach may be deliberate or inadvertent; it may consist of an actual misappropriation or misapplication of the trust property or merely of an investment or other dealing which is outside the trustees' powers."* There are a number of trust duties which we looked at the previous topic but to just recap, they include:

I. The duty to invest wisely as per the requirements of the Trustee Act 2000 & what is included within that; the standard investment criteria & the duty to take advice, as stated in Section 4 & Section 5 respectively.
II. The trust assets must be dispossessed to the people who are entitled to the trust property; it must not be given to anyone who is outside the class of beneficiaries. One of the duties of a trustee is to determine the class of beneficiaries as per certainty of subject matter.
III. As per Section 31 & Section 32, there is a requirement for the trustees to ensure that no trust property is given to the wrong identities. Capital income must be given to the remainder tenant, whereas income must go to the life interest holder. Not doing this

will mean that the trustees are in breach of trust. Trustees will be personally liable for any systematic looting as per the case of *Re Paulings*.

This is covered by the standard common law duty of care which is the requirement as per an ordinary prudent businessman & the standards set by that concept which we looked at the previous topic.

Fiduciary Duties

Not all trust duties are fiduciary. However, all duties are trust duties as such. It is important to note that not all trust duties are fiduciary but at the same time, not all fiduciary duties are held within a trust. It was actually stated in a case that fiduciary duties are notoriously vague to define, and the categories of fiduciary duties are growing. The concept of a fiduciary duty was defined by Finn in 1977, as "*'a fiduciary is expected to act in the interests of the other – to act selflessly and with undivided loyalty.*" You must act in the best interest of the trust property even if this is to a detriment to yourself; everyone & everything comes after the interest of the trust property when you are a trustee & this is effectively the core of a fiduciary duty.

The first significant rule to note when considering fiduciary duties is the concept of the no conflict rule. This is the idea that there must not be a conflict of interest between the two parties. An example of a fiduciary relationship could be the relationship between a solicitor and their client, or the relationship between a doctor and his patient. There is a trust which has been placed in the doctor or the solicitor in both specific situations for them to subsequently ensure that they get the best possible result for the clients/patients. The best way to highlight the requirement for there to not be a conflict between the two parties, is to look at the fiduciary duties of a lecturer in relation to their students and their responsibilities to their organisation.

So, Emma has a fiduciary duty to SOAS to not disclose the exam question(s) to us. This means she has to put this fiduciary duty before everything else, including her own interests. If she tells us the questions, she would probably be the most popular lecturer & everyone would love her. In fact, we might

## The Foundations of Property Law

even get her presents, money etc. & this must be really appealing for a lecturer to be loved by their students to that extent. However, she has to quash that because of her fiduciary duty to SOAS – as per above, this has to come first every single time.

The simple matter is, there must be absolutely no conflict between the fiduciary and the principle and there must not even seem like there was or even could be any sort of conflict. Even the idea of there potentially being a conflict will mean that the courts may consider it to be contrary to the no conflict rule. This was considered in the case of *Keech v Sandford* [1726] where the defendant held a lease of the profits of a market on trust for the plaintiff, a minor. The lessor, concerned about difficulties of enforcement against a minor, refused to renew the lease in favour of the trust, whereupon the trustee renewed the lease for his own benefit. The plaintiff sought an account of profits made since the renewal of the lease and to have the lease assigned to him. It was impossible for the infant to ever get that lease & in order to protect the lease of the infant, it could be said that the trustee decided to take the lease for himself. Lord King LC in his judgement said, *"I must consider this as a trust for the infant; for I very well see, if a trustee, on the refusal to renew, might have a lease to himself, few trust estates would be renewed to cestui que use; thought I do not say there is a fraud in this case, yet he should rather have let it run out, tan to have had the lease to himself. This may seem hard, that the trustee is the only person of all mankind who might not have the lease: but it is very proper that rule should be strictly pursed, and not in the least relaxed; for it is very proper that the rule should be strictly pursued, and not in the least relaxed; for it is very obvious what would be the consequence of letting trustees have the lease, on refusal to renew to cestui que use (the person for whom the trust is created.) So decreed, that the lease should be assigned to the infant, and that the trustee should be indemnified from any covenants comprised in the lease, and an account of the profits made since the renewal."*

In essence, what the court ruled here is that this was held by the trustee on Constructive Trust for the beneficiary, the infant to the extent that the only person in the whole wide world who cannot benefit from the lease is the trustee, because of the requirement of there not being any conflict, the no

## The Foundations of Property Law

conflict rule. The trustee cannot put themselves into a potential conflict position with the trust – they must do everything to ensure that they avoid even a hint of a conflict position.

This was further considered in the case of *Boardman v Phipps* [1967] which is a case where a testator died in 1944, left his residuary estate, which included 8,000 share, about 27% of the total issued shares in a private company. Tom was one of the beneficiaries of the trust and what happened was that as beneficiary & solicitor, Tom (Phipps) & Boardman went to the board meetings often & quickly learnt that the company was no longer doing as well as it should or could have been. What Boardman & Tom decided to do, was to buy shares in the company insofar that they became the majority shareholders & took control of the business because they felt that there was a problem with the running of the trust which was the reason for its inherent failure. They then over a period of time, turned the company into a failing business into a very successful one.

Now what happened next, was that John, Tom's brother, who was also obviously a beneficiary to the trust, decided that he didn't like what had happened & said that this amounts to a conflict of interest on the trust property; how can a beneficiary & a trustee buy out a whole company with their own money, surely this gives rise to a conflict of interest and so when the opportunity came up, it should have been rejected by Tom. What was sought, was that as per the above case, it would be ruled that because there appears to be a conflict of intention, all profits which were made by Boardman and Tom should be determined to be held as a Constructive Trust for the beneficiaries of the trust, it was all trust property. The thing to note here however, is that their argument was literally that they did not hide, not attempt to hide anything that they were doing from the beneficiaries of the trust; everything was in the open & all were aware of what Boardman & Tom were doing. Despite this, the beneficiaries had not explicitly consented to the activities in which they were engaging.

The majority took the *Keech v Sandford* approach in that it was not conflict as such, but they may have had a conflict. The minority said that if you want people to take on the position of a trustee, then you need to be a little bit more lenient & realistic about the pressures you put onto them. The trust could never have done what was done, so there was no chance of any potential conflict & thus the minority believe that a real conflict must be found, not the risk of a potential conflict.

The whole purpose of introducing fiduciary duties was to increase the standard of behaviour of trustees. In light of this, it was held by the courts that although there may not have been an actual conflict, there could seemingly be a conflict & wanting to increase the standard of behaviour, there needed to be a set principle; where it appears that a conflict of interest could arise, it will be seen as being a conflict of interest. The courts realising that this was actually a considerably harsh decision, allowed for Boardman to be generously remunerated and compensated with a large sum of money. Rumour actually has it that in this case John found out that Tom was sleeping with his wife & needed a way to get back at him!

In the case of *Regal Hastings v Gulliver* [1942] is a case where Regal owned a cinema in Hastings. They took out leases on two more, through a new subsidiary, to make the whole lot an attractive sale package. However, the landlord first wanted them to give personal guarantees. They did not want to do that. Instead the landlord said they could up share capital to £5,000. Regal itself put in £2,000 but could not afford more (though it could have got a loan). Four directors each put in £500, the Chairman, Mr Gulliver, got outside subscribers to put in £500 and the board asked the company solicitor, Mr Garten, to put in the last £500. They sold the business and made a profit of nearly £3 per share. But then the buyers brought an action against the directors, saying that this profit was in breach of their fiduciary duty to the company. They had not gained fully informed consent from the shareholders. Lord Wright had a quote in this case, *"It is suggested that it would have been mere quixotic folly for the four respondents to let such an occasion pass when the appellant company could not avail itself of it; Lord King, L.C., faced that very position when he accepted that the person in the fiduciary position might be the only person in the world who could not avail himself of the opportunity."*

Directors of a company owe a fiduciary duty to the company for which they work for; there can be no conflict between the company & the directors. If you as a director of a company come across information or an opportunity as a director, then subsequently resign to take up that opportunity, it will be determined that you were in a breach of your fiduciary duty to the company, because you only received that information because of your position & this was privileged information you received solely because you were a director of the company otherwise you would not have received that information.

Likewise, in the case of *Don King v Warren* [1999] the boxing promoter, where Frank Warren wanted to leave the partnership after it was being wound down after failing. During the wind-up period, it became apparent that Warren had signed a few boxers to promote. This was seen to be a conflict of interest because he was still tied down with the partnership & he had a requirement to offer the boxers to the partnership first; it was imperative to do this regardless of whether or not the partnership would've accepted the boxers or taken them on. Warren was arguing that because of the friction, they would never have accepted him taking the boxers on & because they were winding down anyways, there was no way that they would've been able to take the boxers on.

However, the courts, as per the Boardman case said that the whole purpose of these fiduciary duties was to improve the standards of behaviour and by not asking and releasing himself from his duties to the partnership, Warren was in breach of his fiduciary duties, which meant that the boxers he signed were held on Constructive Trust for the partnership! This was all done to try & ensure that is a high standard of corporate behaviour.

Remuneration, Payment – Fiduciary Duty

It will automatically be held that there is a conflict of interest if a fiduciary can make a profit from his position. However, as we discussed previously, because the obligations and work of a trustee can often be so intense so much so that many people do not actually want to become a trustee. Therefore, Section 29 of the Trustee Act states that trustees can now be entitled to reasonable remuneration for their work:

(1) Subject to subsection (5), a trustee who—

    (a)is a trust corporation, but

(b) is not a trustee of a charitable trust,

is entitled to receive reasonable remuneration out of the trust funds for any services that the trust corporation provides to or on behalf of the trust.

(2) Subject to subsection (5), a trustee who—

(a) acts in a professional capacity, but

(b) is not a trust corporation, a trustee of a charitable trust or a sole trustee,

is entitled to receive reasonable remuneration out of the trust funds for any services that he provides to or on behalf of the trust if each other trustee has agreed in writing that he may be remunerated for the services.

(3) "Reasonable remuneration" means, in relation to the provision of services by a trustee, such remuneration as is reasonable in the circumstances for the provision of those services to or on behalf of that trust by that trustee and for the purposes of subsection (1) includes, in relation to the provision of services by a trustee who is a deposit taker and provides the services in that capacity, the deposit taker's reasonable charges for the provision of such services.

This reasonable remuneration concept suggests that there is a requirement that the trustee is a professional trustee in that this is their full-time job. This is a part of the move from family to commercial trusts. This will allow for a reasonable remuneration. If it has been discovered that you have been reasonably paid, then there can be a duty on you as a trustee to pay money back to the trust; you must account for the profit you made from that money from that unreasonable amount & that will all be held on constructive trust for the trust property because one cannot gain anything from the trust.

With Directors Fees, their salaries are agreed at shareholders meetings & are agreed by all the beneficiaries. However, in the case of *Barclays Bank v Bartlett* [1980] there is an encouragement to become involved in the management of a trust. In the case of *Re Macadam* [1946] if you become a director of a company and are only there because of a trust vote, then it will be held that your entire salary will actually be held on constructive trust. This is because you are only in that position because of the trust documents/trust itself & without it you really wouldn't be there nor in that position. I personally disagree with this whole concept because if there was no trust, then there would be no requirement for me to be there & if there was no need for me to be there, then I wouldn't be there. I am only there for the benefit of the trust, not for its detriment & have been asked to do a job on behalf of the trust; I am being paid for my services, not for my being there for the trust.

This is set out in the case of *Re Gee* [1975] if you can be appointed independently & do not need the vote of the trust, then you can keep your salary.

Secret Profits

This is a concept which was considered in the case of *AG Hong Kong v Reid* [1993] where Reid was actually an AG for Hong Kong, but in his position, took bribes to obstruct prosecution of some criminals, and used the money to buy land in Hong Kong. Some was kept by Mr Reid and his wife, Mrs Judith Margaret Reid, some conveyed to Reid's solicitor. The Hong Kong government argued the land was held on trust for them. The courts said, *"if the bribe consists of property which increases in value or if a cash bribe is invested advantageously, the false fiduciary will receive a benefit from his breach of duty unless he is accountable not only for the original amount or value of the bribe but also for the increased value of the property representing the bribe."* The argument in this case was that the government was never going to have an opportunity to use that money. But the problem with this argument was that it doesn't matter – your conscience was affected & that is enough to deem you in breach of duty. By taking the bribe, your conscience was affected & the money will now belong to the trust & therefore the property will be traced back to the trust too. Current law is based on *FHR European Ventures* [2014] which says that a bribe is held on CT trust for the trust.

Information – Fiduciary Duty

Information belongs to the principal and should not be used to gain your own advantage. This was epitomised in the case of *IDC v Cooley* [1972] in which a business opportunity came up wherein the company that was proposing the business opportunity said that they would never work with the IDC but would happily work with Cooley. Cooley, knowing this, resigned from his position at the IDC by saying that he was unwell and joined the business/architecture venture to make a significant amount of money. Roskill J held that even though there was no chance of IDC getting the contract, if they had been told they would not have released him. So, he was held accountable for the benefits he received. He rejected the argument that because he made it clear in his discussions with the Gas Board that he was speaking in a private capacity, Mr. Cooley was under no fiduciary duty. He had 'one capacity and one capacity only in which he was carrying on business at that time. That capacity was as managing director of the plaintiffs.' All information which came to him should have been passed on.

Breaches

In relation to a breach, the first thing to do is identify the breach in that:

I. Is it a common law breach?
II. Is it a statutory breach?
III. Is it a trust duty that has been breached?
IV. Is it a fiduciary duty which has been breached?

Having determined what kind of a breach it is, the next question is to determine what the remedy of that breach is:

I. Is it a personal remedy?
II. Is it a proprietary remedy?

Personal Remedies

The potential remedies available for breaches are as follows:

I. Pay Compensation – this roots from the case of *Brudenell-Bruce v Moore* [2014] wherein Lord Cardigan is the 49% beneficiary of a bare trust established in 1951 with the remainder being held for the benefit of a trust established for Lord Cardigan's son upon him reaching the age of 40. The Trustees of the 1951 Trust were John Moore, a senior barrister's clerk, and Wilson Cotton, a highly experienced professional trustee and founder of STEP. Following the Trustees' decision to sell a number of the paintings belonging to the 1951 Trust, Lord Cardigan embarked on a course of conduct designed to remove the Trustees by alleging substantial breaches of trust, dishonesty and a breakdown in the relationship of trustee and beneficiary. In addition, Lord Cardigan sought in the region of £4million in compensation for alleged breaches of trust, the most significant of which was an alleged failure to maintain the Stable Block of Tottenham House. It was held by the courts in this instance that the trustee will need to pay back the money which he had received.

II. Disgorge benefit – this is a situation where make profits from the money which you received as a result of a breach, and I turn around & want a value/portion from the profits which you have made. This is a restitutional property remedy as per unjust enrichment.

The requirement for any breach is 2:

- What is the nature of the breach?
- Is it a trust duty or is it a fiduciary duty?

If there is a breach of a trust duty, then:

I. What is duty that has been breached?
II. Who has committed the breach – is it a primary or a secondary breach?
III. What is the loss caused by the breach? The causal link as per *Target Holdings v Redfern* [1995] It must be noted that if one breach causes a loss, then another breach which causes a profit will not offset the balance. Each individual breach must be treated as its own separate breach & dealt with accordingly. This concept differs from the idea of a whole portfolio approach which we looked at earlier in that the whole portfolio must be considered as being one

entity. One can choose to take profits which are made but sue for any losses that have arisen.
IV. Are there any defences?

So, for example...

Paul is a trustee. Emma is a beneficiary of the trust and encourages Paul to buy shares in a high-risk investment, which actually turned out to be worthless. What breach has Paul done?

Paul can be sued as per Sections 4 & 5 of the Trustee Act 2000 wherein he has breached the requirements of the standard investment criteria & the requirement to take advice from professional advisors as per the requirement laid out in Section 5 discussed above.

Defences

There are a number of defences which can be used in situations where the trustee has breached their fiduciary duty & they are as follows:

I. Checking the actual trust document – this may sound stupidly simple & basic but considering that the first point of all information in relation to a trust is held in the trust documents, it is worth making sure that these must be checked. It is vital because as per the case of *Armitage v Nurse* [1998], anything & everything can actually now be excluded from being a breach, in order to capacitate for the growing burdens on trustees. However, as per the case of *Walker v Stone* [2000], fraud cannot be excluded because it must be noted that it is the fine line between dishonesty & negligence but who determines that line? That is something which can be confused very easily.

II. Consent – If the beneficiaries have all consented to the actions of the trustee, so long as the consent is fully informed & they are sui juris, then the consent will be valid based on the case of *Re Paulings* [1962].

III. Section 61 of the Trustee Act 1925 – This no longer applies due to the increased standard in the duty of care however, so long as they acted honestly, reasonably and acted fairly, then they have a valid defence against claims of a breach.

IV. As per Section 21 of the Limitation Act 1980 which considers that a breach must be claimed 6 years from when the breach occurs, or when it falls into the possession, as in when they are sui juris. However, it does not apply to self-dealing or any fraud or proprietary claim.

Primary & Secondary Liability

As a trustee, you will be under personal liability, not a vicarious liability. This is where you may have more than one trustee, but not vicariously liable for other trustess. The best way to understand this is by way of example:

Matthew and Harriet are trustees of a trust. Harriet is busy with her teaching and babysitting responsibilities so leaves all the investments for Matthew to deal with. Matthew, with one of the beneficiaries decides to make an investment without consulting Harriet (he thought he was a man!) The investment fails and subsequently all the funds of the trust are lost.

Harriet has now realised that, when she decided to check her emails, she has been informed of this via her monthly review on the investments & she wants to know if she is liable because Matthew has decided to disappear abroad.

Well, in answer to Harriet's worries, her lawyers won't be much help! There is a duty on her to keep trust assets under joint control & she should have supervised her co-trustee, Matthew, as per the case of *Bahin v Hughes* [1886]. Her failure to supervise Matthew will amount to a breach as well as not making sure that the trust property was under joint ownership. It must however be noted, that the beneficiary who colluded with Matthew cannot claim his share as per Section 62 of the Trustee Act 1925.

Disgorgement Remedy

This is the concept that remedies will be based around what has been gained by the fiduciary rather than what was lost by the trust/principal. This is because often, as we've seen above, gains made by the fiduciary can be excessive & to have those held on Constructive Trust for the trust property can be extremely beneficial & significant.

# **Proprietary Remedies & Tracing**

  I.   What is Tracing?
 II.   Basic Principles
III.   Examples
 IV.   Equitable Tracing
  V.   Foskett v McKeown
 VI.   Banking Rules
VII.   Innocent Mixed Funds

This links in with remedies, as tracing is the process by which you determine which remedy is best to use. If you can prove a proprietary interest, then you can have a proprietary remedy, where you vindicate your property rights & require them to be returned to you. It is not a remedy as such; tracing is merely the process by which proprietary interest is identified. Cohen & Bentham last year considered that property is the rights in a thing, rather than a thing.

What is Tracing?

Tracing is the process by where you assert your property rights in something; the thing may change, but your property rights in that thing will still there & it is that which will be protected because you are trying to find the asset in which the property rights of the claimant belong so that they can get them back. The property itself may change, but the interest one has in the property will not change. This is what is identified in the case of *Boscawen v Bajwa* [1996] by Lord Millet in his judgement. The purpose of tracing is you trace the asset back to whoever is in possession of it and where you find the person who has possession of it, the interest in it will end. This is linked in with the concept of a Resulting Trust, where if you buy trust property which has been mixed with someone else's property assets, then tracing will allow for a process to figure out who owns what percentage share of what – it's like maths, literally! It may seem difficult, but it's important to just remain logical throughout.

What tracing allows for, is a decision to be made as to whether the remedy pursued will be a proprietary or personal one. The property in an asset will be traced & based on what is more beneficial for the claimant to claim, a decision will be made. A proprietary remedy has the added benefit when claiming from bankruptcy. What this means, is that what will happen is that all the assets will be divided amongst all the creditors but before this happens, you can stake a claim and say, hey listen, that's my property so I have first dibs to the amount which I am owed. In a personal remedy, under a bankruptcy claim, it will mean that when the property is divided amongst all the creditors, you will just merely receive a share from it. This mean that at times, you can receive as little as 10p for every £1 that you're owed which is only 10% whereas in a property right you'll always be allowed to stake claim to your property before everyone else.

In a personal breach, you will only get back your exact property. So, let's say there was a breach of £10,000 of my personal property, which was spent on a wedding, then I will only have a claim to that £10,000. But, with a proprietary remedy, I can trace back the actual property or the interest in the property and stake a claim to that. So, let's say with that £100,000 breach, Katie goes and invests in some property that she buys & is now worth some £300,000. Because I now have a proprietary interest in that property, I can say no hold up Katie, that's actually my property because you would not have had that property without the breach, so that actual property now worth £100,000 will be mine; I won't have a claim on only the £100,000 breach but rather trace back what happened with my money & stake a claim in that property.

According to the case of *Foskett v McKeown* [2000] which we look at in more detail later, there is no limitation to a proprietary claim insofar that a proprietary remedy can be claimed, or a lien can be placed over the asset. This means that even if for instance the value of Katie's property fell to £50,000, I'd have a lien which would then give me the choice; do I want the property, or do I want to get my money back. It gives me the freedom to choose what is best for me as a result of the breach.

This is best exemplified by the example that we looked at earlier in the term. Katie takes £100 from me as a result of a breach of duty; maybe she took the money from the Bespoke Hoodies Trust Fund. Using that £100, she

# The Foundations of Property Law

spends £2 on a lottery ticket with which she ends up winning £3 million. Now, I have a choice:

I. If I stake a personal claim to that property, I will be entitled to get my £100 back & she will need to pay me.
II. However, let's say I stake a proprietary claim to that property, then I will say that listen, my property is £98 & the lottery ticket because you used my money to buy that lottery ticket. Without my money, you would not have been able to buy that ticket. So, I will have traced my property back to the £98 and the lottery ticket. This means that as soon as I stake this claim, the lottery ticket too will become my property and subsequently the £3 million she won from the lottery will also become mine! (HAHA! ☺)

Obviously if the lottery ticket had lost, well I wouldn't want it because it's worthless, so I would stake a personal claim to my property & just ask for my £100 back. Simple! What this differentiation does, is allow me as a claimant to choose which remedy will give me the best result for my property & for me to profit from the most; I have a choice of 3 – proprietary, personal or placing a lien.

It will be the complete choice of the claimant to choose which remedy he chooses to pursue based on what will give the best result to him for his property.

Basic Principles

One of the most important things to note is that the Common Law cannot trace into a mix fund because, as we looked at last year, the Common Law does not recognise the concept of divided ownership. This roots from when we look at co-ownership last year & the whole idea that at common law, there is no such thing as Tenants in Common, only Joint Tenants. What this means, is that in common law, assets must work wholly as direct substitutions. Direct substitutions are known to be followed, not traced. My money was used to buy a house, which was sold wholly to buy a horse which was sold wholly to buy a car. So long as it was constantly unmixed, I would say that my interest lay in the car. Whoever's hands I find it in, so long as it is unmixed, I'll be able to say sorry mate, that's my property & I'll have that back please, thanks!

This was considered in the case of *Lipkin Gorman v Karpnale* [1988] where a partner in a firm of solicitors stole money from them, and spent it gambling with the defendants. The firm sued also their banker, who had been held to be aware of the defaulting partner's weaknesses and activities. The plaintiff firm of solicitors sought to recover money which had been stolen from them by a partner, and then gambled away with the defendant. He had purchased their gaming chips, and the plaintiff argued that these, being gambling debts, were worthless, and that therefore no consideration had been given.

The courts held that the casino's defence succeeded. The defence against a restitutionary claim that the defendant had altered his position was available to a person who had changed his position acting in good faith so that it would be inequitable to require him to make restitution. This is a form of wholly strict liability because it is a chose in action. Restitution based on unjust enrichment is the idea that one just has to have the property; knowledge of where it came from etc. is not needed much like herein where the casino did not have knowledge where the money had actually come from as such.

A common law claim can be made only in two instances:

I. You are the legal owner of the property
II. The Property is proven to be unmixed

What needs to happen in this instance, is that the property needs to be followed to determine who holds your property & once that has been discovered, they have to give it back to you.

The change of position defence is something we look at in more detail in the forthcoming topics, but it is effectively where the recipient will argue that I have changed my position on the property and therefore I do not need to give you back all the money which makes it a partial defence. What happens is, because of the property which I have received, I have changed my lifestyle to such an extent that to go back from it, will be difficult for me

& because of this change of position, I have a valid defence as per the claim of *Phillip Collins v Davis* [2000].

So, let's say that Katie took that £100,000 from me & she used it to become a fashion artist to launch her own brand of clothes. As a result, she becomes very successful, makes a lot of money & buys a new house, a new car & changes her whole lifestyle. She could then argue that her whole life has changed as a result & therefore does not need to give me back all of my money. She would say, look Matthew but for receiving that money, I would never have changed my lifestyle & it would've stayed the same. This change obviously must be one in good faith in that she must have genuinely believed that she was entitled to my £100,000 & didn't just splash the cash knowing it wasn't her money!

All in all, for common law, it is imperative to know that a right to claim is lost if the property is mixed before receiving it as per the case of *Aqip v Jackson* [1990]. Can only make a claim at common law if the property is received unmixed but generally it is much more favourable to trace in equity anyways.

Example 1

Emma takes £10,000 from the Company bank account and then gives this to Paul. He puts the money in his bank account, where he has £5,000 and then spends the money on a world cruise he had always dreamt of.

In this instance, Paul received the money unmixed and as a result, there is a direct substitution which means the company can make a claim against Paul of unjust enrichment. However, because he has spent the money on a holiday & not property as such, there is no property to have a proprietary claim against, which means that the company's remedy will be merely personal & will be entitled to get the money back.

Example 2

Emma takes £10,000 from the Company bank account, puts this in her bank where she already has £5,000 and then gives this all to Paul. He then spends the money on a world cruise he had always dreamt of.

In this instance, because the money gets mixed before Paul receives it, there is no claim against Paul. However, at Common Law, there can be a claim against Emma.

Equitable Tracing

Unlike the common law, equity can trace into mixed funds & mixed assets. This again links into what we looked at in previous topics & how equity recognises the concept of Tenants in Common as a form of co-ownership. This too is based on the Resulting Trust principle wherein it will be determined how much of my property is in that final property as per the case of *Foskett v McKeown*. There are two requirements for equitable tracing to be considered & they are:

I. There needs to be a fiduciary relationship
II. There needs to be a beneficial interest – the beneficiary will be the one claiming, not the legal owner.

So, let's say for example, Harriet spends £100,000 of trust money & then £300,000 of her own money (you baller!!) to buy a boat for £400,000. It's clear here that 25% of the share of the boat belongs to the beneficiaries based on the Resulting Trust Principle. With proprietary interests, there is no consideration of anything other than the actual state of the property. Someone's state of mind will not be considered; the beneficiaries will have 25% interest in the boat regardless of what Harriet's state of mind was when she brought the boat. Then, the beneficiaries have two (or three) options again:

I. If the boat goes up in value, they would want to stake a proprietary claim so their property's value would go up too meaning they get more money.
II. If the boat goes down in value, they will seek a personal claim in the £100,000 to ensure that they get their money back from Harriet regardless of the value of the boat falling – she'll have to take that L and just deal with it.
III. This is the wildcard option – they can put an equitable charge/lien on the property to protect their £100,000 all the time which makes you a secured creditor against all situations.

# The Foundations of Property Law

## Foskett v McKeown

This is a case where in breach of trust, Mr Murphy took £20,440 from a company he controlled. Over 200 investors (including one Mr Foskett) had invested in the company for buying land in the Algarve, Portugal. The land had been bought, but not developed as promised.

Mr Murphy used the trust money to pay off the fourth and fifth instalments on his life insurance policy. He had already paid the first three premiums with his own money.

Mr Murphy committed suicide. His children ("the Defendants") were paid the £1,000,000 under the insurance policy. Mr Foskett and the other investors ("the Claimants") sued the Defendants, claiming a 40% share in the policy monies.

The Claimants argued they had a proprietary interest in the insurance monies: the insurance policy had been purchased using a proportion of misapplied trust funds. The Defendants argued that only an equitable lien was available, and the beneficiaries should only receive the amount taken.

The Court of Appeal in their judgement that said this was a personal claim for as per the value of contribution. However, the House of Lords on appeal held that it was all about vindicating the proprietary interest/rights rather than about unjust enrichment. It was deemed that they had owned a proportionate share of the property.

## Banking Rules

A question is then raised as to what happens if money is paid into a current bank account, where it is likely that the funds will be mixed & the money in the bank account belongs to both a trustee &/or a beneficiary.

If money is paid into an overdrawn account, then the property rights will have ceased to exist on your property, as per the case of *Foskett v McKeown*. This would be the case unless the principle of backwards tracing is taken advantage of. This is where the question is effectively asked, why did you borrow the money in the first instance from the overdraft account. If the money was borrowed for an asset, then once the overdraft has been paid off, then the claimant would have an interest in that property/asset; how much would be determined by the concept of tracing. Although this is slightly illogical because the property/asset was actually brought before the breach, it literally seems like the right thing to do, because the breached property was used to pay off the debt which occurred as a result. This roots from the case of *Bishopsgate v Harman*.

There is also the concept of the presumption of honesty which effectively states that the trustee will be presumed to be hone at all times & not in a breach of trust which is considered in the cases of *Re Hallets* & *Re Oatway*.

The starting position for the presumption of honesty will be that the trustee is acting in an honest manner & he will not be breaching his trust.

So, let's say for instance, Donald takes £40,000 of trust money and mixes it in with £20,000 of his own money in his Current Account. He then spends £15,000 on shares & £45,000 on his dream wedding with Melania. Now the question is, who's money was spent where? Was Donald's money spent on the shares & the wedding, or was it the trusts money that was spent buying the shares first & then the wedding? Well, there's two options:

I. **Re Hallets [1880]** – this would say that the first money taken from the account will belong to the trustee. So, in this example, Donald's £15,000 would be spent on buying the shares & then £5,000 on the wedding, whilst trust money will have been spent on £40,000 of the wedding. Here, there can be no proprietary remedy for the trust because there is no property which roots from the wedding – all the trust will have is a personal claim against Donald to give them their £40,000 back!

II. **Re Oatway [1903]** – this case is the other way around so the trust will have a proprietary claim to the shares because their money was used first. So, they'll have the following options:
    a. Proprietary or personal claim on the shares £15,000 based on the value of the shares. If it goes up, they'll seek a proprietary claim but if it's gone down, they'll seek a personal claim.
    b. Personal claim on the £25,000 spent on the wedding.

The trick for this is to take the problems in chronological order & always think what will be the most beneficial for the claimant; where can they get the most money back for the breach against their property. This is known as cherry picking – one can choose whichever of the two cases is better to give a remedy to the interest. Which will give a bigger return to my stolen trust property?

## Example 3

Emma takes £5,000 from the trust and pays this into her account which already has £5,000 in it. She then takes £8,000 out to buy shares which are now worth £16,000 & then she spends the balance on a holiday.

Re Hallet's would mean trust lost £2,000 because it would be said that £5,000 of Emma's money was spent on the shares & then another £3,000 on the shares was from the trust. But £2,000 was spent from the trust on the holiday which has no proprietary remedy to it. So, they'll only get £6,000 of the shares (3/8$^{th}$) as this is all they own.

Re Oatway would mean the trust has all their money in the shares because their £5,000 would be spent on the shares which would mean they'd be in line for a return of £10,000 as they own 5/8$^{th}$ of the shares.

## Example 4

Emma takes £5,000 from the trust and pays this into her account which already has £5,000 in it. She then takes £8,000 out to buy shares which are now worth £5,000. She spends the balance on a holiday.

Re Hallet's would mean trust lost £2,000 because it would be said that £5,000 of Emma's money was spent on the shares & then another £3,000 on the shares was from the trust. But £2,000 was spent from the trust on the holiday which has no proprietary remedy to it. So, they'll only get £6,000 of the shares (3/8$^{th}$) as this is all they own.

Re Oatway would mean the trust has lost all their money in the shares as the value of the shares falls. So, what they do is they place an equitable charge/a lien over the shares for the value taken (£5,000) to protect their

£5,000 as this is the best remedy for them as this becomes like a security for them, much like a mortgage.

Example 5

Donald this time decides to take £20,000 of trust money & mixes it with £5,000 of his money in his bank account to spend all of it on his wedding with Melania. After this, Donald wins the lottery & wins £30,000. With this £30,000 he spends £25,000 on shares. Now for the trust, none of their property/money was spent buying the shares because all their £20,000 had been spent on the wedding & this £30,000 was unrelated. This would mean that all they have is a restitutional personal remedy against Donald to get their £20,000 back but would by no chance have a proprietary remedy in the shares.

Example 6

Emma takes £5,000 from the trust and puts in her bank account with £5,000 of her own money. She then takes out £10,000 and spends on a holiday. Thereafter, she wins the lottery and pays the £100,000 she wins into her bank.

This money from the lottery will not need to be spent on repaying the trust – no proprietary interest in the winnings. All the trust has is a personal claim on the £5,000 which was taken from them.

Innocent Mixed Funds

Example 7

This is based on the concept of *Re Claytons* & the case of *Barlow Clowes* which is **only** implemented between two innocent parties. This principle is that the order in which the money went in, will be the order by which it was spent. So, money that goes in first, will be said to be spent first.

So, let's say for example, on Monday, money from Trust A was put into a bank account & then on Thursday, money from Trust B was put into the bank. On Friday, I purchased shares & then on Saturday, I spent money on my dream wedding. Here, the logic will be that money from Trust A will have

## The Foundations of Property Law

been spent on the shares because it was put in first & money from Trust B will have been spent on my wedding, because it went in next!

However, in circumstances where this would lead to a clear unfair result/outcome, then the case of *Barlow Clowes v Vaughan* will step in & say no, this isn't fair & so the application will need to be proportionate – each will contribute as per the amount of money put into each task. So, let's look at it like this:

- Trust A's money = £20,000
- Trust B's money = £10,000
- Shares = £18,000
    - Trust A = £12,000
    - Trust B = £6,000
- Wedding = £12,000
    - Trust A = £8,000
    - Trust B = £4,000

> Top Tip: draw out a tree-diagram for this to help understand which method needs to be used in which circumstance

# 3rd Party Liability – Personal Claims

I. Basis of the claim
II. Baden Criteria
III. Recipient Liability
IV. Alternative Remedy at Common Law
V. Defences
VI. Equitable Remedy
VII. Consequences of Liability
VIII. Activities

This element of 3rd party liability looks at the whole concept of people that are not subjected to the trust itself. They are people who get involved with the trust due to external sources/reasons which we will consider throughout the topic.

Basis of the claim

Claims in relation to 3rd party liability can be made at both common law and at equity. As we know from previous topics & everything, we looked at last year, claims made in equity are a lot more flexible and make a lot more sense too. This is because of the fact that co-ownership and the concept of Tenants in Common etc. is recognised at equity, not at common law. Let us however first consider equitable liability.

This roots from the case of *Barnes v Addy* [1874] which lays out two rules under which liability can extend beyond the trustees and into 3rd parties. This is through:

I. They receive or become chargeable or in charge/manager of some part of the trust property
II. They assist with the breach with knowledge that they assisted the breach knowing that it was a breach which was fraudulent & dishonest.

If it can be proven for that they engaged in such an action, then it will be such that they will be treated like trustees – they were known for a while as constructive trustees, however, this was changed in the case of *Williams v*

*Central Bank of Nigeria* [2014] is a case where a bank was party to a fraud which was committed by a solicitor in terms of holding back some money. We are interested in this case because it is this case which looks into changing the concept of them being known as constructive trustees, following the ideas which are rooted from the case of *Westdeutsche*. Lord Neuberger states that *"it is unreal to refer to a person who receives property dishonestly as a trustee, given that the trust is said to arise simply as a result of dishonest receipt. Nobody involved, whether the dishonest receiver, the person who passed the property to him, or the claimant, has ever placed any relevant trust and confidence in the recipient."* Basically, what impact this is meant to have, is that rather than even giving them the term trustee, they should be referred to as a wrongdoer, because this is exactly what they are. There is no element of trust placed in them at all & therefore they should not even have the benefit of this term. The effect is that these wrongdoers are treated as trustees but change from a constituted trustee relationship.

This was built on by Lord Millet in his judgement of *Paragon Finance v Thakerar* [1999] states that, *"the expressions 'constructive trust' and 'constructive trustee' are misleading, for there is no trust and usually no possibility of a proprietary remedy; they are nothing more than a formula for equitable relief."* It is deemed as misleading because let's be honest – they're not really trustees, are they? There is no trust property as such.

### Baden Criteria of Knowledge

This criteria assess the steps that must be taken by a 3rd party to then be referred to as a wrongdoer. This roots from the case of *Baden, Delvaux & Lecuit v Societe General* [1983] which comes out with the following requirements which need to be fulfilled:

I. Actual Knowledge – there must be knowledge from the 3rd party that what they are doing will indulge a breach of trust
II. Wilfully shutting eyes to the obvious – this is the idea that the 3rd party has on his own accord, chosen to ignore what was obviously going to be a breach of trust property; not asking too many questions. This has been referred to as Nelsonian blindness. This is where Nelson was blind in one eye & when given the commandment to put the telescope to his eye to look at something,

he wilfully put it to her blind eye & said "Soz mate, man can't see nothing so I ain't following your orders LOL!" This was a willingness from Nelson to engage in that activity of saying he couldn't see anything.
III. Wilfully & recklessly failing to make enquiries to the same degree that an honest & reasonable person would have – something would've triggered a reasonable person's conscience, but it didn't trigger yours therefore you'll have acted in a manner which can allow you to be held liable.
IV. Having knowledge of certain circumstances which would indicate facts to the honest & reasonable person – similar as above.
V. Knowledge of circumstances which would put honest & reasonable person on enquiry; it would make them ask questions & these questions would have indeed been asked by a reasonable person.

The final two points are quite difficult to properly appreciate because they're looking specifically into the state of the mind of the defendant & as we saw all of last year in Criminal Law, this can be very difficult to apprehend. How do you really know what someone is actually thinking?

The first three points all constitute actual notice and according to the case of *Montagu* there is a requirement that this element of actual notice must be present in order for there to be a liability. If there is no notice as such, then there cannot be liability.

In the case of *Agip* it was considered all every single form of 3$^{rd}$ party liability would actually consider all of these elements which was additionally considered by *MacMillan Inc v Bishopgate* [1993] which said that liability would exist where an honest and reasonable person would enquire about something but the 3$^{rd}$ party didn't, therefore liability should exist. The problem, however, is that the courts have significantly found it difficult to understand and determine what level of knowledge you need to have in order for liability to be imposed. How much knowledge do you need to have? Who determines that you have too much knowledge & therefore you should be a wrongdoer?

## The Foundations of Property Law

Recipient Liability

Tracing is a process through which it can be found out who has your property and it will be held that that individual person(s) will be responsible for the breach personally, so they will need to return the property to you. This will be the case so long as evidence can be found that they were aware, then they will be personally liable for that breach. This was considered in the case of *Agib v Jackson* where Lord Millet said that liability could be found where 'an honest and reasonable person would have been aware' there was no need for actual knowledge. With the relevant knowledge, they would be liable to return that property to the owner. However, the constitute notice, it is the idea that one should have known, but you were incapable of making that decision.

There is a constant battle the courts face in finding out just how much knowledge is required, such that Megarry VC says that often there can just be an honest muddle, but still this can be enough for liability against a 3$^{rd}$ party. This approach was accepted by Lord Browne-Wilkinson in the case of *Westdeutsche* too which we looked at in detail a few topics ago.

The case of *BCCI v Akindele* [2000] was a case where the liquidators of BCCI sued Chief Labode Onadimaki Akindele, a Nigerian businessman, for $6,679,226 that he got in divestiture payments in 1988. ICIC Overseas Ltd, in the BCCI group, had agreed Akindele would buy shares in BCCI Holdings, and be guaranteed a 15% pa return for a $10m investment. BCCI in fact gave him $16.679m to do this, thus leaving $6.679 over. Akindele did not know this was part of a fraud scheme to enable BCCI Holdings to buy its own shares. The liquidator argued he was a constructive trustee, for both knowing receipt and knowing assistance. The liquidators argued his dishonesty could be inferred from his knowledge of the artificially arranged loan transactions and his unusually high interest rate of 15%.

Basically, he gave £10 million and over 3 years, was paid £7 million in interest. When the bank went through the financial crisis & was under administration, the creditors wanted the £7 million back because they were saying that he was wholly dishonest in his approach. The question for the courts however was whether or not Chief Akindele was aware of this 'wrongdoing' as such.

What the Chief continued to say was that he quite simply did not have the knowledge & just did not ask questions about the high return. He held that he saw it as a really profitable investment & like any other investor, this was an investment which really made sense & was very attractive, therefore was happy to invest & not ask too many questions.

The courts said that there are 3 requirements which would deem it unconscionable for a 'wrongdoer' to be labelled as such & not be able to retain the benefit & those 3 things are:

I. It must be a breach by a fiduciary
II. There must be a beneficial receipt by the Defendant; the receipt must have benefitted them
III. There must be requisite knowledge – the Defendant should have had some form of knowledge that would make it unconscionable to retain the property

Obviously point 3 again, like discussed above is very vague & something the courts have constantly struggled with, but it is wholly unclear as to whether or not this will include the situation where a person should have been suspicious. In a situation where things seem too good to be true, can it be determined that that you should have asked questions to decide whether this constituted a breach or not.

These 3 points were questioned in the case of *Critereon Properties v Stratford* [2004] wherein Lord Nichols said that we shouldn't even need to ask about the level of knowledge; we should just consider the first 2 points & so long as these 2 have been satisfied, then it can be held that there would have been a breach and the individual can be labelled a wrongdoer.

This section of recipient liability considers those recipients who are innocent & those purchasers who are not bona fide.

What this means, is that Akindele can just turn around & say that nope, I really was not suspicious; I thought it was a really good return on investment, so I just didn't ask why I was getting such a high rate of interest.

## The Foundations of Property Law

The reason Akindele can argue this point, is because of the change in the law from the old Baden Criteria because he was not acting in an unconscionable manner.

### Activity 1

Emma takes a Picasso painting belonging to the trust and sells it to Paul for £1000. Paul has no knowledge of art, but the colours went with his study. Paul is an art dealer in Old Masters

In this one, it is clear that Paul really does not have any sort of expertise in Art that is related to Picasso. You could argue that how can someone in Art not know about Picasso, but truth is, it is very simple to fall into that & therefore, him having no expertise in this, can make it very easy for him to argue this defence by saying sorry, I really just had no idea that this was actually Picasso's work, I just thought it looked good!

### Activity 2

Paul is an art dealer in Modern Art

Well in this instance, he really cannot argue this defence – he is a dealer of modern art & it would be unreal for him to now know Picasso whilst dealing in modern art! What nonsense!!

### Activity 3

Emma gives Paul £1000 – he thinks she won the lottery and he buys himself a holiday

Well here again, Paul is under the genuine impression that she has won the lottery & he has no reason to doubt her. Therefore, his lack of questioning will not give rise to him having some sort of knowledge.

### Activity 4

Emma gives Paul £1000 – he wonders where she got it from so buys himself a holiday

The simple fact that he actually wondered where she got the money from, is enough of a reason to give rise to some sort of knowledge. His conscience was affected & this quite simply cannot be ignored.

## Alternative Remedy at Common Law

If a person has received property in an unmixed form, then they can make use of this remedy. Remember, if this property has been mixed before it has been received, then this remedy cannot be used. It can only be used if the property is received unmixed. Once the property has been received, it does not matter if they mix it, the only requirement is that when it is received by them, then it must be unmixed. The remedy is quite simple when thinking about it; the mere element of unjust enrichment can be used – you have unjustly received my money as a matter of fact & therefore, you owe it to me to return it to me because you have received this unjustly & do not have a right to it; restitution. There is no consideration of the state of mind.

The liability is strict however, it is subject to defences which we look at below.

## Defences

There are a number of defences which can be used, which include:

I. The Change of Position defence can be used at common law which is exactly what we looked at a couple of topics ago too. This is the element that when you innocently, meaning the 3$^{rd}$ party innocently receives a piece of property, then so long as they have done something that they would not have done but for the receipt of that trust money, then they can claim this defence. So long as they have acted innocently & in good faith as per *Abou Rahmas v Abacha*, then they can stake claim to the defence, as per the case of *Lipkin Gorman v Karpnale*.

II. Bona fide purchaser – this is the situation where I am an innocent purchaser of the property in that I gave it its proper value. If I am bona fide, then I can stake a complete defence.

III. Dissipation – this is a defence to a proprietary claim but in a personal claim, they will still be liable to it. In a personal claim, they will have to give back the value of the property, but in terms of property, well the property no longer exists so there can be no proprietary claim anymore as such.

### Equitable Remedy

This is a remedy against a person who has not received trust property, but rather they have merely helped in the breach of the trust. They have provided an assist to breach the trust! Previously where they had been labelled a dishonest associate, now they are labelled under the remedy of accessory liability.

Accessory liability was considered in the case of *Royal Brunei v Tan* [1995] wherein Royal Brunei Airlines appointed Borneo Leisure Travel to be its agent for booking passenger flights and cargo transport around Sabah and Sarawak. Mr Tan was Borneo Leisure Travel's managing director and main shareholder. It was receiving money for Royal Brunei, which was agreed to be held on trust in a separate account until passed over. But Borneo Leisure Travel, with Mr Tan's knowledge and assistance, paid money into its current account and used it for its own business. Borneo Leisure travel failed to pay on time, the contract was terminated, and it went insolvent. Royal Brunei claimed the money back from Mr Tan.

The Judge held Mr Tan was liable as a constructive trustee to Royal Brunei. The Court of Appeal of Brunei Darussalam held that the company was not guilty of fraud or dishonesty, and so Mr Tan could not be either. The case was appealed to the Privy Council.

In this case, the Privy Council said that honesty is not an optional case, rather is it per the moral standards of each individual. Lord Nicholls in his decision said that, *"Acting as an honest person would in all the circumstances, with regard to personal attributes, such as experience and intelligence."* Both experience and intelligence are taken into account when considering the level of liability against someone.

It must also be noted however, that there is a subjective element to honesty which will be judged by your standard of expertise – how much do the people of your field need to be honest.

In the case of *Twinsectra v Yardley* [2002], there's a clear division between the court itself & this just goes to prove the extent of the problem which we face in trying to understand the extent of this subjective element. So, in this case, the majority decision was that there is indeed a subjective element to it. It was held that D must not act in a way that a reasonable person would think dishonest & he must have understood that to act that way was dishonest.

The minority decision in this case however was that led by Lord Millet, who was very loud, passionate & honest in his dissent; this was one of the strongest dissents ever. Like he literally did not hold back at all. Lord Millet said that the test was not subjective & the majority in the House of Lords had misinterpreted the decision of Lord Nicholls from the Privy Council case. Millet was adamant that the Lords in this case had quite simply just got it wrong – this was not the law which Lord Nicholls had intended to have in the Privy Council decision. This was proven by Lord Nicholls himself by saying that the decision reached by the majority in this case was indeed wrong & the interpretation of his decision was correct by Lord Millet, not by anyone else.

In the case however of *Barlow Clowes v Eurotrust* this was allowed to be revisited however, this is another privy council decision. They reviewed the decision. Lord Hoffman, who was part of majority in the previous case, confirmed that Lord Millet was right & altered his belief; he agreed that it was indeed wrong in the previous case. He was able to clarify where the majority judgement was wrong.

Now the Court of Appeal is bound to follow the House of Lords decision; the House of Lords decision will be given preference over the Privy Council. But in this instance, the Court of Appeal actually chose to follow the Privy Council decision. The problem here is that by following the Privy Council decision, is that there is no way for it to go all the way up to the supreme court & for our laws to be properly verified and laid out properly for us. There is no certainty; the law of the House of Lords is one thing, but the courts in the land are actually using another law, the law of the Privy Council.

Since the case of *Wilers v Joyce* [2016] allows for decisions to be made to be binding on domestic courts if it is expressly stated as intended to be binding. But hey, right now, the law is all over the place & there is absolute confusion – literally no one knows what will happen on a case by case basis! Nonsense!!

In the case of *Williams v Central Bank of Nigeria* [2014] the courts determined the following:

I. Recipient liability of a stranger to the trust, a 3$^{rd}$ party, arises independently of any fraud on the part of the trustee.
II. Accessory liability of a knowing assister will depend on the unconscionability of his conduct. So, there is a suggestion that there must be a suspicion of the breach – will my conduct be unconscionable.

What we have now, is a position of law where we really just don't know what will happen on a case by case basis; how do we know what liability will be imposed. Baden criteria may have been bad, but at least there was a set element of questions that needed to be answered & by answering them, you could come to a conclusion to know of the liability that you'd be faced with.

In the case of *Brinks Ltd v Abu-Saleh* [1996], the wife believed that they were transporting money in order to evade tax. She had absolutely no idea that the transporting of money was actually transporting stolen money. In this case, there will be absolutely no liability on her because she quite simply just did not have any knowledge – her unconscionability was not affected.

### Activity 5

Emma takes 100K from the trust. She is able to do this because the cleaner lets her into the trust office when Emma explains (fraudulently) that she has lost the key.

In this case, the question will be whether the cleaner will be liable or not? Has the cleaner acted in an unreasonable manner? Well it can be argued that a reasonable cleaner would not just allow anyone into an office, but rather say sorry you've got to get your own keys. If it was a subjective test, the questions will be how long has she been a cleaner? If she's been on the job a long time, then she definitely should not be allowing anyone in, whereas if it was her first day on the job, then of course potentially she can be forgiven.

## Activity 6

Emma takes 100K, Paul the company accountant had paid over the money when Emma presented invoices to that amount. Paul thought this was unusual but could not be bothered to check.

An honest & reasonable accountant would not just hand over money – this is the subjective part of the current test therefore; Paul would be liable because he has failed that subjective standard.

## Activity 7

Emma takes 100K, Paul the company accountant had paid over the money when Emma presented invoices to that amount. Paul was Emma's best friend and although it was unusual knowing Emma needed money, he thought it best to pay quickly then check later.

Here he is definitely liable. If you apply this to the Baden criteria, you will come to the same decision. They are still the guiding light when deciding if someone's conscience is affected or not.

The Baden Criteria can still be deemed as being the guiding light in terms of defining what is & what is not conscionable behaviour.

## Consequences of Liability

If a person receives property as a knowing recipient, then the remedies can be personal (hand over the money) or they are proprietary (continue the tracing process.) Now the tracing process used against them, will be altered based on whether they are an innocent recipient or if they're a wrongdoer. If received with knowledge, different tracing rules will be applied.

So...

If the recipient has knowledge, money placed into their account which already has money in it & then using that money, shares are brought and the balance spent on a holiday, then the rules applied will be from *Re Hallets/Oatway* which we looked at the previous topic.

If the recipient has no knowledge, and money is placed into their bank account which already has money in it & then using that money shares are brought & the balance spent on a holiday, then the rules applied will be from *Re Claytons/Barlow Clowes v Vaughan* again which we looked at the previous topic.

There will also be a common law claim against the recipient potentially. As long as property has been received unmixed, then their liability does not need to be concerned with their behaviour being unconscionable.

If, however, a person assists in a breach, there is no need to prove that the trustee was dishonest, but rather only the accessory as being dishonest, the only remedy available is personal. The assister will be liable for the amount which they helped to be breached – they are treated just like trustees.

# Recommended Readings

Below, I thought it important to list a range of books which are particularly useful for the study of Land & Equity Law, and from which the foundations of this guide are based on. If you wish to further develop your knowledge of any topic, these books are the place to start.

## Land Law

Mark Davys, *Land Law*, Palgrave Macmillan, 2017.

Martin Dixon, *Modern Land Law,* Routledge, 2016.

P. N. Gravells, *Land law: text and materials*, Sweet & Maxwell, 2010.

Paul Kohler and Alison Clarke, *Property law: Commentary and Materials*, Cambridge University Press, 2005.

## Equity & Trusts

Alastair Hudson, *Equity and Trusts,* Routledge, 2016.

Jonathan Garton, *Moffat's Trusts Law: Texts and Materials,* Cambridge University Press, 2015.

Printed in Great Britain
by Amazon